D1167947

TOURISM, LEISURE AND RECREATION SERIES

Series editors
Gareth Shaw and Allan Williams

Urban Tourism

Also available from Continuum:

Urban Tourism Second Edition
The Visitor Economy and the Growth of Large Cities

Christopher M. Law

continuum
LONDON • NEW YORK

Continuum

The Tower Building
11 York Road
London SE1 7NX
www.continuumbooks.com

370 Lexington Avenue
New York
NY 10017-6503

First published 2002

British Library Cataloguing-in-Publication Data
A catalogue record for this book is available from the British Library.

ISBN: 0-8264-4928-X(hb)
      0-8264-4926-3 (pb)

Typeset by YHT Ltd, London
Printed and bound in Great Britain by Cromwell Press, Trowbridge

Contents

List of figures

List of tables

List of plates

Preface

The origin of this book goes back to 1984 when I was asked by the Planning Department of the former Greater Manchester Council to write a report on what at that time appeared a novel idea, namely, that Manchester might become a tourist destination. Old industrial cities like Manchester had only just cleaned the soot off their buildings and the thought that people might want to visit scarred cities was strange, but if Bradford just down the road was attempting to attract them, why not Manchester? There was very little literature on the topic, but a grant enabled me to visit cities in North America and Europe and assess what they were doing and achieving. The research was essentially empirical and practical. Data about the nature and scale of urban tourism were presented, and prescriptions offered. I discovered from the demand for the working papers from the project and the requests to give talks that there was an audience that wanted to know more about the subject and eventually this led to the first edition of this book. The book followed on from the research report; to map the nature and scale of urban tourism, but in addition to use theory to interpret the phenomenon. Readers who expected a highly theoretical treatise with little grounding in reality would have been disappointed. In preparing the second edition I have followed the same lines, seeking to balance an account of the subject against interpretations that can be made using theory. In the nine years since the first edition was published there has been an explosion in the literature on urban tourism and this has made it difficult to do justice to all the material that has been written. The topic is now so wide that probably several books would be necessary to encompass all the research that has been undertaken.

A large number of people have helped me in my study of urban tourism. They include many officers employed in the planning and development departments of cities and in the promotional organizations who have either given time to allow me to interview them or answered my written, telephoned or e-mail requests for information. They are too numerous to mention, but I need to thank them. I am also grateful to academic colleagues such as Greg Ashworth, Rick Ball, Paul Bull, T.C. Chang, Andrew Church, Myrian Jansen-Verbeke, Gareth Shaw, Karen Thomson, John Tuppen, Duncan Tyler, Jan van der Borg, Alan Williams and others for discussion on the topic. Special thanks are due to Gustav Dobrznski for drawing the figures and to Carol Goddard and Moira Armit for helping me in various clerical matters, all in the (late) Department of Geography at the University of Salford. Finally, thanks to my family, Elizabeth, Kate and Nick for their tolerance and help in letting me disappear at frequent intervals to visit foreign cities. I am still trying to convince them and others that visiting exotic foreign cities is work!

Chris Law,
School of the Environment and Life Sciences,
University of Salford,
Salford, Manchester,
May 2001

Introduction

Two key propositions underlie the reasons for writing this book, namely, first, that large cities are arguably the most important type of tourist destination and, second, that tourism has become an important and significant component of the economy of most large cities. Only a few years ago in the early 1980s, these two propositions would not have been recognized or accepted. Subsequently, with the growth of tourism in cities they are more likely to be recognized but many academics and planners have still to absorb their implications. There is still a great deal of misunderstanding as to what constitutes tourism and, as a consequence, a lack of appreciation about its scale and ramifications. This is partly because tourism is a very fragmented industry and partly because tourism is often only one component of a multi-purpose project. Thus, a new concert hall may have the aims of providing cultural opportunities for the local population, raising the profile of a city, assisting the transformation of the image of the city, attracting tourists through the events which it hosts, and be offered as part of the lifestyle opportunities that a city has when seeking to attract mobile executives. Notwithstanding these cognitive problems, over the past twenty years, most city councils have come to value the role of tourism such that part of their strategic vision encompasses the idea of creating a city that will attract visitors.

The aim of this book is to describe and explore the state of tourism in large cities. It will seek to interpret the role and impact of tourism. In the words of John Rennie Short, 'our aim is to be theoretically informed and empirically grounded'. Tourism studies are often criticized for lacking theory, which is perhaps not surprising in a subject area that is relatively new. As with Geography, the theories that are used are often borrowed from other disciplines. Theory and critical approaches are highly valued in the academic world today but frequently the authors of new ideas make little effort to evaluate the relevance of their theories to the real world. By the time they have been evaluated by others, another set of theories is being put forward. Theoretical approaches therefore should be developed on a secure understanding of the shape of the real world. However, the latter may be a phantom as our perceptions of reality are shaped by the cognitive maps in our heads. This book will seek to balance theory and description. It will also try to suggest how tourism can be developed in cities, although it is not written as a manual of good practice.

This chapter will discuss a number of issues which will provide some background for the rest of the book. These include a brief history of urban tourism, a definition of urban tourism, measuring its scale, a listing of the major urban tourism centres, the tourism system, and the types of urban tourism.

DEFINING TOURISM

The use of the term tourism is not unproblematic. In popular usage tourists are people who travel on leisure trips and are most likely to visit the seaside. Only gradually has the meaning of the word broadened to include visits to towns and cities. In the United States the term is used for leisure trips only, as the convention industry is categorized as a different industry. Other terms used in the United States include the visitor industry, the hospitality industry and the travel industry. The term business tourism is used to cover both ordinary business travel and travel to conferences and exhibitions. The latter is sometimes referred to as MICE – meetings, incentive (travel), conferences and exhibitions.

The World Tourism Authority (WTA) definition of a tourist is someone who moves away from home on a temporary or short-term basis for at least 24 hours, whether travelling in their own country (domestic tourism) or going to another country (international tourism). The restriction of the use of the term to people who are away from home for at least 24 hours is considered by many to be too narrow. Most writers on tourism would want to include day trippers or excursionists. In Britain these are defined as people spending at least three hours away from home and involving a round journey of at least 20 miles which they do not regularly make, thus moving outside the area of their normal travel (OPCS, 1991). However, any distance used is open to discussion. As travel has become easier, the range of commuting has become wider. For some cities this may be up to one hundred miles, although for most people 10 miles might be a more appropriate figure.

Excluded from the WTA definition are students and workers migrating temporarily. Some people in the industry in an effort to avoid these definitional problems have resorted to using the word 'visitor' to cover both overnight stayers and the day tripper. Unfortunately the word visitor has a very common usage and cannot be so easily redefined. Chadwick (1987) has attempted to define and classify tourists (Figure 1.1). Tourists are classified by the primary purpose of their travel into four types, namely, business, pleasure, visiting friends and relatives, and other personal reasons. Chadwick also recognizes that while there may be a prime motive for travel, there may also be secondary motives and activities and these may be a significant factor in the decision to travel. Thus the decision whether to attend a conference may not be made solely on the basis of the conference programme but on its location and the interest of the place and the opportunities it affords. Similar considerations may apply when visiting friends and relatives.

At first glance these discussions may appear academic and irrelevant, but definitions are important when assessments are made of the impact of tourism. Thus it is necessary to define a tourist in order to count their number and to use surveys of expenditure to estimate their economic impact. It is possible to debate any particular definition which is why different studies use different definitions and comparisons and compilation of statistics may be difficult. The focus of this book is cities and for this purpose a tourist would generally be a person coming from outside the metropolitan region which might be defined on the basis of commuting flows. But how is this to be operationally defined? By detailed survey? By the use of a simple distance radius from the centre of the city and, if so, what distance? And how would one city compare with another?

Given these definitional problems, it is not surprising that collecting tourism statistics is fraught with problems and that there can be great debate as to their meaning. The most easily collected and available statistics are those counting travellers crossing national borders, as shown in Figure 1.2. Since 1950 there has been 26-fold expansion and

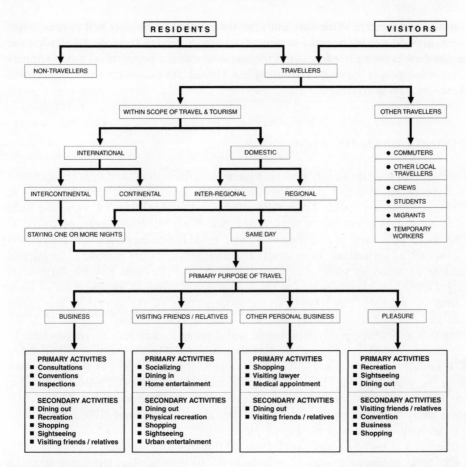

Figure 1.1 Classification of travellers
Source: After Chadwick (1987)

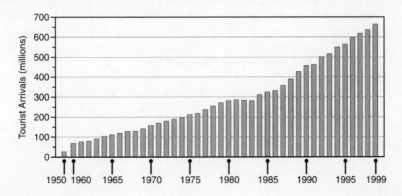

Figure 1.2 Growth of world tourism, 1950–99

this is projected to continue. These figures only count international tourists and ignore domestic ones, which are very large in a country the size of the United States. Because

European countries are often small in area the number of tourists will appear large. These figures do not distinguish overnight stayers from day trippers. In Europe the large numbers crossing borders could include a significant proportion of day trippers whereas most people leaving or entering the United States (except for Canada) will probably be staying overnight.

DEFINING URBAN TOURISM

The term urban tourism simply denotes tourism in urban areas, and begs the question what is special about urban areas? The urban–rural dichotomy has been around for at least two centuries ever since census takers and governments intent on reforming local government sought to categorize settlement types. Rural settlements were perceived as on the small scale with the majority of their inhabitants dependent on land-based activities such as agriculture. In contrast, urban settlements were considered larger and dependent on activities such as manufacturing and services and possibly large-scale mining. Definitions of minimum size for a place to be classified as urban varied from one study to another. Law (1967), in a rigorous study of the growth of the urban population in England and Wales in the nineteenth century, used a figure of 2,500, arguing that agriculture production would not support a settlement above this size. In the twentieth century conditions changed dramatically. The agricultural labour force shrank initially, causing many villages to decline. However, the possibility of commuting, the growth of the retired population and new methods of teleworking have meant that settlements are no longer dependent on local employment. Many rural dwellers enjoy the benefits of an urban lifestyle and the urban–rural dichotomy may no longer be useful as means of classifying places.

Settlement size may be a more useful way of thinking about places. A town of 5,000 has very little in common with a metropolis of 10 million. The latter will have an economy which is very complex and very diversified with many linkages between activities. Each activity will have connections around the world. In the case of the former, there will often only be a few activities and possibly one of these may dominate the economy. Accordingly, most discussions of population and economic change classify places by size and observe the changes taking place. Categories used might include up to 25,000, 25,000–100,000, 100,000–500,000, and so on.

How does this relate to a discussion on the definition of urban tourism? The basic question is whether all places classified as urban should be included. With regard to tourism, is it meaningful to discuss tourism in places as varied as the small town of 5,000 and the metropolis of 10 million? At least one author has used size to define his topic. George Cazes in his studies of urban tourism in France used 25,000 as the lower limit of urban size (Cazes and Potier, 1996). This of course still means that a very wide range of settlements are included. The Federation of European City Tourism Offices uses the figure of 100,000 as the basis for membership (Wober, 1997). Page (1995), in his book on urban tourism, recognized the variety of place types and presented a typology as follows:

- capital cities (e.g. London, Paris and New York) and cultural capitals (e.g. Rome);
- metropolitan centres and walled historic cities (e.g. Canterbury and York);

- large historic cities (e.g. Oxford, Cambridge and Vienna);
- inner city areas (e.g. Manchester);
- revitalized waterfront areas (e.g. London Docklands and Sydney's Darling Harbour);
- industrial cities (e.g. Bradford);
- seaside resorts and winter sports centres (e.g. Lillehammer);
- purpose-built integrated resorts;
- tourist-entertainment complexes (e.g. Disneyland and Las Vegas);
- specialized tourist service centres (e.g. spas and pilgrimage destination areas);
- cultural art cities (e.g. Florence).

While this typology points to the tourism differences between different types of urban centres, the justification for the classification is not always clear. How do cultural capitals (e.g. Rome) differ from cultural art cities (e.g. Florence)? How can Oxford and Vienna be put in the same category? Is it right to call Canterbury and York metropolitan centres? Should parts of a city, e.g. waterfront areas or the inner city, be separated off from the rest of the city? But, above all, is it meaningful to study tourism under one generic title (urban tourism) in places as varied as Canterbury, Lillehammer and London?

Judd and Fainstein (1999) presented a three-fold classification:

- tourism urbanization – specialized resorts which have been created, either planned or unplanned (after Mullins, 1991)
- tourism historic cities, ancient cities – which because of their historic, architectural and cultural identity attract tourists (after Ashworth and Tunbridge, 1990)
- converted cities – places which have set about constructing an infrastructure to attract visitors.

This classification is simpler but ignores size; thus within tourism urbanization a seaside resort might vary in population size from 5,000 to 250,000 and visitor numbers likewise. However, the large resort is likely to be more diversified in its economic structure and to have more opportunities to develop its tourism, as well as possibly more problems. It is also not clear from this classification where large metropolitan areas like capital cities fit in.

The focus of this book will be on large cities, generally those with over one million population, although cities with between a half a million and one million may share many characteristics. In these large cities tourism will be generally only one component of the economy. There are only a few created and specialized resorts, notably Las Vegas and Orlando, which have grown to exceed one million.

In the large city the tourism economy will have several components. Many of these sectors will serve the local population as well as visitors. There are issues concerning the relationship between visitors and residents which are more complex than in a place with a mono-tourism economy. Tourism will be linked to the rest of the economy through a series of linkages, not least the selling of the city both to visitors and to other economic activities.

THE STUDY OF URBAN TOURISM

Until recently the study of tourism in large cities had not attracted much attention from academics. Books and articles written about the economies of major cities such as London and New York, where tourism employed very large numbers, hardly made mention of the industry (see Fainstein *et al.*, 1992). Only one report, that by Llewelwyn Davies *et al.*, (1996) on four world cities, included tourism as one of the main drivers of the metropolitan economy. While recent interest may be explained by the expansion of tourism, the earlier lack of interest needs some explanation. This lack of attention almost certainly arises from contemporary fashionable methodological approaches. In the past the economic/export base theory suggested that the prime sector of the economy was manufacturing which attracted income from the rest of the world (Williams, 1997). More recently it was recognized that parts of the long-neglected service sector was capable of generating export income, but interest quickly focused on producer services such as finance and business services. One reason for the lack of attention given to tourism was its invisibility. Employment generated by tourism does not appear within one Standard Industrial Classification order or minimum list heading. Whereas statistics, say, for the motor car industry can be quickly plucked from the regular statistics this is not possible for tourism. This is because generated employment occurs under several headings and then often only as a part of these headings. Tourism employment estimates require large and expensive surveys. Academics have also frequently written off tourism wrongly, perceiving the jobs to be seasonal and part-time. In fact, tourism is a very important export industry for cities and most of the jobs in this industry are permanent and not seasonal.

Academics studying tourism have also neglected the large city as a type of destination, while perceiving it mainly as the origin of tourist flows. This neglect may be because most attention was given to holiday tourism and its end point in seaside resorts. Trips for business and conferences and to friends and relatives were hardly recognized in the past, nor were short breaks and day trips, all areas important for the city. While it has been recognized that cityscapes and museums attract tourists, it has often been difficult for the tourism researcher to distinguish the locals from the visitors and therefore to evaluate precisely the importance of tourism. Pearce (1989, p. 180) suggested that tourism researchers were more interested in the delights of resorts and mountains and therefore neglected cities. However, this surely must be a personal view and not borne out by the widespread interest academics have shown in cities. It also ignores the fact that most universities are based in large cities. Pearce himself has more recently shifted his interest towards urban tourism with several articles on Paris (1997, 1998a, 1998b, 1999).

While the academic world may have ignored urban tourism until recently, many reports have been produced for and by the industry and by consultants. Unfortunately most of these reports are not easily available to the outsider, sometimes because only a few copies are produced or because their contents are considered confidential. This is a problem for anyone studying the industry. These reports may be of interest either because of their empirical content or because of the strategies and action plans proposed. Access to them is essential if an evaluation of tourism management is to be made.

There has always been some tourism in cities as the next section will detail. In 1989

Ashworth (1989a) and Pearce (1989, p. 84) both drew attention to the imbalance in studies of tourism which virtually ignored the large city. There were a few case studies of tourism in large cities, some of which were brought together in a book edited by Vetter (1985). During the 1980s, following the severe recession of the early part of the decade, older industrial cities became interested in the potential of tourism to assist regeneration, particularly in the city centre and the inner city. The English Tourist Board encouraged local authorities to consider the potential of tourism to create employment. A few academics were involved in research to explore the potential of tourism and various works appeared from these studies (Buckley and Witt, 1985, 1989; Jansen-Verbeke, 1986, 1988, 1989; Law and Tuppen, 1986).

During the 1990s there was an explosion of publications on urban tourism, either textbooks, edited volumes or journal articles. As a consequence, there is now a burgeoning literature which deals with the issues and also provides detailed case studies. General textbooks have been produced by Law (1993), Page (1995) and Cazes and Potier (1996). Conference proceedings and collections have been edited by Judd and Fainstein (1999), Law (1996), Murphy (1997), and Tyler, Guerrier and Robertson (1998). Other volumes bringing together research have appeared by Berg, Borg and Meer (1995) and Mazanec (1997). Since the beginning of 1999 a new quarterly journal, *TTI City Reports*, has appeared which contains five case study reports in each issue. As could be expected, the quality and depth of the reports vary considerably but they all provide up-to-date statistical information (where available) for the individual cities. When these are combined with the steadily increasing number of case studies published in the ever expanding number of academic tourism journals plus the data for places obtained from the Internet, it becomes possible to survey the state of urban tourism in a way that was not feasible only a few years ago without extensive fieldwork.

A BRIEF HISTORY OF URBAN TOURISM

Towns and cities have always been visited by people living outside their areas, but generally these people would not have been considered as tourists. The essential function of towns, as described by many geographers including Christaller, was that of a service centre for the surrounding area, as a market or central place for the exchange of goods and services. Most people using the town in this way would have travelled only a short distance but for higher order goods and services much longer distances would have been covered. The cities at the top of the hierarchy would thus have attracted visitors from a distance for business (including administration), for shopping and for other reasons.

In the past it was generally only the wealthy who could afford to travel. Often the wealth of such persons was based on country estates where they resided for much of the year. Leisure and shopping may have taken place in local towns but probably at least once a year trips would have been made to the capital city, particularly in the period known as 'the season'. Before the twentieth century there were many small states in Europe, each with their own capital, as well as larger capital cities such as Paris and Vienna.

In Britain county and regional centres such as York provided a range of facilities for the aristocracy from racecourses and theatres to assembly rooms. Visits might be for a day, but in some cases houses were owned so that visits could be longer. Capital cities, often the seat of royalty, would generally be larger, attracting more visitors from further away and with a wider range of facilities. In places like London there were a large number of town houses for the aristocracy mainly found in the West End. The influx of these wealthy people provided a significant boost to the economy and stimulated the development of facilities that would be the basis of tourism in later years. During the eighteenth century there was a significant development of spas. Although initially established for medical reasons, the larger ones like Bath attracted visitors because of their social and entertainment activities.

Another feature of the eighteenth century was the Grand Tour. Young aristocrats completed their education with a tour of the main cultural cities of Europe, a tour which might last several years (Towner, 1996). British travellers frequently went to Paris and thence Italy where they visited Venice, Florence, Rome and Naples. During their stays in the different cities they would purchase souvenirs which were brought back to Britain to adorn their houses. Perhaps the most significant of these souvenirs would be paintings, particularly of Venice by artists such as Canaletto and Guardi. Woburn Abbey in Bedfordshire has 23 of Canaletto's views of Venice. Through these souvenirs images of certain foreign cites would become familiar to the aristocracy and this in turn would encourage them to visit those cities. The construction of the railway network in the mid-nineteenth century facilitated easier travel and stimulated travel for leisure purposes. The wealthy could now visit Europe's major cities as well as journey to warmer resorts on the Mediterranean.

From the mid-nineteenth century European and later North American cities began to organize large exhibitions to display arts and crafts as well as modern technology. The first of these was held in London in 1851 in the Crystal Palace. These were later to evolve into 'world expos' and become special events, a topic that will be discussed more fully in Chapter 7. These general exhibitions were held in capital cities and in major provincial cities such as Manchester and Glasgow which aspired to world status. A feature of these large-scale events was that they often left behind a legacy of resources such as parks and museums which later became important with the growth of tourism.

The expansion of trade in the nineteenth century was accompanied by the growth of business travel, whether on a regional, national or global scale. Businessmen travelled to purchase materials and components and to sell goods. They mainly travelled to cities and towns and their overnight stays provided a stimulus for the development of hotels. From the late nineteenth century onwards specialized trade fairs or exhibitions evolved, particularly in continental Europe drawing participants, both exhibitors and customers, from a wide area. In the twentieth century the emergence of the multinational company and more recently the global corporation has increased business travel. This is now undertaken for much more than merely the purchase of materials and the sale of goods; it involves bringing company employees together from around the world to share ideas, develop strategies and to be trained. Corporate meetings of this type are now an important feature of the tourism business.

Until the 1950s travel to foreign cities was restricted to a small segment of the population. It is only in the past forty years and perhaps in the past twenty years that there has been a massive expansion of visiting cities, mainly for short breaks. By the 1990s the travel supplements of newspapers were featuring a different city every week and TV quiz programmes were offering city visits as prizes. In publishing there was an explosion in the number of city guides while the tour companies were offering a wider variety of destinations from a wider variety of airports within a country and giving a wider choice of hotels in the destination cities. It is easy to say that this has been facilitated by easier travel, greater affluence and more leisure time, but the explanations need to be deeper and will be discussed later in this book, whether they come from the demand or supply side.

MEASURING THE SCALE OF URBAN TOURISM

As a prelude to the detailed accounts of the different aspects of urban tourism which appear later in this book it would be useful to provide an overview of the state of tourism in the major cities of the world. Which are the most important tourist cities? What is the ranking of these cities? In recent years, many more statistics have become available which might make this possible. However, comparability and reliability are major problems (see Wober, 1997). Figures are not always comprehensive, so that, for instance, the statistics for hotel bednights may cover only large hotels in some cities whereas in other cities they are fully comprehensive. Some statistics cover only tourists staying in hotels while others include visitors staying with friends and relatives. In a large city the latter may represent up to 50 per cent of the total. Another issue concerns whether the statistics are for the central city or the metropolitan area. In some cases there could be a significant difference between these two sets of figures. The origin of the statistics may also affect their interpretation. In some countries city statistics are obtained from the disaggregation of national survey data such that the sampling error is sufficient to make year-to-year changes unreliable. A final issue is, what are the key statistics: income, jobs, overnight arrivals, overnight numbers, foreign tourists vs. domestic ones, or daytrippers?

Bearing in mind all these caveats, Table 1.1 attempts to list the major tourist cities in the world. In this table cities are ranked by the number of tourists whether they come from the same country (domestic) or from another country (international). Some cities such as Las Vegas have a very large number of visitors, but most come from the United States, including a third from nearby California. In contrast, other cities such as London and Paris draw a significant proportion of their visitors from around the world and thus might be described as 'world tourist cities'. Using this idea, an alternative ranking based on the international dimension could be produced. The basis of this hierarchy would be as shown in Table 1.2 (see Law, 1996, p. 15 and Butler, 1991).

THE TOURISM SYSTEM

The basic features of the tourism system have been described diagramatically by Leiper (1990) (Figure 1.3). Tourists move from an originating or generating region to a destination region passing through transit regions which may or may not be affected. With a high level of urbanization in the advanced countries it is not surprising that most originating areas are also urban. The urge to travel may arise from either push or pull factors; from the felt need to escape from a place or the pull of another place. The crucial issues around the demand for travel will be discussed in Chapter 2. Destination

Table 1.1 The leading tourist cities in the world

| City | Year | Overnight arrivals (millions) | | |
		Total	International	Domestic
London	1999	28.3	13.2	15.7
Las Vegas	1999	25.3	2.3	23.2
Los Angeles	1999	23.8	6.0	17.8
Orlando	1999	23.1	3.5	19.6
Tokyo	1994	22.3	2.3	20.0
New York City	1999	18.4	6.6	11.8
Chicago	1997	15.5	1.2	14.3
Paris City*	1999	14.5	9.5	4.9
Ile de France*	1994	19.7	10.9	8.8
Atlanta Metro	1998	17.1	0.6	16.5
San Diego	2000	15.2	0.9	14.3
Boston	1997	11.1	1.1	10.0
Hong Kong	1996	11.7	11.7	0
Washington, DC	1999	8.6	1.6	7.0
Greater Toronto	2000	8.6	4.6	4.0
Vancouver	1999	8.3	3.5	4.8
Sydney	1998	8.0	2.1	5.8
Singapore	1997	7.2	7.2	0
Rome*	1999	6.3	4.0	2.2
Montreal	1998	6.0	2.1	3.9
Melbourne	1997	5.8	0.9	4.9
Madrid*	1999	5.5	2.5	3.0
Amsterdam	1999	5.3	4.4	0.9
Dublin	1999	4.4	3.2	1.3
Berlin*	1999	4.2	1.0	3.2
Munich*	2000	3.7	1.6	2.1
San Francisco City*	1996	3.5	–	–
Venice (including mainland)	1996	3.5	–	–
Greater Manchester	1998	3.3	0.6	2.7
Barcelona*	1999	3.1	1.8	1.3
Vienna*	1999	3.1	2.1	1.0
Prague	1998	–	2.1	–
Edinburgh	1997	2.5	1.2	1.3
Milan*	1999	2.5	1.0	1.3

Notes: *Visitors staying in registered hotels only.
These figures are not strictly comparable, see text.
Source: Various including visitor and convention bureaux (and the Internet) and *TTI City Reports*

Table 1.2 Ranking of major tourist cities

Rank	Category	Origin of visitors
1	World	Significant share from world
2	Continental	Mainly from the same continent
3	National	Mainly from the nation in which the city is found
4	Regional	Mainly from the macro-region of country
5	Local	Mainly from local region

areas are of many types, from those based on natural resources such as the coast, scenery and mountains to ones based on cultural resources such as the built environment, to visitor attractions and special events. It is these latter resources which form the basis of tourism in cities. Jansen-Verbeke (1988) has divided them into primary and secondary elements (Figure 1.4); primary elements which have the ability to draw tourists and visitors and those secondary elements which are used by the traveller either to get to a destination or as a service when they are there. This distinction, while generally valid and used in this book, is not watertight. While most travellers do not go

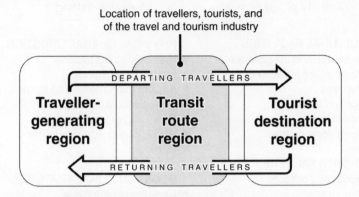

ENVIRONMENTS : Human, sociocultural, economical, technological, physical, political, legal etc.

Figure 1.3 The tourism system
Source: After Leiper (1990)

to a place because of its shops, although they use them when they are there, for some tourists the range of shops may be part of the attraction of a place, and for a few they might be the main reason for going there.

The collection or the supply of resources at the destination can be described as the product or the bundle of products. The use of the term 'product' illustrates the importance of marketing as a device for selling cities to potential visitors. Until recently cities merely advertised the resources which they had and in a low key way. With the recognition that attracting tourists is important, not least because of the income which it generates and the jobs which it creates, marketing methods are being used to develop products which can be sold to different markets, and these are defined by demographics, lifestyles or geography. Existing resources can be bundled together to sell the city as a cultural city, a sports city, a fun city, etc. At the same time the product is reviewed and deficiences noted with action plans launched to create new components which will strengthen the attraction to the tourist. While tourism planning is developing, it is still haphazard because of the disparate nature of the activity, the fact that different actors are developing their own products independently and without regard as to how their contribution might link up with a wider strategy.

There has been much discussion in the literature as to whether there is a tourism industry as such (Gilbert, 1990). This is because, compared to, say, the motor vehicle industry, the boundaries are not very clear-cut. Many of the firms associated with tourism supply both tourists and residents, and there is no way of recording the division of trade between these two markets. Many firms which supply tourists do not think of themselves as being part of the tourism industry. Again, an industry is usually defined in terms of its product, but this can be defined in different ways. Some writers have avoided the term tourist industry and taken cover in what is described as the tourist system (Gunn, 1988). Other terms used are tourism complex and tourist cluster. This

PRIMARY ELEMENTS

| Activity place | Leisure setting |

CULTURAL FACILITIES
- Museums and art galleries
- Other visitor attractions
- Theatres
- Concert halls
- Cinemas
- Convention centres

SPORTS FACILITIES
- Indoor and outdoor

AMUSEMENT FACILITIES
- Night clubs
- Casinos
- Bingo halls
- Organized events
- Festivals

PHYSICAL CHARACTERISTICS
- Historical street pattern
- Interesting buildings
- Ancient monuments and statues
- Ecclesiastical buildings
- Parks and green areas
- Water, canals and riverfronts
- Harbours

SOCIO-CULTURAL FEATURES
- Liveliness of the place
- Language
- Local customs and costumes
- Cultural heritage
- Friendliness
- Security

SECONDARY ELEMENTS

- Hotels
- Catering facilities
- Shopping districts, centres and malls
- Markets

ADDITIONAL ELEMENTS

- Accessibility
- Internal transport
- Parking facilities
- Tourist facilities: information offices,
  signposts, guides, maps, leaflets, etc.

Figure 1.4 The elements of tourism
Source: After Jansen-Verbeke (1988)

suggests a group of firms which have their own distinctive objectives but which are linked in some way such that they gain strength from each other. Most obviously this might be by way of demand. Either a cluster of visitor attractions has greater pulling power than an individual one or tourists drawn to a visitor attraction spill over to other firms such as shops and restaurants. They may also be joined via promotional agencies since collective marketing will be stronger than the sum of individual advertising.

The adoption of the concept of the product from marketing literature invites other questions. The model of the product lifecycle has been widely used in other disciplines including tourism. Its basic premise is that demand will grow for a product until a mature stage is reached and then fall away, although this declining stage is debatable and depends on the notion that new competing products will take away demand. Can this be applied to individual tourism products such as visitor attractions and/or the whole city product as in Butler's (1980) destination area lifecycle model? These issues will be discussed in later chapters.

Different products vary in their popularity and this clearly applies to the city product. Within tourism the concept of a hierarchy of attractiveness is well established in the popular mind and guide book practice as illustrated by the starring system in the Michelin Guides where three stars are for a journey/highly recommended, two stars for a detour/recommended and one star is for interesting. Butler (1991) has suggested that there is a hierarchy of attractions as follows:

1 International recognition. Many elements appeal and this tourist city attracts people from all over the world, e.g. London and Paris.
2 International recognition. Limited or special appeal, such as the Pyramids.
3 National recognition with wide appeal.
4 National recognition with specialized appeal.
5 Regional appeal.
6 Local appeal.

OVERVIEW OF THE BOOK

Large cities have always attracted visitors but in recent years tourism to cities has increased and the visitor economy has become more important to them. The significance of tourism to cities clearly varies but even where it is currently on a small scale there is usually recognition that it is a growth industry and should be encouraged. The aim of this book is to explore the processes which result in an increasing flow of visitors to cities. Chapter 2 examines the demand side, how individuals and in the case of business travel, organizations, come to make decisions to visit cities. What is the context in which these decisions are made and what is the appeal of cities? How does the consumer decide which city to visit, how far is it related to their own personality and how far to societal influences such as the impact of the media? Most of the book is concerned with the supply side. Urban public authorities are heavily involved in the development of tourism, from the provision of general infrastructure and services, the operation of visitor attractions, and the promotion of cities. Chapter 3 examines the context in which city authorities operate, from changing economic fortunes, the framework provided by national strategies with respect to tourism in more detail, including ideas of product development, public–private partnerships and promotional organizations. The following chapters examine the main components of tourism in cities, from visitor attractions in Chapter 5, conferences and exhibtions in Chapter 6, culture, entertainment, sport and special events in Chapter 7 to the secondary elements in Chapter 8. In discussing these elements, various themes will be considered from the different roles of the public and private sectors, the multi-objective nature of many of the projects and the critical factors for success. Chapter 9 examines the impacts of tourism on cities, in individual ones as well as some of the more general effects. The concluding chapter will attempt to draw the various threads together, considering the inter-relationship of tourism with other activities in cities and the critical factors for success.

Understanding tourism involves many disciplines, but the perspective of this author is primarily that of a geographer. In many respects tourism is the geography of consumption outside the home area, it is about how and why people travel to consume, whether it be historic buildings, landscapes, art and museum collections, or sport and entertainment. It is concerned with what makes tourists travel, what determines how far and in what direction they move. On the production side it is concerned with the process or processes whereby some cities are able to create tourism resources and a tourism industry. How far is this primarily a political process and to what extent do existing resources and potential ones influence the outcome? These and many other questions will be considered in the rest of this book.

Chapter 2

The demand for urban tourism

This chapter will examine the demand for urban tourism from the perspective of the consumer. Why do people want to travel? What are the principal motivations? To what type of places are they attracted? What is the appeal of cities? What are the principal characteristics of cities? As always there are push and pull factors. The push factors are usually personal while the pull factors relate to the features of the destination. People do not have to travel so the motivation to travel has to be strong. Often this is the result of stimulation from the potential destination. Strong images are created which persuade consumers that travel is highly desirable. The way these images are created will be discussed in a later chapter but for the moment it is necessary to be aware the demand does not simply arise from within an individual but can be a created or constructed demand. Most of the material in this chapter will be concerned with leisure travel but it is important to remember that some of the demand for travel comes from business reasons. This will briefly be considered at the end of the chapter.

Discussion on the demand for leisure tourism has stressed the importance of increasing leisure time, greater discretionary income and easier travel. These are very important considerations and provide a context in which tourism takes place. However, they should be seen as enabling or facilitating factors. Consumers do not have to travel because they now have the time, the money and because travel has become easier. They need to have the motivation. The chapter will begin by considering these enabling factors bearing in mind this qualification.

INCREASED LEISURE TIME

Leisure or discretionary free time is usually defined in terms of the time that is left over after we have taken into account work and work-related activities such as the journey to work, time spent on essential activities such as shopping for food, cleaning and personal business matters, and sleep. When these are deducted from a normal working weekday there is about 15 per cent free time, although this does differ between men and women, to the advantage of the former. The main reason for increasing opportunities for leisure during the twentieth century has been the reduction in the working week and the increase in holiday entitlements. However, it can also be noted that the shortening of the working life including earlier retirement, accompanied by better health, has enabled the affluent elderly to have many opportunities for leisure including travel.

For most of the twentieth century the number of hours in the working week has been falling although because of overtime this does not always equate with the number of hours worked. Thus, in 1990, in the United Kingdom the official working week averaged 38 hours, but the number of hours actually worked averaged 43. This compares with 44.4 and 47.8 hours respectively in 1951. There was a tendency for the actual hours worked in the 1990s to increase, mainly because of either the competitive pressures experienced in industry or the increased bureaucracy in the public sector. These pressures were particularly felt by managers and other white-collar workers. This group is sometimes referred to as the time-poor, money-rich in contrast to the time-rich, money-poor group of the unemployed, the elderly and single parents. The number of hours worked in the week varies from one country to another. In some cultures, such as Japan, there has been an expectation that employees will work long hours, well beyond the official hours. One of the main consequences of the fall in the length of the working week in the twentieth century has been the reduction in the number of days worked from five and a half to five, thus creating a clear two-day weekend. This can be used for a weekend break involving one or two nights away with the possiblity of extension by using days from holiday entitlement. In Britain this weekend became effective in the 1960s.

The concept of holidays developed in the late nineteenth century. The word holiday is derived from 'holy day' and concerned the main religious festivals such as Christmas, Easter and Whitsun (Pentecost) and in some countries saints days. People stopped worked to celebrate the festival and develop their spirituality. It was not related to any concept of travelling away from home. Gradually, from the nineteenth century on-wards, the term has come to mean simply cessation from work. Initially it was probably seen as a time for rest, relaxation and recovery perhaps involving travel to a different place. The need for such refreshment was probably connected with the transformation of society following the industrial revolution. In rural and agricultural societies the rate of work would not necessarily have been even throughout the year. There were busy times and slack times. The coming of the factory system transformed this type of regime with a change to regular working hours and a more even flow of work throughout the year, although workers could be laid off when there were no orders. Gradually in the late nineteenth century firms began giving their workers a paid one-week holiday. This was linked in time in Britain to the introduction of national one-day holidays through the 1871 Bank Holiday Act which provided an extra day to the main Christian festivals plus a one-day national holiday in August (August Monday). While many firms did grant their employees paid holidays, it was not until 1938 in Britain that the first Holidays with Pay Act was passed, giving workers the right to have holidays. By the 1950s over 90 per cent of workers had two weeks paid holiday and by 1990 over 90 per cent had four weeks holiday in Britain. This pattern may vary from one country to another (Clark, 2000). In the United States holiday lengths have generally been shorter, the average being only 10 days, while in Japan the average holiday entitlement is 17 days, but only 9.5 days are taken.

The concepts of work/non-work and time have changed dramatically during the second half of the twentieth century and it may not be useful or relevant to talk of these matters using the old terms. In 1950 most people worked a five and a half day working week, approximately from 8 o'clock in the morning to 6 o'clock in the evening for 50 weeks in the year. They had a two-week holiday away (if they could afford it) which was usually taken in the same relatively close seaside resort every year and perhaps the odd bank holiday weekend away, usually visiting family or friends. By 2000 society had changed greatly. With factories often working three shifts a day and six days a week and shops opening for longer hours including Sunday, the week had become much more shapeless. The concept of the working week and the weekend is disappearing for some. It may be more appropriate to talk simply of hours worked in the year rather than hours worked in the week. Likewise the shape of leisure time is no longer of short evenings in the week, a very short weekend as in the past and a longer period of paid holiday. People can plan their leisure in different ways to create discrete time periods to be used for particular purposes. Some of these can be used for travel outside the home area whether for a day trip, a short break (no longer necessarily at the weekend) and a longer holiday which might be of any length from one week to four. One year it might be concentrated (to permit a long-haul trip, say, to Australia) while in another it might consist of several week holidays and numerous (three night) short breaks.

The increase in leisure time and its availability in different shapes have undoubtedly facilitated the growth of tourism. Overall, there has been a move towards shorter, more frequent and more intensive holidays spread more evenly throughout the year (Clark, 2000). The increase in short breaks is perhaps the significant factor for urban tourism. Most visits to cities take the form of a short break (one to three nights) rather than a long holiday although the large number of day trips should not be forgotten. In discussing the increase in leisure time, it is easy to think that this is universal, that is that it applies to everyone. In fact, there are many groups in society for whom leisure is an unknown concept. Some of the poor have to work long hours for low wages just to earn enough to survive. Others have family responsibilites, whether young children or elderly parents, which leave them with little free time. This is before economic factors are taken into account.

INCREASED DISCRETIONARY INCOME

Participation in leisure and travel activities has always been dependent on wealth. This appears so obvious as to hardly need further comment. However, some elucidation may help us to understand the demand for urban tourism. The key factor affecting leisure spending is discretionary income, that is, the income that is left over after all the essential needs have been met. These will include housing costs (including gas, water, etc.), food, basic clothes and other costs such as travel to work. These will often include the costs not only for the earner but for his or her dependants. As such, discretionary income cannot simply be related to gross or disposable (net after tax) income. Two people with the same disposable income may have very different amounts of discretionary income. Thus single people can often have more free income than, say, a person with a family. Some commercial organizations have discovered the significance of the pink pound, that is the spending power of the gay community. The creation of gay quarters in cities may not just be a matter of granting rights to a group previously denied them, but recognizing a marketing opportunity. In recent years the significance of young adults who have yet to start families and 'empty nesters' whose children have left home, has been noted by many commercial organizations, not least those selling short and long breaks. Changing demographics can have a significant effect on tourism flows. These groups have another advantage for the travel industry in that their holiday patterns will not be constrained by school holidays and as such can be used to extend the season and reduce seasonality. As cities may not be the most exciting places for children, it is these other groups which form the core markets for urban tourism.

Discretionary income is also related to the size of income. Poor people spend most of their income on basic items and have little discretionary income, both absolutely and relatively. In contrast, the higher income groups will spend a lower proportion of their income on basic items with discretionary income forming a larger share of the net income and of course being much larger absolutely. Given these considerations not surprisingly taking holidays is related to income. About 40 per cent of the British population do not take holidays and these people are strongly concentrated in the lower income groups. Of course, for some of those not taking holidays there are other reasons such as being disabled, having work responsibilities and needing to care for relatives. At the other end of the range of holiday taking, those that have several holidays a year, these groups show a strong correlation with high incomes. Most probably high income groups will take many short breaks and city destinations are likely to be prominent among these.

Discretionary income has a tendency to increase faster than the real rise in incomes. As the standard of living increases, so the proportion of discretionary to total income will increase and in absolute terms it will become more significant. These funds can of course be used in various ways, from local leisure activities (including eating and drinking out), more consumables for the home (and more on the basic house itself), on clothes, and many other uses as well as for activities outside the home area which involve travel. There is intense competition among firms operating in these areas to obtain a share of the growing discretionary income and it is by no means certain that individuals will necessarily maintain their spending on travel and tourism. In any one year a household may decide to spend a large chunk of their discretionary income on a particular large purchase and sacrifice their holiday. In this kind of market place destinations and the providers of holidays must make a big sell to persuade consumers of the merits of spending their money in this way. Even when consumers have been persuaded to travel, there is intense competition among destinations to attract them; this will be by type of destination as well as by geographical location. As will be discussed below, in order to understand the resultant patterns it is necessary to appreciate the motivations of tourists.

EASIER TRAVEL

The expansion and form of tourism have been closely related to developments in transport. In the nineteenth century the construction of railways opened up many previously remote and isolated areas to tourism. Travel became easier and cheaper. In the twentieth century the motor car and coach have provided a much more flexible means of transport, opening up rural areas to the influx of visitors, particularly those within easy reach of the major cities. In the late twentieth century the development of large aircraft, of air routes and charter services has widened the range of areas that can be considered by the tourist. In particular, long-haul routes enable travellers to escape from their own climatic zone and thus spread their holidays over the entire year. Together with the innovation of the all-inclusive package tour, these developments have opened up many new areas of the world to tourism, particularly around the Mediterranean which was previously remote from the cities and urban areas of northern Europe.

There is a tendency to think that these developments have opened up the whole world, that it has shrunk in some way and that everywhere is accessible, almost on an equal basis. In fact, for long-distance travel places near airports are much more accessible than those places some distance away and for which a change in the mode of transport is necessary. Similarly, the frequency and directness of flights to airports may vary as may the cost, the latter depending on the competition on the route. So a place at or near a major airport is much more accessible than one which is not. Most major cities have important airports which are well connected. This is because they are usually important for business and it is business travellers who often in the first instance provide the basis to establish an air route. Major cities are likely to have a large population and be the gateway to a region, both of which form a strong catchment area for the airport. With this infrastructure cities have the opportunity to develop tourism markets, providing of course they have some good reasons why visitors should come to them.

MOTIVATION FOR LEISURE TRAVEL

As was mentioned above, the term holiday or break usually means not just stopping work but travelling outside the home area and going to a different place. People are often heard to say that they 'need' a holiday, they 'need' a break, they 'must' go somewhere to escape, they 'want' a holiday. But the use of the words 'need' or 'must' is different from its use in connection with, say, food, clothes or shelter. It is not necessary to travel to another area in order to survive and for centuries people did not do so. However, modern people have become so accustomed to holidays that they have come to expect them. In a society where everybody else has a holiday and where the media is constantly discussing holidays, not to have one is to feel deprived. A person's values and desires are shaped by the society around them, that is, they have been socially constructed. This will affect everything they do and in this sense taking a holiday is an act of consumption which will fit into a pattern of a lifestyle, a topic which will be discussed later.

In a well-known work Maslow (1970) suggested a hierarchy of needs, which was portrayed in a triangular diagram (Figure 2.1). At the bottom are the basic needs for food, water and air. Then, above them is the need for safety, security and protection. After these needs have been met, an individual has a need for love, affection and friendship. When these have been satisfied an individual may seek status and self-respect and, finally, at the top of the pyramid is the need for self-actualization or self-fulfilment. All these terms require definition, but overall the individual moves from needing material things to needing more inner or psychological elements. Such a shift

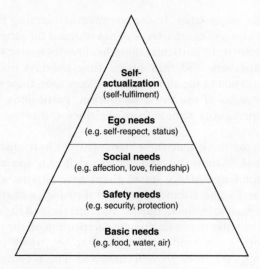

Figure 2.1 Maslow's hierarchy of needs
Source: After Maslow (1970)

could be correlated with economic development. For centuries humankind struggled to satisfy basic needs. By the late twentieth century in the advanced countries most people had met these basic needs and could move up the hierarchy to search for self-fulfilment, whatever this might mean for the individual.

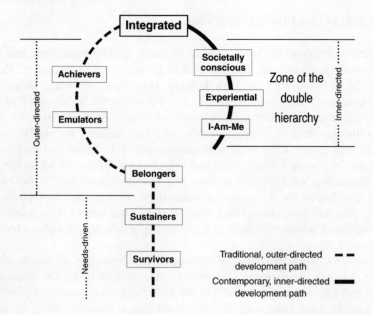

Figure 2.2 The values and lifestyles hierarchy (VALS)
Source: After Shaw and Williams (1994)

There have been many attempts by psychologists and marketeers to classify people according to their behaviour with a view to its use in advertising and maybe counselling. The VALS (values and lifestyles) classification originally developed in North America by Mitchell (quoted by Shaw and Williams, 1994) is shown in Figure 2.2. Here individuals are divided into four groups. At the bottom of the diagram is the needs-driven group seeking to satisfy basic needs including that of being with other people. The outer-directed group seeking status and achievements is likely to be influenced by those round about in terms of values and how life should be lived. The third group, the inner directed, is seeking to explore and have stimulating experiences and is motivated by particular values which may be different from those which society in general propounds. In general, the needs-driven group is likely to be comprised mainly of the

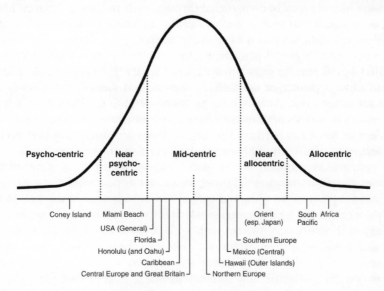

Figure 2.3 Personality and travel destination choice
Source: After Plog (1987)

working classes while the other two groups consist of the middle classes.

Another personality classification which has had great influence on tourism thinking is that by Plog (1987) (Figure 2.3). Plog classified people's personalities on a continuum from psychocentric to allocentric. Psycho-centrics favour the familiar and being with people they know. They are more likely to travel short distances and return to places they know. At the other end of the scale, the allocentrics are people who are often seeking new places and novel experiences and who are prepared if necessary for long journeys and possible discomfort to achieve their objectives. By the nature of the normal distribution, most of the population would find themselves in the middle classified as mid-centrics.

Sociologists studying tourists' motivation have suggested that this type of behaviour should be placed in the context of general patterns of consumption, which is affected by class and status. Bourdieu (1984) has emphasized the importance of education and upbringing which varies across classes. The middle classes grow up knowing about history and art, they have, in Bourdieu's phrase, 'cultural capital'. They can appreciate and obtain pleasure and satisfaction from visiting heritage sites and art galleries. Accordingly, such behaviour is likely to be part of their leisure activities, in contrast to other groups without cultural capital. Baudrillard (1988) emphasized that consumption patterns shape and reveal our identity. An individual constructs their own identity by consuming signs and images. When a purchase is made, what is important is the signs that go with it, rather than whether the product functions well. When a purchase is made it must convey an image that confirms or reaffirms the identity which the consumer wishes to have. Thus the importance of designer clothes. Visits are made to places, visitor attractions, restaurants and hotels which help construct the consumer's identity.

A person's identity may be constructed through visits to 'famous' places. MacCannell (1976) has suggested that tourists authenticate their lives by making such 'pilgrimages'. Urry (1990) has elaborated this idea of the tourist 'gaze'. Through the media some places become well known. When a news item appears on the TV about Paris a picture of the Eiffel Tower may be shown to represent the city. Films taking place in Paris will be sure to show a picture of the Eiffel Tower so that viewers can identify the place. Likewise for other cities. Although in contemporary life the individual is bombarded with thousands of images of different places, some locations constantly reappear. A city such as Venice has been portrayed in art for three centuries so that it becomes well known and it is constantly reappearing in films and travel programmes. These are 'organic' images as opposed to 'induced' images which have been projected by destinations to attract tourists. Through continual appearances these places become destinations people want to visit, and perhaps would say they 'must see'. In the major cities of the world there are numerous iconic sites that a tourist would say he or she must visit. Many of these are very ancient such as the Colosseum in Rome. Visiting heritage attractions is a way of authenticating one's self with the past. Seeing great (famous) art is another. No matter how many reproductions there are of the Mona Lisa, it is necessary to see the authentic and original painting. Sociologists have examined the paradoxes surrounding this search for the authentic. Many heritage or cultural sites have been so altered or sanitized that what is left is hardly authentic. Similarly, with local cultural events which today are preserved and 'put on' solely for the tourists.

Not all the sites that the contemporary visitor 'must see' have a long history as tourist attractions. The use of sites for films and events can cause them to become instant and possibly temporary tourist magnets. Thus, following the filming and showing of the stately home of Lyme Park in Cheshire in a BBC version of Jane Austin's *Pride and Prejudice*, it experienced soaring visitor numbers. The death of Diana, Princess of Wales, directed interest to places such as Kensington Palace in London, with which she was associated. Again, visits were made by people wishing to link their lives to that of a famous person.

CHANGING AND DIVERSE MOTIVATIONS

There has been a tendency in writings on the motivations of tourists to develop a sophisticated theory and suggest that this is overwhelmingly important for travel to all types of destination, notwithstanding that this would appear contrary to evidence, none or very little of which is usually provided. While these meta-theories are full of insight, it strains credulity to think that one theory can explain all trips to tourism destinations in the present as well as the past. As suggested by Maslow, there do appear to be changes in the motivations of tourists. In the past, as described by Krippendorf (1987), many holiday-makers were escaping from hard toil and were looking for rest and relaxation which they might find at a seaside resort. This may still be true for many holiday-makers today. However, increasingly, tourists approach their leisure time more proactively, they positively want to do certain things on vacation. Voase (1995) has suggested that holidays are a time when a person can set their own agenda, they can discover their true selves and can realize a dream. But of course any individual may have many dreams and many aspects of their personality to explore. If they wish, they can use their various holidays and free periods to travel to do a variety of things, from a beach holiday, a skiing holiday, a city visit, shopping, pursuing a hobby to developing relationships. This could be described as self-actualization. Aristotle wrote that the aim of education is to equip us to make noble use of our leisure time (quoted by A.C. Grayling, in the *Guardian*, 5 February 2000). With increasing education, and the gaining cultural capital according to Bourdieu (1984), it is not surprising that cultural and heritage tourism has become important. Many people are using their leisure time to practise and explore the arts, to deepen their understanding of life and civilization, and to further friendships. All of these may involve travel. But this is using the term culture in its most profound sense. It can mean many things and not necessarily just visiting the 'marked' sites. There is often a simple motivation to go to strange, foreign, different and novel places. This desire for novelty has the consequence that repeat visits are less likely and that spatial and temporal patterns are more volatile. Maybe this is part of what Gray (1970) called 'wanderlust' (as opposed to sunlust).

For many tourists there is no such underlying serious purpose. Holidays are a time for pure fun and entertainment, whatever form that may take. The media encourage ideas of hedonistic relaxation and being indulgent to oneself. This is not to suggest that cultural travellers do not enjoy themselves. But there has been a tendency to downplay travel for entertainment, this in spite of the fact that theme parks, pop festivals and casinos are attracting millions of visitors. Through this pure escapism and fantasy individuals can find refreshment and relaxtion to return to a world which may offer little in the way of satisfaction and personal fulfilment.

Sexual motivations for travel are similarly often downplayed. Many people seek to use their leisure time and opportunities for travel to find sexual partners. Certain types of holiday, particular types of activity and distinctive places may offer greater opportunities to meet potential partners. Nightclubs are one such type of meeting ground. They are often found in abundance in cities and in larger resorts, but some places have established a reputation for the vitality of their nightclubs. Prostitution is another activity found in cities, often clustered in 'red light' districts. Gay sex is another aspect of this topic (Holcombe and Luongo, 1996; Hughes, 1997a, 1997b; Clift and Forrest, 1999). Gay areas are now found in a number of cities where gay men can escape and find freedom from a homophobic society. Such districts can attract visitors from far-away.

THE IMAGE OF CITIES

The role of image in the mind of the potential tourist is considered to be critical in their choice of destination, albeit it is not the only factor as price and quality will also play a part. The concept of image is difficult to grasp. Image gives identity to a place. It is linked to the idea of a place product which can be suggested in the image. In this section we shall look at the general image of cities and then the image of individual cities.

Cities in general often have a negative image. There is an anti-urban bias in society. Rural areas are seen in a very positive way: quiet, peaceful, beautiful, healthy and uncrowded. In contrast, cities are perceived to be dirty, crowded and congested, ugly, noisy, unhealthy, unsafe and full of unpleasant people. They can be seen as immoral, with youths being destroyed by evils such as prostitution. They are anonymous, where people can be lonely and there is no sense of community. The city can be a battleground between groups, a veritable jungle in which it might be dangerous to be caught. These are not the characteristics that are likely to attract visitors. Against this, there is a very positive set of images; the city is seen as lively, exciting, civilized, cosmopolitan, and full of opportunities. It is in cities that culture is created and found at its highest levels. There are theatres, concerts, art galleries and a wealth of publishing. There are many opportunities to meet other people and social life can be sophisticated. The city offers many types of entertainment, sufficient to meet the needs of all tastes. The city offers many types of spectacle and as with sport there can be much excitement. Within the city there are opportunities to shop, from department stores to markets. There are also opportunities to make money and become rich. The city can also be a place of fine environments and townscapes, of grand and imposing buildings and of skyscrapers. In short, the city is rich and diverse with many attractions for the tourist. These mixed images of the city make it difficult to generalize about its appeal to tourists. The strong positive features will apppeal to many and attract them while others will be put off by its negative aspects. Differences between individuals may reflect gender and age, with a presumption often made that women and older people will be more deterred by the negative aspects of cities.

Of course, the image of the individual city may and usually will vary from the general image of the city. For some cities the positive features will outweigh the negative attributes and it will be relatively easy to attract visitors. This is likely to be those cities described above which feature regularly in the media and which have strong icons. Some cities will be known for particular attributes, fine art galleries, good shops, or great sporting spectacles, and these may attract visitors on their own. These are usually the large and capital cities where the media are based and which receive much more attention than other places (Avraham, 2000). In this sense the city may be offering a number of different products and be catering for different markets. However, many visitors may be attracted by several features, illustrating the idea that cities offer a joint product. Against these cities which have a strong positive image there are other cities which may either have a low profile or a negative image. Cities which appear in the media as industrial and where crime is always occurring are likely to find it difficult to attract visitors, unless they can change their image, a topic discussed in a later chapter.

THE DEMAND FOR BUSINESS TRAVEL

Business travellers form an important component of travellers to cities. While their share of total visitors may be only 15–20 per cent, because they are high spenders, they make a larger contribution to revenue. Included in the business traveller category are delegates to conferences and exhibitions. This topic will be dealt with more fully in a later chapter. Business people travel to make contact with other business people for a variety of reasons, for sales, to oversee lower management, to discuss business matters with professionals and experts outside their company such as bankers, accountants, lawyers, scientists, government officials as well as to attend larger meetings (conferences) and exhibitions. There are no long-term trend figures for business travel, but it is highly likely that it has been steadily increasing. One reason for this is the growth of very large companies through mergers and takeovers. From the late nineteenth century to the middle of the twentieth century this took place largely within countries, resulting in a concentration of the head offices of the large companies in capital cities. The process of globalization in the late twentieth century has created a vast increase in cross-national takeovers and mergers to form transnational corporations. Despite improvements in telecommunications there appears still to be a need for executives to travel to meet each other, and now over longer distances.

The distance and direction of business travel are very varied and can be almost over any distance and in any direction. However, it is certain that the main flows are between the major financial, business and government centres of the world. These can be defined by the number of banks headquartered in the city and the scale of financial trading, the number of major companies headquartered in the city, and the scale of business services. Much of the recent literature on world cities has been in terms of these major command and control points in the urban system and how they can be defined. Generally capital (government) cities are also major business centres although there are a few exceptions such as Washington, DC (USA) and Canberra (Australia). Some cities combine several national and supranational administrative functions and so attract more travellers, Brussels being an example. Although the business and administrative functions may appear separate, the need for the two sectors to deal with each other ensures that there is much interaction and travel between them. These major central places attract large flows of business travellers. In contrast, places lower down the urban hierarchy and with branch plant characteristics in their manufacturing and service sector economy will attract much smaller flows, far less than from the population size one might expect. The significance of these flows is more than the income and jobs which are generated. Business travellers often provide the base or core business for activities such as hotels and airline operations and leisure tourism frequently develops on the back of these resources which have already been created.

THE DEMAND FOR PERSONAL TRAVEL

The third component of travel to cities is that of personal travel which can include travel to visit friends and relatives (VFR) as well as to undertake personal business such as visiting professions such as doctors and lawyers. It would appear obvious that the flows in the VFR sector are strongly correlated to population size. A large city will attract large flows as many people will have friends and relatives there. Notwithstanding this hypothesis, it is also suggested that flows may be affected by the attractiveness of a place to visitors. If there is strong demand for leisure visits to a place, some visitors may combine seeing friends and the place. A person with a house or flat in the centre of London may find themselves very popular! With the emergence of the weekend, the possibility of short breaks, and the ease of travel, plus the scattering of friends and family as a result of having to move for work, it is highly likely that travel to friends and relatives has increased.

CONCLUSION

The demand for travel to cities has grown greatly in the second half of the twentieth century and this has arisen for all of the three main types of travel: leisure, business and personal. The demand by leisure tourists to travel to cities also has various elements from culture to entertainment, although in some cases there may be joint demand. Potential tourists have become more proactive in what they want to do in their leisure time, to use it positively to achieve their particular aims. This may vary from wanting to 'live it up', to find excitement, to visit different/strange/foreign places, to do novel things, to see the great and famous sights or develop one's special interests. All of these objectives have become possible with more leisure time, more money and easier travel, which opens up the possibilities for a new range of experiences. Some of them, such as visiting the world's cultural heritage and pursuing special interests, have become more significant in recent years and are likely to continue to become more important as the population becomes more educated. These impulses can arise quite naturally within the individual, or be created (or constructed) by the society in which they live or be stimulated by destinations and travel companies seeking to capture their spending resources. This latter topic, the supply side of tourism, is one which we shall discuss when the tourism strategies of cities are considered.

Chapter 3

The urban context

The aim of this book is to examine the role which tourism can play and might play in the economy of large cities. Within North America and Western Europe there are over 60 metropolitan areas with a population of over 1 million and probably as many again in the rest of the world. The focus here will be on those cities in the developed part of the world. It is important to understand how cities are changing and how they are responding to change, in order to place tourism in this wider context. In this chapter the changes that are taking place to cities, their relationships to each other, and the internal spatial changes, will be reviewed. The response which cities are making to this changing environment and how successful their policies have been will also be examined. Very little mention will be made of tourism in this chapter as this is the subject of the rest of the book, but an understanding of the urban context is essential if the rise of tourism in urban economies and its impact are to be evaluated.

CHANGING PATTERNS OF URBAN GROWTH

Geographers have long sought to understand the pattern of cities, why some places are important and others less so. While there have clearly been some chance factors, it is also possible to discern general forces at work. Two influences in particular can be mentioned. First, there is the importance of what is called the urban economic base. Cities grow because they are able to export goods and services and the income derived from this enables them to import materials, manufactured goods and services, sustain a high standard of living and invest in further growth. For many centuries cities depended primarily on the basis of trade, either over a short distance or over a longer distance. However, from the late eighteenth century onwards, industries evolved and developed to be of great importance in the economy of cities. It was the growth of manufacturing and associated activities in the nineteenth century and the first half of the twentieth century that caused most cities to expand, and the terms industrial city and industrial age were used. The exact character of industry varied from place to place, depending on local resources, communications and the characteristics of the population, including the skills and innovative abilities available. Thus, there were steel towns, shipbuilding towns, cotton towns, motor vehicle towns, and so on. Because the resources used by industry, both natural and human, were unevenly distributed, there was no simple geographical pattern of cities. While there was some concentration of urban growth on coalfields and other natural resource sites, industry was also found elsewhere at ports, existing large cities and new centres where innovators lived.

A second influence on the pattern of cities focuses on what is technically called 'central place theory'. As mentioned above, towns and cities developed to trade with their surrounding areas. They provided services such as retailing, which could not be justified in every village because of the small population. A regular pattern of towns developed every few kilometres to serve rural areas. However, these small market towns could not supply all the services needed and so larger towns emerged less frequently to meet the need for these 'higher order' goods and services. Most countries do (or did) exhibit an urban hierarchy, moving down from the largest city supplying a very wide range of goods and services over a very extensive area, to the lowest level of town, offering a limited range of goods and services to a small area roundabout. As the population grew in the nineteenth and twentieth centuries, this urban hierarchy both changed and was reinforced. In some regions industrial cities grew rapidly in size and moved up the urban hierarchy, overtaking or supplanting older cities as with Manchester and Chester and Leeds and York in Britain. However, many existing cities maintained their status helped by the arrival of railways which gave them increased accessibility and made possible the attraction and development of industry. This was the case in Germany and other European countries where the main wave of industrialization occurred after the creation of the railway network. Existing large cities were often the first places to receive other types of new infrastructure such as gas supply and telephones and this too helped them to attract new forms of economic development. Pred (1966) has also shown that the larger the city, the more innovative it was likely to be, as shown by the number of patents. For these reasons, by the end of the nineteenth century and the beginning of the twentieth century the urban hierarchy appeared more stable. Once a city had achieved a certain size and status in the urban hierarchy, it appeared able to maintain this role without threat from neighbouring rivals and relatively safe from the competition of cities further away because of the friction (cost) of distance. Generally, the larger the city and the higher its position in the urban hierarchy, the more diversified its economy was likely to be and this would include the importance of and the range of services provided.

Since the mid-twentieth century these truths have been changing, owing to a number of factors. First, the economic structure of cities and national economies has been evolving. Overall, manufacturing employment is far less important than it used to be. Increased mechanization and automation ensure that goods can be produced with much less labour than in the past. This increased productivity has affected the primary and secondary sectors far more than the tertiary or services sector with the consequence that a growing and majority share of employment is found in the latter. One response to this shift is to talk of a post-industrial society and the post-industrial city.

While jobs in manufacturing overall have tended to decline, there have been also shifts within the sector. Within the advanced countries older industries, such as textiles and clothing and some branches of heavy engineering, have experienced a very steep decrease in production and employment which may be a consequence of either a fall in demand for the product world-wide or a shift of production to the developing countries. The decline of industries in an area usually has knock-on effects; suppliers of components and services are also hit. At the same time certain types of chemicals and electronics industries, the so-called high technology industries which require much research and development, have been growing. The history of the period since the industrial revolution with regard to the types of manufacturing industry has been likened to a series of innovative waves throwing up new industries. According to the theory put forward by Kondratieff, these waves occur every 50–55 years. The current wave, it is suggested, involves advanced electronics and biotechnology.

Another change within industry involved occupational shifts. The structure of employment within manufacturing firms has shifted away from blue-collar shopfloor manual workers towards white-collar non-manual and professional workers. This in part reflects the increases in productivity on the factory floor discussed above. It also reflects the greater importance of activities like marketing, research and development and also corporate changes taking place involving takeovers and mergers and the creation of large firms. The different units of the manufacturing firm which once co-existed on the same site may now be located in different places, with the factory on one site, the head office somewhere else and the R&D laboratory in yet another location, all reflecting their particular locational requirements. Whereas the factories can be found in settlements of different size, head offices and R&D laboratories tend to be drawn to large cities. The changing occupational structure of the economy provides a partial explanation for the high levels of unemployment that are found in some places. When the old smokestack industries decline, they make a labour force redundant which does not have the requisite skills for jobs in the new economy, which are likely to be found within offices.

The tertiarization of the economy, or the growth of services, has not been without spatial implications. Not all services have experienced employment growth. Jobs in railways and ports have disappeared rapidly, while the location of other activities such as wholesaling has changed. For many years after World War II, the main expansion of services involved public services, especially education and health. In the last quarter of the twentieth century the rate of expansion in these sectors slowed down as governments shied away from raising taxes to pay for these services. In recent years the most notable growth of services has been in finance and business services. While education and health services are widely distributed in space according to the population, finance and business services are more concentrated.

Notwithstanding the apparent locational flexibility of many financial and business service activities, there is a tendency for the higher level functions to cluster. High-level decision-taking can be risky and face-to-face discussions with knowledgeable individuals can inspire confidence about the right course of action. Those cities with advantages for finance and business services have gained jobs at a rapid rate, although this has been tempered by some dispersal of more routine jobs to places with lower labour costs. Leisure and tourism jobs have also grown and these will be discussed later in this book.

Another factor which has affected city growth in recent years has been improvements in communications, both physical and telecommunications. This has undermined the local base of cities, enabling them to compete against each other through widening spheres of influence. Previously cities would have been protected from competition because of the cost of movement. Now companies may be able to serve distant markets using the telephone or dispatch goods from a few central warehouses rather than a large number of small ones serving each local area. With computers and telephone lines, work that was previously done locally can now be done centrally. Improvements in physical communications also enable greater locational flexibility. As a consequence, economic activities can take place over wider areas and firms have a greater choice of location. While economic factors will always be important, non-economic factors may play an increasing role in the decision of firms concerning where to locate their facilities whether it is a head office, factory or R&D laboratory. Firms may be influenced by the image of a place, the attractiveness of the physical environment and the lifestyle opportunities that would be available to its executives if it located there. The latter may include theatres, concert halls, museums and art galleries, sports, restaurants and clubs.

General trends in the distribution of population and employment within countries are also affecting cities. Two broad trends can be distinguished. First, there is the shift away from large cities towards rural areas, sometimes called 'counterurbanization' (Berry, 1976; Champion, 1989). In North America and Western Europe aggregate statistics show that the very largest cities (or conurbations) are either losing population or growing less rapidly than other types of (smaller) settlements. Surprisingly in view of the demographic history from 1850 to 1950, many remote rural areas after decades of decline, are showing growth again, often at the highest rates. Because of this reversal of roles, Berry also used the term 'the inversion of geography'. The outcome of these trends is that many large older industrial cities are experiencing population decline and stagnation. Any explanation of these trends must involve many factors and their changing significance over time. In the past, cities had many advantages over rural areas which enabled them to attract economic activities, such as good communications, public utilities, a large labour force with varied skills and a complex of industries and services which could provide external economies. In contrast, rural areas offered few of the facilities needed by industry. However, today rural areas have all the basic utilities, are often near motorways and have plenty of land for development. Living in rural areas today does not mean cutting oneself off from the benefits of civilization as it was once perceived to do. Television at least gives access to the rest of the world. Meanwhile, conditions in cities have changed. Land and labour are expensive and traffic congestion may add costs. At least for a period in Britain up to the 1970s land was often in short supply as greenbelts encircled cities. These conditions may have encouraged firms to move out of cities. For the residents, cities often appeared expensive, congested, polluted and crime-ridden, a contrast to the perception of the rural idyll to which they increasingly moved.

A second trend within countries has involved inter-regional shifts, frequently described as the shift from north to south. In the USA this is seen in the difference between the sunbelt and the frostbelt (or rustbelt). There has been a shift in the distribution of population and employment from north and east to the south and west, from the states like New York and Pennsylvania to states such as California and Texas. In Britain there has also been a shift from the north and west to the south and east. A similar shift has occurred in Germany where the southern areas of Bavaria and Baden-Württemberg have gained, while in France the southern areas have again experienced high rates of growth. Superficially all these shifts appear to suggest the importance of environmental factors in determining where people live and work.

At least two conclusions can be drawn from the above analysis. First, economic activities are much more locationally footloose than they were in the past and as a consequence firms have a greater choice of locations. Cities have to be competitive to retain firms and to attract new activities. Today they are not just competing with cities and towns 'down the road' but with cities around the world. Globalization means that many firms operate at the world level in competition with other global firms. To be competitive cities have to offer a high all-round quality environment, involving not just the traditional economic factors such as infrastructure, land and property, skilled labour, etc. but also a good quality environment and lifestyle for the executives. To be able to attract firms, cities need a good image, which suggests that it would be a suitable place for both the company and its executives. Given the wide choice which firms have and the lack of time to examine all possibilities, it is likely that firms only consider those place which have a good image. Those cities with either low visibility or a poor image will not even be considered.

A second conclusion is that there is a great variety in the experience of cities in the developed world. The worst affected have been the older industrial cities in the 'northern' parts of their countries, cities such as Glasgow, Liverpool and Manchester in Britain, of Cleveland, Detroit and Pittsburgh in the United States and the cities of the Ruhr in Germany. These cities are sometimes described as 'spent' or 'struggling' cities. Their urban areas have been severely affected by deindustrialization whether this is the decline of output or employment resulting in high long-term unemployment and accompanied by serious social problems. New jobs in the service sector have been on an insufficient scale to mop up the unemployment and in any case, as mentioned above, the unemployed are unlikely to have the skills for these new jobs. Industrialization and deindustrialization have left behind poor environments which reinforce the bad image many of these cities have and make it more difficult to attract new economic activities. Outmigration to rural or less urbanized areas is also affecting these cities. Turning these cities round, reinventing themselves is inevitably a difficult task, made harder in a globalizing world where competition is so intense. A second type of cities is found in the 'southern' parts of their countries. It would include cities such as Bristol, Munich, Barcelona and San Francisco. These places have suffered less from deindustrialization than the first group and they probably had an economic structure that was more predisposed towards growth. Their main advantages have been a location in the 'right' part of the country coupled with a relatively favourable image which has enabled them to attract new economic activities. A third group of cities are referred to as 'world cities' and include places such as London, New York and Tokyo. These cities have benefited from the structural changes in the economy and have been the beneficiaries of globalization, attracting business from an increasingly interconnected world. This of course is particularly apparent in the areas of finance and business services. The three cities mentioned are the most important ones dealing in currencies and derivatives as well as stocks and shares and also as the location for head offices. There are perhaps another dozen cities which can claim to have the attributes of a 'world city' (see Beaverstock *et al.*, 1999). These other cities are seeking to join the top three and possibly displace one of them.

There is no doubt that cities are affected by global economic forces but questions can be asked as to what extent their future is immutably determined by these forces and to what extent policies developed locally can have real consequences for cities (Schimmel,

1995). Advocates of the structuralist position argue that the local state can have little impact on global flows of businesses, while those arguing for the importance of agency point to examples where local politics have made a real difference to the economic fortunes of a city.

INTRA-URBAN PATTERNS

The post-war period has also witnessed significant changes in the internal geography of cities. From being relatively compact and monocentric (i.e. focused on the city centre) cities have decentralized and become polycentric with consequences for the core areas. Cities have always been focused on the city centre and the coming of the railways reinforced this tendency. They gave the city centre great nodality both for people and goods, and as a consequence cities were often structured around this core of accessibility. Shops selling comparison goods and offices which needed to draw in people from a wider area, and which could outbid other land uses in paying higher rents, came to dominate the city centre. Around them were found warehouses and manufacturing industry which needed to be near the railway goods yards from where goods were dispatched by horse and cart. Further out were the residential areas, with the poor living near the centre in high densities to be near their work, while the rich lived on the periphery in larger houses and gardens and were able to afford to travel back to the centre. Of course, cities did not show an exact concentric pattern or complete segregation of land uses. Without planning the mixing up of land uses was inevitable and the physical geography of cities meant that transport and industry were often pulled towards particular areas such as river valleys.

During the twentieth century there was an increasing trend towards decentralization, made possible by easier transport and in particular the use of motor vehicles. This allowed cities to sprawl outwards. Initially the predominant form of decentralization was of people, thus introducing a longer pattern of commuting back to the core area. Later as jobs decentralized, some people moved out to be near their work. But at the same time journey to work patterns became more complex, with movements from suburb to core, core to suburb and suburb to suburb. Many expanding industries found that their central city sites were too constricted with no room for expansion and thus looked for sites on the periphery. Similar trends affected warehouses, where the change from vertical to horizontal buildings and the congested inner city streets encouraged firms to relocate to sites in the periphery and particularly near motorways. For a long time office-based activities appeared to prefer to remain in the centre, where there was good accessibility, the possibility of face-to-face contact with firms in ancillary businesses and external economies, but the high rents, the difficulty of recruiting staff and sometimes the need or the wish to use the car regularly have now persuaded many firms of the benefits of the suburbs. Finally, there has been the decentralization of retailing. As the population increased in the suburbs, shopping centres evolved to meet their needs. Initially these sold convenience goods but as the population grew so the range of goods offered widened until it was not necessary for the suburbanites to return to the city centre to shop.

The social patterning of cities is also important in understanding the 'inner city' problem. The more modern and spacious housing of the suburbs has inevitably drawn the higher income and family groups to these areas, leaving the poorer housing stock of the inner city to the less affluent. Here a cycle of deterioration has often occurred as low returns on investment discouraged landlords from undertaking repairs so that the standards of the housing declined even further. In Britain slum clearance led to some of these houses being replaced by social housing, which increasingly has become the housing of the poor. Falling household size and lower density housing have ensured that the population of the inner city has fallen considerably from its peak at the beginning of the twentieth century. In general, inner city areas are occupied by the poor, but one counter-trend has been 'gentrification', with a few middle-class households moving back to these areas. The areas of gentrification are generally fairly limited and discrete and may involve the conversion of warehouses to flats, the upgrading of edge of city centre old housing areas with character and new build on derelict sites including old docklands. The type of households moving back are usually those without children, either young adults or 'empty nesters' (older people whose children have left home), some who work in the city centre and wish to avoid the commute from the suburb, some who want to enjoy the lifestyle opportunities of the city centre of the theatre, concerts, clubs or eating and drinking. In some cities the gay community is well represented.

Most large cities have some problems in their core areas, although the scale, nature and intensity vary considerably. In the city centre, retailing faces competition from suburban and out-of-town shopping centres, and it also suffers from the population decline in the surrounding inner city which was a captive market. As a consequence of these circumstances, trade in the city centre has often declined and in some cases seriously so. This is particularly the case in many North American cities where some traditional downtown shopping districts have almost disappeared. In most city centres office activities remain important and may have grown significantly, although in most cities they face competition from suburban complexes. The wholesaling and manu-facturing functions on the fringe of the city centre have generally declined significantly, together with transport and public utilities. This has often resulted in derelict building and vacant land being left behind. What was once expensive land has now become much cheaper, although the owners are not always ready to accept this and keep the land underused while they hold out for an unrealistic high price. For several years in many city centres one of the main challenges for planning was to find new uses for these redundant fringe areas.

In the surrounding inner city areas there are similar problems. Industry and ware-housing have declined. Many firms have gone out of business, others have relocated to the suburbs, while others which were parts of large organizations have been closed as part of a rationalization process. There are now sites for industry but these are not always perceived favourably as skilled workers no longer live locally and there may be problems of crime and vandalism. As regards housing, there may be a mix of old housing sometimes in need of renovation and modern housing, such as high rise flats, which are deteriorating rapidly and forming zones where there are often severe social problems. In a situation of low overall demand, some of these areas are being deserted as those with the resources or the ability to move leave them for 'better' areas, with the result that there is housing abandonment in some parts of the inner city. Investment in private sector housing is difficult to obtain but may be possible in a few zones where land has been cleared and a new start is being made and the location is favourable such as a waterfront area or one with proximity to the city centre.

There is no one universal model of decay of inner cities just as there is no one cure for it. In general, it could be argued that decline in the inner city is greatest in the USA, less so in Britain and least in continental Europe, but within each of these regions there is considerable variation. Detroit does provide the example of the (ringed) doughnut city where the city centre has virtually closed down particularly as regards retailing, but there are many US cities such as Boston where the downtown area is still vibrant. In continental Europe the city centre has remained successful for several reasons. It has historic buildings and associations which attract people. The wealthy and affluent still live in central area apartments and have never moved away as they have done in North America and Britain. The city centre and the whole urban area continue to be served by a regular and efficient public transport system. Good shops and cultural activities continue to thrive in the city centre. Notably there is lively social life. People delight to come to the area to eat and drink often sitting outside in the open air, which creates the appearance of an animated city life. This pavement culture has become the envy of many British cities, and the objective of 'becoming a European city' often involves the idea of having a similar lively street scene.

So far this section has emphasized the problems facing the core areas of cities, but the news is not all bad. Mention has already been made of a movement to move back to live in the city centre. Another activity in the core which has grown is higher education. Many institutions were founded in this zone many decades ago and have remained on or close to their original sites. A few have relocated to the suburbs to find more and cheaper space. The great expansion of higher education in the last quarter of the twentieth century has seen relatively small institutions with a few thousand students expand to have more than 20,000. Not only do the students study in or close to the city centre but they also live close by, often in university-owned accommodation. Given the existence of more than one university in or close to the city centre, the residential student population of the core area can easily reach 50,000 or more. The impact of the spending power of such a group on the leisure functions of the city centre can be considerable, affecting bars, clubs and cinemas. Students may also find employment in these facilities.

The combination of problems in these core areas, dereliction, low investment, poverty and unemployment, plus the desire of cities to revitalize their city centres to present a good face to the ouside world, has meant that these areas have become the focus of public policy since the late 1960s. The occasional riot has kept these zones in the news and reinforced the policy emphasis. In the USA central cities were the recipients of several types of federal grants and urban development action grants in the 1970s and 1980s, including community block grants and urban development grants. In Britain a strong inner city policy has existed since 1978 and has included enterprise zones, city grants, urban development corporations and task forces. Inner city areas are often the potential recipients of grants from other tiers of government from the level of the region to the supranational, such as the European Union.

POLICY APPROACHES

Urban policies to deal with these issues have been evolving since the 1960s. They have been developed to deal with the economic and social problems which cities face, whether these are competing for economic growth in an increasingly globalizing world or dealing with the problems of the core which have arisen either from the effects of economic restructuring due to globalization or from the processes of decentralization operating within urban areas. As some of these problems first emerged in the United States, it is not surprising that many policies were first developed here and have been copied in countries such as Britain. However, cities are looking for inspiration in urban policy and creativity and there is no simple answer. Urban success stories, such as the impact of the Guggenheim Museum in Bilbao, Spain, quickly become news and are copied elsewhere. Of course every city faces a slightly different set of problems with a slightly different set of advantages and disadvantages and must put together a package of measures that will achieve the most for the particular city. In the section below the general ideas and approaches which have shaped urban policies in many cities will be discussed.

Entrepreneurial Cities and the Emphasis on Economic Policies

Commentators on the history and politics of urban policy have suggested that the approach of city governments is often dominated by a particular viewpoint as to what are the major issues and priorities, and how they should be tackled. From among competing claims a coalition of interests emerges (Stoker, 1995). From time to time this viewpoint will change and it is suggested that city policy will pass from one 'regime' to another. The reasons for the change of regime will almost certainly reflect the external environment, but internal politics, the rise and fall of individuals and groups, may affect the timing of the change of regime. In times of steady economic growth and when there are perceived to be few major problems, city governments tend to focus on welfare and managerial issues, that is ensuring that services such as education are well organized and provide quality. In recent years the rise of economic problems, discussed above has forced a change of 'regime'. The continued existence of cities, particularly the central city, that is the administrative unit covering the core area, has been under threat, and without new jobs the city will die. This has caused a shift of emphasis away from social policies to economic ones. The general approach adopted by many urban governments has been described as entrepreneurial (Harvey, 1989; Hall and Hubbard, 1996, 1998). The entrepreneurial city is pro-active, opportunistic, pragmatic, initiatory, innovative, speculative and competitive. Many examples of this approach will be given in the rest of this book as it is very pertinent to any understanding of developments in tourism, here just the general features will be described. It is possible to argue that there is a long history of entrepreneurial cities. In the United States this is associated with the idea of 'boosterism'. Cities like Atlanta have been competing to attract economic growth almost from the time they were established, their first initiative being to attract the new railway lines. In Britain the industrial cities of the nineteenth century competed with one another when they built new town halls, organized large exhibitions and opened their new museums and art galleries. These were all statements of how important they thought they were and this was also expressed in the architecure. At the end of the century cities again showed their entrepreneurialism when they took over gas companies and tramways, and established new elecricity supply companies, all so that the city functioned smoothly and could attract new investment. Later on, they were to lay out suburban industrial estates so that firms from inner city areas could relocate, but also so that new firms would be attracted to the city. In Britain after World War II many functions were removed from local authorities, such as gas , electricity, water and health and put into national (and nationalized) corporations. In the immediate aftermath of the war, unemployment was low and the main problems concerned housing and schools so that economic issues appeared less important. As the Labour Party gained control of many cities, other ideological issues, such as equal opportunities, became a dominating concern. However, from the late 1970s and particularly from the early 1980s on, unemployment rose and it was only a matter of time before local politicians were forced to return to economic issues and adopt approaches which they previously considered to be anathma. In Britain this coincided with the third election victory of the Conservative Party under Mrs Thatcher. Henceforward the local authorities would emphasize economic success including the success in obtaining private investment. Hitherto, they had been very much concerned with public investment, in schools, housing, etc. but to attract private investment they would need a different approach more akin to that found in the private sector and that might only be obtained by working more closely with that sector.

Public–private Partnership

The concept of public–private partnerships was one that was pioneered in the United States in the early post-war period and has been borrowed by public bodies in Britain and elsewhere. One of the earliest examples was the American city of Pittsburgh which, typically, was a city suffering from the effects of the decline of its basic industry, steel. In 1947 the Democratic Mayor and Party met the leading businessmen including the Mellon banking family, to plan the renewal of the city and in particular the downtown area, the Golden Triangle. The success of this first Pittsburgh 'renaissance' was an inspiration for other cities.

Public–private partnerships can take many forms. Joint committees of the city council and representatives from the private sector can develop strategies for the whole city or small parts of it which the public sector undertakes. Sometimes when the public sector has improved the infrastructure and purchased land to allow suitable sized holdings to be created, there is a commitment on behalf of the private sector to buy and develop the land. At other times it is merely putting the land up for sale and leaving the private sector to develop it. In some cases public–private partnerships involve joint companies, with a shareholding from the city council and, say, the Chamber of Commerce. Such companies may organize the redevelopment of an area, be concerned with the promotion of the city to attract inward investment or, of relevance to this book, be concerned with the promotion of the city to tourists. Joint companies may also run particular facilities as is the case of the National Exhibition Centre in Birmingham, or organize special events such as the Olympic Games. In Britain in recent years joint companies have been established to manage the city centre, particularly the shopping and tourist zones, where ensuring that the environment is attractive is extremely important in attracting people to these areas.

Public–private partnerships have been very important in the United States where they have often been referred to as 'growth coalitions', a phrase which indicates their purpose. One of the reasons for their success has been the importance of locally based businesses which have a very real interest in the success of the city region economy. These firms may be in utilities, banking or property development. In the United States until recently, many of these firms were unable to become national firms so they depended to a very large extent on the local economy. Other companies, such as multinational manufacturing firms, still had a loyalty to the city where they were originally established and where their headquarters were located. Unlike many other countries, in the United States major company headquarters are not as nearly concentrated spatially so that most large cities have at least a few major firms based there. Consequently, there is often a large group of firms wanting the local city to be successful, willing to be involved in local public–private partnerships, and willing to invest in order for this success to be achieved.

In Britain and in some other European countries the situation is very different. The public utilities, as mentioned above, have been brought under national control, although the privatization of water and electricity in the 1980s did to a certain extent return some control to the regions. In Britain most local banks disappeared at the beginning of the twentieth century with the emergence of a national banking system. Similarly, other activities such as retailing also operate through national companies that have little interest in local economies. If trade shifts from one area to another, they will pick it up through other branches. Accordingly, the local business community with a real interest in city growth is limited. One sector where this does not apply is construction. For their business, which often has a limited geographical basis, they want to see investment taking place and therefore are willing to participate in joint committees. This also gives them the advantage of knowledge about what contracts are likely to come up. The structure of the tourist industry is slightly different and the implications for public–private partnerships will be discussed in the next chapter. Some commentators have therefore suggested that this has meant the city authorities are more dominant in Britain and that there is weak private sector involvement (Boyle and Hughes, 1994).

The operation of public–private partnerships has been the subject of much scrutiny and critical commentary by academic writers. The private sector clearly has an agenda which may be either general, in wanting to encourage growth, or specific in regard to particular schemes which would benefit individual firms or industries. The composition of the private sector to the partnership may influence the proposals which are forthcoming. It is highly probable that its ideas for growth will require greater public sector investment. This is likely, if accepted, to change and shift public sector spending priorities away from welfare budget headings towards capital expenditure. In Birmingham it is alleged that the funding of the International Convention Centre resulted in the underfunding, as determined by national government criteria, of education. Leaving aside the merits or otherwise of any individual decision, it can be argued that the private sector can, through partnerships, exert an undue influence on the allocation of public resources and undermine the democratic character of local government. Evidence for this statement from Birmingham and Indianapolis will be discussed in later chapters.

Assessment of the exact influence that the private sector has on decisions made in these partnerships will always be difficult to evaluate. What contribution can a businessman knowledgeable about one sector of the economy make to the running of a complex city economy? Do they have any grand vision for the direction of the city? Work by Peck and Tickell (1995) on Manchester would suggest that the business community does not have any grand design and that they can easily be infatuated by grand or 'big ticket' projects which are put before them (see also Schimmel, 1995). These projects are relatively easy to comprehend while more sophisticated analyses and detailed proposals for the city are not.

Re-imaging and Selling the City

The mobility of capital and the wide choice of locations offered to firms have already been discussed above. While the actual resources of a place are important, whether they are its infrastructure, economic factors or lifestyle opportunities for the executives, they are useless unless a firm can be persuaded to look at a place. With a wide choice of locations executives are often influenced by the visibility which a place has and then by its image. Cities may have either a positive image, a weak image, a negative image or a contradictory image (Kotler *et al.*, 1993). Many older industrial cities have a poor image, or an image problem, usually based at best on out-of-date perceptions (Holcombe, 1993). In the case of cities such as Liverpool, historical images can overshadow present reality (Madsen, 1992). Images of old factories, polluted skies, dirty blackened buildings and century-old terrace housing do not encourage firms or make people want to move to (or even visit) that place. Potential investors need to have confidence that the area is moving forward. Not surprisingly, then, the re-imaging of cities is often high on the agenda of local governments, public–private partnerships and development agencies. Surveys are undertaken of the image held by businessmen in other places, with a view to understanding more clearly both the negative and positive perceptions. Frequently marketing companies are set up to sell the city and, as will be discussed in the next chapter, these are often linked to the selling of the city to tourists. Place marketing is concerned to construct a new image to replace either vague or negative images previously held. According to Gold and Ward (1994), it is 'the conscious use of publicity and marketing to communicate selective images of specific geographical locations or areas to target audiences'. It also involves the hyping of success stories and the creation of place myths (Goodwin, 1993). According to Watson (1991), 'Places have always been as much about myth as they have been about reality, but this is particularly so when they are for sale.'

Selling a city is fraught with difficulties. Unfortunately the media have a habit of recycling old images so that cities have a problem trying to escape from their stereotype (Avraham, 2000). A good selling job can be done, but then the media may be full of bad news about the city, an example being drug wars in the inner city, and all the old stereotypes are rehashed again. There can be no such thing as news management for a city. The traditional method of trying to change the image of the city is through newspaper and television advertising, using photographs, place logos, slogans and lists of positive facts (Ward, 1998). Photographs can encapsulate the favourable parts of the city and in addition a slogan can be coined. In the case of old industrial cities, these often attempt to convey ideas which can replace the old images. So the city is changing, it has experienced a renaissance, a rebirth, it is the comeback city. Slogans are also a way of place positioning by suggesting success and importance; it's an international,

European, capital city, etc. Slogans are difficult to formulate, particularly now when so many cities are playing the same game in what is sometimes referred to as 'place wars' (Haider, 1992). Because the same ideas and the same words are constantly being used, there is a tendency for all cities to become similar (Griffiths, 1998). A slogan should be memorable and distinctive so that it can easily be associated with a place. It should not raise expectations too far so that the reality is too different from that offered. An important point to note is the target market of the advertisment and slogans. Given the widely varying markets from businessmen to tourist, and, within the latter, several types, it may be difficult to find one slogan that fits all. However, multiple marketing may lose overall impact. This question of selling the city will be discussed again in the next chapter in connection with tourism. Slogans are also aimed at local people as much as outsiders. They attempt to show locals that change is taking place and that they should be part of that process. However, in some cases the new identity connoted by the image is contested (McInroy and Boyle, 1996).

In recent years it has been realized that two of the most important ways a place can change its image is through special events and the construction of landmark buildings, both topics which have great relevance to urban tourism. Mega-events like the Olympic Games place a city before the world and enable it to sell its favourable features and, as a result, raise its visibility and change its image. Two cities which have benefited from this process have been Barcelona and Glasgow. Barcelona hosted the Olympic Games in 1992 and drew attention to itself as a place that was good for both business and the tourist. As seen in Chapter 1, as a result it has become one of Europe's leading tourist cities. In 1988 Glasgow hosted a Garden Festival and in 1990 it was European City of Culture. Both events raised the visibility of the city and briefly uplifted tourism. However, the main impact was probably on the image which was transformed. Previously perceived as an industrial and working-class city the events showcased the cultural resources of the city and this has made it attractive to firms seeking locations for branches. Given these experiences it is not surprising that the entrepreneurial city is pro-active in seeking to capture mobile special events as it is in developing its own special events.

Architecture has always been symbolic as well as solely functional. It has the power to mediate perceptions of urban change and to mobilize images of vitality (Crilley, 1993). As mentioned above, the grand town halls built in the nineteenth century were meant to be visual statements about the cities where they were built. This is done through the general style, often classical, and the extent of ornamentation. In the middle of the twentieth century architecture appeared to lose some of this symbolic significance. Buildings in 'modern' style appeared less able to carry these symbolic meanings and the post-war austerity meant that there was little money available to spend in this way, even if the city wanted to. All this has changed in the late twentieth century, no doubt for a variety of reasons. There is more money for landmark buildings in both the public and private sectors. Architects have emerged who both want to and are capable of designing these landmark buildings, which in some cases are the 'architecture of fantasy' (Hannigan, 1998). But in particular it can be noted that cities want to have a building (or buildings) that are easily recognizable, will give identity to a place and thus will establish an image for that city. This has long been true; witness Paris and the Eiffel Tower. Such buildings have been described as iconic. There are many cities which have demonstrated this idea in recent years from Sydney's Opera

House (adding to its well-known bridge) and St Louis' Gateway Arch. However, the media impact of the 1997 opening of the Guggenheim Museum in Bilbao, Spain, designed by Frank Gehry has added power to this idea and every new landmark building opened subsequently will be judged by this standard. The 'Guggenheim' has put a relatively unknown Spanish city before the world and transformed its tourist industry. Not surprisingly, the entrepreneurial city is seeking to emulate this example.

Semi-autonomous Regeneration Agencies

A frequent criticism of municipal authorities is that they are slow, bureaucratic, frightened of taking risks with the taxpayers' money and not sufficiently market orientated. Earlier projects to regenerate small areas of the inner city involving the demolition and clearance of old properties were undertaken with the aim of redeveloping the zones for publicly owned properties, notably social housing. The situation has changed and the proposed regenerated areas which will not necessarily involve demolition and clearance, are designed to attract private investment. To avoid the perceived weaknesses of local government semi-autonomous agencies or agencies at arm's length from local authorities have been established in many cities. In the USA many cities have set up these agencies, provided them with land obtained by compulsory purchase and also with the necessary finance, after which they have functioned as a private development company. There are numerous examples of this, but one of the best known is Baltimore's Charles Center Inner Harbor company which had a dramatic and succesful effect in redeveloping part of the city centre and the decaying harbour around which the city had originally been built. In Britain the 1979 Conservative government established the principle that urban development corporations (UDCs) could be established to regenerate inner city areas and initially two were established in the London and Merseyside docklands. Later UDCs of varying size were established in many British cities (Imrie and Thomas, 1999). They incurred the disapproval of the local authorites as they were not under their control and initially at least they appeared unresponsive to the needs of the local population. This was a consequence of the narrow brief given to them which was to regenerate the land within their boundaries and attract private investment. More recently the 1997 Labour government has allowed local authorities to establish regeneration companies, one example being East Manchester.

Leveraging Private Sector Investment

The role of the local authorities and semi-autonomous agencies in the regeneration of inner city areas is to create an environment such that the private sector will want to return to and invest in the zone. There are many reasons why there has been a lack of private sector investment. Redeveloping old areas (called brownfield sites) is usually more expensive than building on greenfield sites. The ownership of the land may be fragmented and unsuitable for the type of development that would be economic. The general infrastructure of the area may be inadequate, a consequence of its age. All these problems may need to be solved before there is any chance of private investment returning. Even then, the lack of confidence in the area may deter would-be investors.

To overcome this problem incentives may have to be given, whether grants or tax abatement. Most agencies responsible for these regeneration zones have some means like this to leverage private investment. Where the agency has not prepared the land, then the grant represents the cost of brownfield development. Nearly always the grants are for property development whether the building erected will be used for business or residential purposes. The lack of any link with employment has been criticized because these areas usually suffer from high unemployment. This property-led regeneration appears to ignore the social needs of the local areas.

City Centre Focus

Although the city centre is only a small part of the inner city, and generally being lightly populated has few social problems, it has tended to receive most of the investment for regeneration, from both public and private sectors. This situation has arisen because this is the zone where private investment is likely to earn its highest return, and perhaps the only place where it will be profitable. The city centre still usually has good accessibility by public transport, although this needs modernizing and improving. It will have offices and shops, plus many other facilities from museums to nightclubs. These provide an economic base which can be expanded. In contrast, the inner city areas may have extensive tracts of poor quality residential areas containing low income groups, where there is the prospect of low return on investment. From a strategic perspective the role of the city centre in the economic life of the urban area is crucial. The city centre usually represents the city to the outside world. A dynamic downtown area will give a good image to visitors and a dowdy decaying zone will do the reverse. If the city centre can be made to grow, this will impact on the surrounding inner city. Residents of this area will be able to find jobs and obtain good services, and people will be attracted to live here because of its proximity to the centre. Planning to improve the city centre is therefore very important and will involve upgrading the environment using landscape architecture. Landmark buildings alone will not be enough, they will need to be set within an impressive urbanscape. Urban design is not a new idea, it has been used for centuries, notably in capital cities. But it is having a renaissance as cities compete against each other to attract investment, jobs and visitors. The components of such urban design are clearly subjective, but might involve fine buildings and streets, impressive vistas, open spaces, public art and pedestrian zones.

Flagship Projects and Public Sector Anchors

A flagship project is a large scheme that will attract attention by its scale and architecture and provide a good basis for the regeneration of a zone by attracting further investment in the sites round about. This may be because the perception of the standing of the area has been improved, and the flagship will have boosted confidence in the future of the area. It may be also because the function of the flagship attracts allied or linked activities. Thus a convention centre will stimulate hotel development. This example is an illustration of the fact that many flagship projects fall within the leisure and tourism sector and as such will be discussed later in this book. Other examples include theatres, museums and art galleries, arenas, concert halls, sports stadiums and shopping centres. Many of these facilities are part of the public sector or part of the non-profit-making sector which often depends on grants from the public sector. It is noticeable therefore that many of the flagship projects in the regeneration zones on the edge of the city centre or in the inner city are in fact publicly funded. In the United States these are often referred to as 'public sector anchors'. In Baltimore there are three public sector anchors around the Inner Harbor, an aquarium, a science museum and a convention centre, while the fourth, the Harborplace festival market, received a large subsidy.

Pro-active Competition for Funds and Events

City governments must now compete for public and private investment and events in a much more pro-active way than they have done in the past. It is not a case of simply advertising a piece of land and hoping that a developer will come along and bid for it. Rather, it is a case of seeking out developers who have a good track record and perhaps of doing the kind of thing that the city wants to do, and persuading them to take an interest in the site. Similarly, for public sector funding which may not automatically come to the city. Central governments and supranational bodies like the European Union have funds which can be bid for in competition with other places. The National Lottery in Britain is another source of funding which requires a pro-active approach. There may also be private or individual donors who are willing to give to projects such as a museum or theatre and these must be found and courted. As will be discussed in a later chapter, some of the larger museums and art galleries are seeking to open branches and are looking for a suitable location and perhaps some assistance with funding. The pro-active city will be on the look-out for such opportunities and quick to make a bid. Finally, there are special events which move from place to place and can be bid for, the most notable example being the Olympic Games. Such events bring opportunities for publicity, possibly profit and almost certainly assistance from national governments. The pro-active city will be therefore looking for such opportunities. Special events will be considered later in this book.

Types of Economic Activity

The changing economy of the city core has been discussed above and it was observed that certain activities such as manufacturing, wholesaling and transport had experienced severe employment decline and that it was unlikely that they would thrive in this zone again. What kind of activities then can be developed in this area to revive its fortunes? The two mainstays of the city centre have been retailing and offices, both of which have been subject to the forces of decentralization with competition between the downtown district and the suburbs. In each case the city centre has held on to aspects of these activities where it was perceived to have a comparative advantage. Thus, professions such as law, accountancy, finance and chartered surveyors and certain business services have tended to stay in the central business district. Factors such as prestige, accessibility and the need for face-to-face contacts are believed to be the reasons for this. In so far as these activities have grown, then the economy of the city centre has thrived, as the examples of the world cities show. However, in other cities declining regional economies and the shift of company headquarters to higher order cities have weakened this sector. City centre retailing has often survived by becoming more specialized, more concerned with speciality goods, luxury goods and other types of comparison goods. Shopping for these types of goods is often described as leisure shopping. Cities will obviously encourage these two sectors but there may be limits to their expansion potential. What other sectors are likely to expand and have potential in the city centre?

The leisure sector, which includes tourism, is an obvious candidate which an entrepreneurial city will seek to encourage. The city centre has always been important for leisure facilities whether they are theatres, cinemas, concert halls, clubs, pubs or restaurants. There has been some decentralization of these facilities in recent years as witnessed by the closure of city centre cinemas followed by the emergence of new multiplex cinemas in the suburbs. There was also a closure of some pubs as the inner city population declined.

The recent expansion of leisure activities generally and in the city centre in particular reflects various trends in society. Greater affluence enables people to spend more on leisure, to move from home-based activities such as watching television and also away from activities provided by voluntary community groups. Commercial firms have moved in to take advantage of the new opportunities whether they are eating out or health clubs. Demographically two groups can be identified. The young adult group, discussed in the last chapter, with their increased spending power, are visiting bars and clubs, while the empty nesters are visiting restaurants, theatres and concert halls. The city centre is able to take advantage of these trends, although it is by no means the only part of the city to do so. It is accessible from all parts of the urban area and region with a relatively good public transport, a key factor for those who do not want to drink and drive. It offers a very wide range of opportunities; for example, a variety of types of restaurant. The recent move back by people to live in the city centre has increased the local market and there is a symbiotic relationship here as the more people choose to live here, the more the range of leisure opportunities increases and this will attract more people to live in the zone. The relationship between these leisure resources which are primarily conceived for local people and their use by tourists is one that will be explored later in this book.

Many city councils have been surprised by the spontaneous expansion of leisure facilities in the city centre and the emergence of leisure-led regeneration. Very quickly these trends have been taken on board and policies to further encourage leisure activities have been developed. As David Harvey wrote in 1989, 'cities that once sold themselves as places of production are now selling themselves as places of consumption'.

As these trends have evolved, the concepts of the evening economy and the 24-hour city have been developed (Bianchini, 1994, 1995; Lovatt and O'Connor, 1995; Montgomery, 1994, 1995a). Until recently planners and policy makers in Britain focused very much on the 9 to 5 (or 6) economy, catering for those activities which operated in this time and dealing with any resulting problems such as the rush hour. City centres could become very quiet after 6 o'clock and the business parts of the district were almost dead. While there were always some evening activities, they were not considered important or contributing to the 'basic' economy. With the expansion of leisure activities in the evening, it is clear that there are many jobs in this part of the economy, although it is not clear how many are full-time and whether some posts are held by people with 'daytime' jobs. As mentioned above, cities are keen to promote the city centre as a lively place, just as many European cities are perceived to be. Here activities do not stop at 11 o'clock, as they used to in Britain under the drink licensing laws, but continue well into the night. The campaigns for a 24-hour city have partly come from pub, bar and club owners with a vested interest in expanding, but they have later been supported by city councils with a view to regenerating the city centre and drawing in customers (tourists?) from an ever wider area. In the case of cities such as Manchester, it is reported that on Friday and Saturday evenings there are over 80,000 people in the city centre, nearly as many as those who work there in the daytime (Law, 2000). These policies are not without potential conflicts: noise affecting the burgeoning resident population and fears for safety (Bromley *et al.*, 2000; Heath and Strickland, 1997; Thomas and Bromley, 2000).

CRITICISMS OF THE ENTREPRENEURIAL CITY

The re-emergence of the entrepreneurial city in the past twenty years of the twentieth century has resulted in a number of critiques concerning the impact and effectiveness of the policy. The emphasis on property development has already been mentioned. The levers of regeneration policy are nearly always concerned with the use of land, getting under-used land back into use, reclaiming brownfield sites, giving grants to achieve these objctives. Of course, it is hoped that new buildings will provide employment (when not residential), but there is no relationship between the scale of investment in a site and the number of jobs created or any certainty about the type of employment created and whether it will be suitable for local people. There is a distinct lack of opportunity to target investment to achieve wider goals. Many of the jobs created in office blocks in renovated docklands are for highly skilled people, and there are likely to be few living locally in the adjacent inner city area. If redevelopments result in some of the employees coming to live locally, the consequences of redevelopment could be a change in the social composition of the area and former inhabitants being excluded.

Entrepreneurial cities are market-led. Of course, the growth of cities has always reflected economic trends and market forces, but the entrepreneurial city is throwing itself more on these forces and this may have particular consequences. Property development will follow market forces very closely. Economic cycles are exaggerated in property development cycles. When the economy is expanding, property developers gain confidence to invest and there can be a boom period. When the economy goes into recession, many new buildings are left empty and until these are filled and confidence returns, there will be very little property investment. Property-led urban regeneration can therefore be stalled and the city's hopes for revival dashed. The type of development will also reflect market forces, for a few years offices or shops and now residential and leisure. Such fashions may not reflect the long-term needs and aspirations of a city. To be too market-led makes it difficult to formulate grand strategic visions and follow them through over a number of years. The entrepreneurial city will quickly be blown off course by market influences.

The entrepreneurial city, as has been suggested above, places most emphasis on economic development and less on traditional welfare issues and programmes. There is a danger that there will be a displacement of funds from welfare to economic policies and that there will underfunding of basic services.

The entrepreneurial city has to speculate in order to have the opportunity to win investment and other benefits. Such speculation always has a cost. Just to bid for the Olympic Games as Manchester did in 1993 may cost several million pounds. While it could be argued that in this case the government gave grants for facilities to support the bid which would not have happened otherwise, there were still costs to the people of Manchester, which might have impacted on other sevices. Hosting a special event is also speculative as the example of the New Millennium Experience at the Dome in Greenwich illustrates. Costs must be covered but if the number of visitors is less than predicted, revenue will be less than the costs and there will be a loss. For cities this again could impact on the provision of basic services.

In the end, development is a zero-sum game. Entrepreneurialism takes place within the context of inter-city competition (Wood, 1998). There is only so much growth to be distributed, just as there are only a certain number of tourists to be distributed among cities. With competition there will be winners and losers. All competitors cannot be winners. Within the capitalist system there is always a tendency towards uneven development, with certain organizations and places which have the most advantages taking the lion's share. All cities may compete but many will not be successful and their speculated investment will be lost. There is no easy answer to this problem, particularly as inter-regional planning has been reduced in recent years. Governments may give greater grants to the more needy areas to help them compete, but few today are prepared to operate controls to restrict development in some areas and switch it elsewhere to prevent the losers doing too badly. In an era of globalization this intense competition between cities will continue. Cities have no choice but to compete, but for some the chances of achieving great success are limited. It is a long-term game and only a few cities may be lucky enough to find the winning number.

Case Study: Baltimore

The container revolution of the 1960s and 1970s transformed the ports of the world. New container ports developed downstream, leaving the old port areas, often near the city centre, redundant. This created the opportunity to reconnect the waterfront zones with the downtown areas (Hoyle *et al.*, 1988). These reclaimed areas became the test-beds for ideas about regeneration, from the use of special agencies, the creation of spectacular cityscapes, the roles of public and private investment, gentrifying inner city areas and, particularly relevant to this book, the use of leisure and tourism in the emerging economy. Baltimore was one of the first cities to successfully regenerate its waterfront and as a consequence became an examplar to the rest of the world (Lyall, 1982; Berkowitz, 1984).

The city of Baltimore lies on the north-east coast of the USA between Philadelphia and Washington, DC. It was founded as a port in 1729 around what is now known as the Inner Harbor, and for most of its history its economy has been dominated by the port and associated industry. Because of this industrial character it was never regarded as a tourist destination, a city to be avoided rather than visited. Like other American cities, the downtown area suffered from the effects of decentralization and in the mid-1950s the Greater Baltimore Committee, consisting of the leading businessmen, commissioned a plan for a small part of this area. In 1959 a public–private partnership was formed to undertake the redevelopment of what became known as the Charles Center project. Early success with this scheme gave the partnership confidence to proceed with a larger project focusing on the Inner Harbor where departing trade had left behind a derelict and often unsafe area very close to the downtown area.

The 1965 plan envisaged a large investment in infrastructure improvement and social housing premised on the availability of federal government grants. When it was discovered that these grants were not available on the scale required, the project had to be rethought and it was then that it was decided to anchor the scheme with leisure activities that would bring people back into the area. In 1976 a museum, the Maryland Science Center, was opened, followed by a convention centre in 1979, a festival marketplace (Harborplace) in 1980, and the National Aquarium and Hyatt Hotel in 1981, all receiving sizable Urban Development Action Grants. Various ships were anchored in the harbour to create a maritime museum. By 1981 the first stage of the remodelling was complete and it was beginning to look like a success. Private investment was beginning to flow into the area with office blocks being built on the north side.

During the 1980s and 1990s the project continued with extensions to the area on the east and west sides, with further investments by both the public and private sectors. On the west side the Orioles baseball team was lured downtown by the construction of a new stadium, Oriole Park opened in 1992, and in 1998 adjacent to it the PSINet American Football stadium was opened for the Ravens football team. Other developments in the late 1990s in what the city describes as a 'second renaissance' have included a children's museum (Port Discovery), the National Historic Seaport, a museum of industry and an extension to the convention centre. In the past twenty years there has been a great expansion of tourism, with many hotels built and over 2.9 million overnight tourists staying an average of 3.3 days (1999). The city believe that the long-term strategy has successfully created a cluster of visitor attractions which has reached a critical mass with significant potential for growth.

The whole project is not without its critics, both from within the local community and from the academic world (Levine, 1987; Hula, 1990). While there can be no doubt about the success of the Inner Harbor, critics would argue that it is skin-deep, with the nearby areas of poverty seemingly unaffected by any trickle-down effect.

CONCLUSION

The aim of this chapter has been to describe the context in which tourism is developing and being promoted in cities. While the emphasis has been on the need for cities to obtain economic growth, it should be remembered the city councils have a wide range of responsibilites and agendas. One topic of increasing significance is the need to plan for a sustainable city, although so far there has been much talk and relatively little action. With regard to the economies of cities, these have been changing rapidly in the past forty years with varying impacts on different types of cities. However, in a

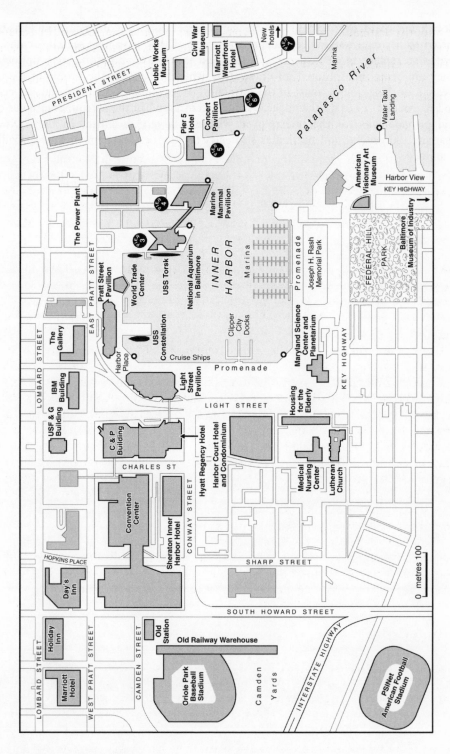

Figure 3.1 Baltimore's Inner Harbor

globalizing world, every city faces increasing competition from other cities and has been forced to become more entrepreneurial. As part of this pro-active search for new activities to replace those in decline, leisure and tourism have become very important. They are being incorporated into a strategy which must raise the profile of the city, create a positive image, assist in the attraction of investment, revitalize the city centre and regenerate zones on the edge of the city centre and in the surrounding inner city, and provide jobs for the unemployed who are largely unskilled. In the following chapters the general and particular strategies for the development of tourism will be examined.

Chapter 4

The strategy of urban tourism

During the 1980s, policies aimed at developing tourism in cities were widely adopted in North America, Western Europe and many other parts of the world. At the beginning of the decade, Bradford in England, a city hitherto only noted for its woollen industry, surprised many people in Britain by advertising itself as a tourist centre. Could they be serious? When other industrial cities and towns attempted to follow the example, the media had so little understanding of tourism that cartoons or photomontages were produced of people sitting on beaches against a background of factories. However, what was considered a surprising development by many at the beginning of the 1980s had by the end of the decade become accepted orthodoxy. The aim of this chapter is to explore the reasons why and how cities came to incorporate tourism into their economic objectives, how they have developed tourism strategies, what the urban tourism product is, what the urban tourism markets are and how tourism strategies are implemented. This chapter provides an introduction to topics that will be considered in more detail in later chapters.

ADOPTING TOURISM AS AN ECONOMIC STRATEGY

The context for the proposal to develop tourism in cities has already been outlined in the previous chapter. Since at least the 1970s cities have found themselves in a more competitive environment. This applies to all types of cities both the world cities and the older industrial cities. The effects of globalization and decentralization have been experienced in the run-down and closure of activities and establishments which have often resulted in derelict and under-used areas on the edge of the city centre and in the inner city. Cities need to attract new and growing activities which will provide jobs and assist the physical regeneration of inner city zones. To many cities tourism has appeared such an activity, destined to grow with increasing affluence, leisure time and easier mobility. Moreover, it was an activity for which cities already had a basis: in their visitor attractions, historic buildings, sports and cultural events. Without much deep thought and analysis political leaders came to the view that tourism did have a role to play in the development of their cities. Tourism was never perceived as a panacea for all urban problems but as part of the solution.

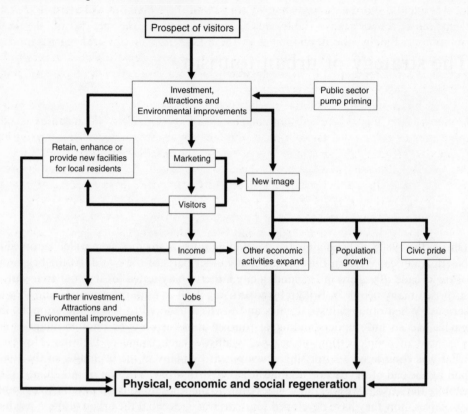

Figure 4.1 The strategy of urban tourism
Source: After Law (1992)

However, it would be too simple to see tourism development as just one component of local economic development policy, similar to either industrial or office promotion (Law, 1991). The advocates for urban tourism have always suggested that it had much greater significance (Collinge, 1989) (see Figure 4.1). Investment in tourism involves the development of facilities, activities, physical environments and infrastructure which will have benefits for the local community. It involves the marketing of the city and the selling of an image which will assist in the attraction of industrial and commercial activities (Ashworth and Voogd, 1990). As discussed in Chapter 3, in order to attract mobile investment and activities cities must first gain attention in an increasingly competitive situation. Advertising the city and engaging in activities which will be described later in this book will raise the profile and visibility of the city and this will be of assistance to those engaged in economic promotion. Many of the functions which could be expanded at least in part because of the desire to attract tourists, such as culture and sport, will help persuade potential residents, such as business professionals and executives, that the city is a good place to live, that it has the right lifestyle opportunities. With the renewal of old districts and the new image that this brings, it will be easier to tempt middle-class residents to come back and live in the inner city. The new facilities which are constructed partly to attract tourists will also be available to local residents, and the money spent by tourists in these facilities will assist in making them more economically viable, maintaining them to the benefit of the local community. Finally, the development of these facilities, the physical regeneration of zones and the arrival of more visitors will increase civic pride which is generally regarded as a desirable quality. It is suggested that local residents who have civic pride will take a greater care of the environment.

Large cities are already tourist centres, but if tourism is to play a larger role in the economy, then it must be substantially increased in size. This will mean attracting thousands of extra tourists to bring in the additional income and encourage further rounds of investment. To attract more tourists the necessary resources must be expanded. As discussed in Chapter 1, these can be classified into two types (Jansen-Verbeke, 1988). Primary elements are those which attract people and consist of historic buildings and urban landscapes, visitor attractions and convention facilities. These can be described as the urban product or products and will be discussed below.

While the strategy of urban tourism has been widely adopted, the path to adoption and incorporation in plans has not always been straightforward. Critics, who sometimes include elected representatives, have suggested that tourism is not a 'proper' industry, and that cities should continue to rely on manufacturing industry to restore their fortunes. Given the near universal shift in employment structures away from manufacturing towards services, this approach appears increasingly irrelevant. Cities must seek to expand the service sector, which is very broad, and thereby create jobs. Tourism is one part of the service sector and, along with finance and business services, is one of the fastest expanding industries. Another criticism of developing tourism concerns the perception that the industry only provides low-paid, and seasonal jobs (Williams and Shaw, 1988). For urban tourism the latter statement is not true, or much less true than for the rest of the industry. Evidence to be presented later in this book will demonstrate that many of the components of urban tourism, such as conferences and exhibitions, experience only minor variations from one part of the year to another, and that the hotel industry in cities has a very different seasonal profile from that in resorts. While some of the jobs are low skilled, this could be in the industry's favour as when it is located in or near the inner city the reserves of labour which are available are predominantly unskilled. The tourism industry does in fact provide many skilled jobs in the high levels of management.

Another a strong argument against the tourist industry is that it involves expenditure on visitor facilities when the priority should be spending on facilities for local residents. For this reason many studies have attempted to show that there are community benefits from tourism and that any public sector investment can be justified.

This ambiguous attitude to tourism held by some city councils has meant that funding sometimes has been either denied or limited so that the expansion of tourism by cities has varied in scale from place to place. Of course, general attempts to cut public expenditure have impacted on the funding for tourism projects and administration, and this again has varied from city to city.

Other critics perceive tourism as having adverse consequences for cities. Bringing more visitors to a city might add to existing congestion. More tourists will add to the wear and tear on facilities and increase the cost of urban management. Furthermore, the influx of visitors may not be welcomed by local residents and the facilities or the specialization of these facilities favoured by tourists may not be those needed by the community. Thus speciality shopping has been described as 'commercial gentrification'. These and other criticisms will be considered later in this book in the chapter on the impact of tourism.

DEVELOPING AN URBAN TOURISM STRATEGY

Tourism, because of its fragmented nature, is one of the most difficult industries to plan. Both the public and the private sectors consist of many components, not all of which recognize that they are or could be part of tourism. As has been mentioned before, the resources which tourists use are also used by local residents and the proportional importance of each market will vary from one activity to another. It may be high for hotels but in many cases, as with retailing, the tourist share may be quite small. Given this situation, it is not surprising that many parts of the sector do not wish to contribute to a tourist strategy.

Within the public sector many local authority departments may be involved with tourism either directly, such as the providers of visitor attractions like museums, or indirectly such as cleansing departments whose role in keeping a city centre clean and tidy could be vital in shaping the image of a city and in forming the initial visitor experience. In the past and often today it has been the planning department which has attempted to research the tourism sector and develop strategies. More recently the restructuring of local authorities has often resulted in large departments such as leisure services where there has been a significant interest in tourism sufficient for it to want to be the lead department in developing a strategy for the industry. Once a strategy has been developed and given political support, it is easier for the sector to implement proposals.

In contrast to the public sector, the fragmented nature of the private sector and its varying levels of interest often make it difficult for the sector to come together in a trade body and to contribute proposals for the development of the industry other than general promotion. It is in the nature of a free enterprise economy that individual entrepreneurs and firms make a decision to enter (or leave) the tourism sector and they may be only slightly influenced by whether there is a tourism strategy or not. The best that can be said about having such a strategy is that it gives confidence to entrepreneurial activity. A city that has an expanding tourism industry is likely to experience independent private sector entrepreneurial activity which may or may not be related to any strategy and which may necessitate subsequent adjustments to any strategies. In contrast, a city with a small base in tourism which it wishes to expand may be desperate to attract private investment but despite its best efforts it may still find it difficult to obtain.

The initial forays of cities into tourism were relatively simple and unsophisticated. Attracting tourists was perceived to be simply a matter of advertising what resources the city had in traditional ways: leaflets, newspaper advertisements, etc. Gradually the idea of target markets was taken on board and then the development of slogans, and finally, the idea that there might be an urban product that could be sold. But this was very much making the best use of the resources that were available. The package on offer might not be of a high quality with gaps in provision, and the existing resource base might not be capable of resulting in the sustained growth of tourists to the city. To achieve this, a strategy for growth would be necessary. In Britain from the late 1980s cities began to prepare tourist strategies. Sometimes these were produced in-house by the local authorities and in other cases outside consultants were brought in. The level of these strategies varied considerably; some were just a few pages long while others were thick bulky documents. The latter were likely to have involved some research, perhaps involving both primary and secondary material and particularly about the current markets.

The cities of Birmingham and Glasgow can be used to illustrate the production of tourism strategies. Both have been pro-active over many years in producing tourism plans. In 1987 Birmingham's Development Department produced an action pro-gramme which ten years later was updated by a study of the tourism sector and a strategy document (Birmingham Economic Information Centre, 1987, 1998, 1999). The latter presented a SWOT analysis, a vision statement, a strategic framework and an action plan. During this period the city also produced an arts strategy, a heritage strategy and a museums strategy as well as more general economic and development plans. The city also has strategies for the conference and exhibition industries which are organized by the NEC Group (see Chapter 6). In Glasgow the City Planning De-partment undertook research into tourism from the early 1980s. A review of tourism was commissioned in the late 1980s (Segal Quince Wicksteed, 1989), and from this a five-year tourism strategy and action plan was developed for 1995–99 (Greater Glasgow Tourist Board and Convention Bureau, 1995). This was sponsored by the City Council, the Glasgow Development Agency and the Tourist Board, who have since gone on to produce a further five-year plan for the period 2001–6. The key aims are expressed as attracting more visitors, increasing their length of stay, encouraging increased ex-penditure, increasing the number and quality of the jobs created, improving the quality of the visitor experience, attracting tourism investment and promoting the city.

The influence of these documents and, indeed, the idea that tourism could make a contribution to the economic development of the city depend to a considerable extent on whether they are absorbed into the thinking of local politicians and city civil ser-vants and whether they are incorporated into the more comprehensive plans of the city. In some cases plans were produced which appeared to be ignored by the other strategy documents of the city, a situation more common in the past. More recently tourism has had a more prominent role in the planning documents of the cities, either explicitly or implicitly. Very often there are references to creating a city fit for residents, businesses and *visitors*. There is still some uncertainty among local politicians about promoting tourism too openly in case voters accuse them of spending scarce resources on tourists rather than the residents.

THE URBAN TOURISM PRODUCT

The selling of cities to potential visitors raises a number of issues as to what is being sold. Marketing is generally about selling a product. In what way can a city be com-modified as a product? Or is it a number of products? What are the characteristics of this product or products? Ashworth and Voogd (1990, 1991, 1996) have made a number of points about what they call a 'place product'. First, in selling a city to tourists, only part of the city is being sold, obviously those components which are thought to be attractive to them. But can the city be so divided up, will not the visitor experience the parts of the city which are not part of the tourism product and could this affect the satisfaction of the experience? Second, even within the tourism resource base, there is a selection of components that are thought likely to have appeal. A package of elements is put together by promotion agencies, tour agencies and perhaps the local authority. Usually this is done on the basis of intuition rather than market research. A city then is a 'composite product' or a 'bundle of products'. Third, it is possible to put together a number of different packages with different appeals, such as culture, heritage, sport, etc. In this way the city is being sold in many ways to the tourist, and when the wider selling of city is considered, such as to business, this multi-selling increases. Could there be a clash between the packages that are being offered? Some commentators have referred to the city as a brand and talked of the rebranding of cities. But a brand has a distinctive, well-recognized identity and represents values and standards. It is not clear that the different products that a city offers have sufficient commonality to fit within this concept of a brand. It may work for a few cities: thus, Florence is able to sell itself under the slogan 'Florence: Centre of the Renaissance' because of its oustanding art and architecture, but it would not work for most cities. Fourth, the tourist is often looking for an experience which just does not automatically emerge from a list of visitor attractions. Visitors are often looking for what is going on behind the scenes, 'the front regions', going to the 'back regions' of the city to find the 'authentic' city (MacCannell, 1976). Finally, there is the problem of maintaining quality control for the product which consists of so many elements, each controlled by a separate organization. If the quality of the product falls, there will be dissatisfaction which may result in fewer visitors.

Hannigan (1998) has argued that one of the key features of the modern economy is the exploitation of synergies which can give value-added to a product. Thus, sports teams do not today merely sell seats for a match, but also TV rights, merchandise, opportunities for sponsorship, corporate hospitality and even the naming of the stadium. In a similar way, cities which attract tourists for one product attempt to sell the other products that the city has, to encourage a longer stay and a greater amount spent. Hannigan has also suggested that through theming, the downtown areas of cities are becoming a fantasy, a characteristic which provides another reason for the tourist gaze (Urry, 1990). Thus cityscapes become stage sets and there are themed streets in shopping malls, themed restaurants, themed clubs, themed hotels and theming in museums. The only danger for the city is that since the same themes are used in all cities, they can all become alike.

The elements which a city puts together to produce a package will not remain constant. As the city evolves and new features emerge, so new product packages can be created. Part of the tourist strategic planning will be concerned about the development of the product. This in turn will depend on which markets a city wishes to attract. If a city is aiming to be in the conference and exhibition marketplace, then it must ensure that it has all the necessary requirements. If it does not have all the resources for a particular market, then it may need to reposition itself.

The elements of the urban product will be described later in this book. They consist of visitor attractions, heritage in the form of buildings and cityscapes, the arts, sports, special events, entertainment, shopping and conferences and exhibitions. But just listing these resources cannot convey the full experience that visitors to the city can have. The urban experience is clearly something very different from the rural experience which might be characterized by words such as natural beauty, peacefulness and calm. Cities have a buzz, an energy, a dynamism, a speed, a liveliness, a cosmopolitanism, opportunities to have a wide range of experiences of a magnitude not found elsewhere, and the chance to meet a wide range of people. Each individual city can add to this list with particular qualities. Thus Paris is claimed to be a city for romance. In particular, cities are associated with nations and national culture and national histories. Capital cities in particular embody these national characteristics. Thus any visit to a foreign city while outwardly to see historic buildings or visit a famous museum is also an exercise in tasting a foreign culture.

URBAN TOURISM MARKETS

Visitors to cities can be classified in various ways. Traditionally, the prime visitor markets for urban tourism have been thought to be:

- business travellers;
- conference and exhibition delegates;
- short-break holiday-makers;
- day trippers;
- visitors to friends and relatives;
- long holiday-makers on a tour, stopping off for a short visit;
- (for some port cities) the cruise ship market;
- long holiday-makers using the city as a gateway to the surrounding region.

With the exception of the last two categories, few visitors stay long in cities and the only types of destination which attract long stays are capital cities and entertainment zones. The importance of passing trade may depend on the location of the city in relation to main routes. A city such as Lyons in France, which is on the main route from the northern regions to the Mediterranean coast, has the opportunity to benefit from passing travellers (Renucci, 1992).

   As discussed in Chapter 2, the growth of tourism has been enabled by increasing affluence, easier travel and greater leisure, and in the twentieth century the range of leisure opportunities has increased enormously. The basic task of cities is to persuade the leisure tourist to visit them. Some assessment of this task can be made by examining the present patterns of leisure tourism, both overall and through the different sub-markets. A study of the US pleasure travel market by Tourism Canada (1986) classified trips into eight types and found their importance to be as shown in Table 4.1. At first sight the prospects for cities do not appear promising, as only 7 per cent of all visits are to cities, but visits to friends and relatives, touring and theme park, etc. may all involve a city location. Thus while the purpose of the trip may not be expressed as a city visit, it very often does include an urban component.

   Of course, the above classification is only one way of segmenting the market; other ways are by interest, age and origin. Visitors coming for a short break may have very diverse motives such as having fun, seeing sport, tasting culture or attending an event.

Table 4.1 The structure of the US pleasure travel market (%)

1	Visits to friends and relatives	44
2	Touring	14
3	Close to home leisure trip (mainly outdoors)	13
4	Outdoor activities in a rural area	10
5	A resort trip	8
6	A city trip	7
7	Theme park, exhibition or special event	3
8	Cruise	1

Source: Tourism Canada (1986)

With respect to age, cities often focus on the young adult and 'empty nester' markets. The former may be more interested in having fun while the latter are more likely to have a strong interest in culture. Markets can be also classified by geography. Places nearby may not be the only places to be targeted. In a continent like Europe there can be strong cultural and historical links between two countries which encourage travel between them, and equally there may be antipathies (Grabler *et al.*, 1996). Markets which attract high spending tourists are also likely to be targeted.

Long Holidays

A long holiday is defined as 4+ nights away from home. British survey figures show that about 40 per cent of the British population do not take a long holiday (Table 4.2). This proportion has not varied significantly over the past twenty years, although as could be expected, there is a small increase in years of recession, and a decrease in years of high economic growth. Again, as could be expected, those who do not take holidays are drawn more from the lower income groups and from among the elderly, the disabled and the poorer regions. Other people may not take long holidays either because they do not wish to go away on their own or because of work commitments. The latter may be able to take their holidays in the form of short breaks. About 60 per cent of the population do take a long holiday and in 1998 this figure was composed of 34 per cent who have only one long holiday, 16 per cent who have two holidays and 9 per cent who have three or more. Over the period from 1971 to 1998 the share of the last two categories has increased from 15 to 23 per cent, suggesting that with greater affluence there will be more holiday taking. Some of this group may consist of comfortably off young retireds. Table 4.2 also shows that more British people are going on holiday abroad. Britain has a stable population and these figures suggest that the main cause of growth in the number of long holidays has been in those taking an additional one, many of which may have been taken abroad.

Most of these holidays took place in the five summer months, 77 per cent for those in Britain and 63 per cent for those abroad. Of holidays in Britain about 50 per cent were self-catering, 30 per cent were in serviced accommodation and 20 per cent with friends and relatives. Of British holiday-makers going abroad, just over half used serviced accommodation, about 30 per cent were self-catering and the rest stayed with friends and relatives. Staying with friends and relatives may serve several purposes: seeing people, having a cheap holiday, and perhaps looking after a sick or elderly person. When families and friends are widely scattered, it may be possible to see them only by

Table 4.2 Long holiday taking by the British

	Frequency of 4 + nights by British adults			
	1971 (%)	1981 (%)	1991 (%)	1998 (%)
No holiday	41	39	40	41
All holidays	59	61	60	59
One holiday	44	40	36	34
Two holidays	12	15	16	16
Three or more	3	6	8	9
British Isles	49	46	43	33
Abroad	13	21	28	36

Source: British Tourist Authority (1991, 1999)

using one's holidays. Long holidays are generally perceived as one stop, but they may take the form of a circuit with stops at several places, thus being the tour from which the word tourism was derived. This type of tourism commonly takes the form of visiting cities, as with the 'Grand Tour' in the past.

Cities have not generally targeted the long holiday-maker. With the exception of capital cities like London and Paris, cities have not generally appealed to the long holiday market. However, this may be changing. There are signs that the growth of the package tour to the Mediterranean resorts has peaked and that tourists are beginning to look more widely both in terms of destination and in terms of the type of place. If the package tour was Fordism, then post-Fordism will involve greater variety and more self-designed holidays. With an ageing population, more people will be interested in cultural holidays (broadly conceived) and it is here that cities will have an advantage. As mentioned above, some tourists take a long holiday in capital cities such as London, but frequently only part of the time is actually spent in the city. Day trips are made to Windsor, Oxford and Blenheim, Bath and Stratford-upon-Avon. In this case London is used as a base and a gateway for visits to the wider region. Many other cities would like to perform a similar role. Whether they can may partly depend on how many attractions there are in the surrounding region, having high class accommodation, having a good environment in the city and good international air links. In other cases the long holiday is broken down into sections, with three or four days spent in a different city. Many American cities are aspiring to gain a share of the coach tour market which often appeals to senior citizens.

Short Holidays

Cities are interested in the short holiday market for a number of reasons. It is a type of business which operates throughout the year and is therefore attractive. It is also a type of business which operates throughout the week but which can be particularly important at the weekends. Given that business travellers come mainly during the week, city hotels are looking for business to fill up their bedrooms at the weekend. Most city hotels offer special cut prices at the weekend and may be willing to arrange tickets for sport and entertainment at the same time. British cities have joined together to form the 'Great British City Breaks' consortium to market these packages more widely. Except for the largest cities, most visitors would only want to visit a city for a short break as they would be able to do all they wanted on a short visit. Many of the other reasons for visiting a city, such as a conference, special event, or seeing friends and relatives, are in fact likely to attract people for only a few days. While cities prefer visitors to use serviced accommodation and thus make a greater economic impact, one of the principal types of tourist to the city is the visitor to friends and relatives who rarely uses serviced accommodation.

A short holiday is usually defined as 1–3 nights away from home although a few surveys have included up to 5 nights. Some surveys cover all short holidays whatever the purpose or type of accommodation used, but others exclude visits to friends and relatives and those not using serviced accommodation. Beioley (1999) distinguishes between the short holiday which includes visits to friends and relatives and those using campsites, caravans and second homes, and the short break which uses commercial accommodation. Care therefore is needed in comparing the available statistics. Another problem is that short holidays have not always been recorded in surveys, and, even when they have, the small samples used may mean that the results are not always reliable or consistent. In 1997 British residents took 37.4 million short holidays in Britain and 3.1 million abroad (Beioley, 1999). The number of short holidays taken has been growing since the 1970s, but there were brief periods of decline in the early 1980s and early 1990s during recessions, giving credence to the idea that short holidays are perceived as additional to the main long holiday and are the first to be cut when money is short However, since 1993 the number of trips has grown by over 5 per cent a year and many in the industry consider that they have become more recession-proof. For some they are no longer a luxury but an essential part of life, enabling people to take a breather, to get away from the stresses of a busy working life. For some they are a time to relax, to have quality time in a relationship, a reward for hard work and a way of celebrating an anniversary or other special event. For others they are an opportunity to explore, to gain new experiences and to meet the need for constant stimulation. On the supply side, the growth of short holidays reflects greater affluence, easier and cheaper transport, the growth of budget hotels, the use of the Internet to obtain information and book holidays and the promotion of special events. Within the short holiday market the main trends in recent years have been the increase in the use of serviced accommodation, the reduction in the importance of the visits to friends and relatives and the increase in the numbers travelling abroad (Mintel, 1999c).

In 1990 44 per cent of those staying in Britain stayed with friends and relatives, 31 per cent were self-catering in some form (i.e. second homes, caravans, camping, etc.) and only 25 per cent used serviced accommodation. Nevertheless during the 1980s, the share using serviced accommodation increased, another indication of increasing affluence causing a shift in the patterns of holiday behaviour (British Tourist Authority and English Tourist Board, 1988a; Trinity Research, 1989). By 1999 the proportion staying with friends and relatives had fallen to 35 per cent and the proportion in serviced accommodation had risen to 37 per cent (Mintel International, 2000c). Not surprisingly, these short breakers tended to be drawn particularly from the professional and managerial groups, childless households and from either younger or older adult (empty nesters) age groups. In Europe there has been a similar growth of the short break market (Lohmann, 1991). Short break holidays take place throughout the year with a higher incidence in the spring and autumn. Similarly, while they can occur during any part of the week, there is a significant concentration at the weekend.

Some research has been undertaken on the location of short holidays. In general, people do not want to travel too far, or at least spend too much time travelling as this will eat into the time available. A distance of up to 150 miles is common. This means that cities are likely to have a predetermined hinterland for packages offered to land travelling visitors. Of course, with air travel short breaks can be offered in foreign cities from Paris to Vienna. Surveys have asked people what type of destination for a short break they would prefer. Table 4.3 shows the results for 1989 and 1998 for UK residents. Cities and large towns have now become the most popular type of destination, overtaking seaside resorts which have lost popularity. A 1999 survey suggested that 20 per cent of the British population had taken a city break in the last five years (Mintel, 2000b). An English Tourist Board survey of 1992 asked people what they were looking for in a short break. It then classified the results into 6 groups, including 'cities and culture' and 'out for a good time' with the former accounting for 20 per cent and the latter 15 per cent of the sample (English Tourist Board, 1993). While a 'good time' might be had elsewhere than in a large city, this is probably the most obvious location.

Table 4.3 Short break destinations in Britain by type of area, 1989 and 1998 (%)

	1989	1998
Seaside resorts	42	25
Countryside	18	23
Large towns	14	28
London	7	
Small towns	14	20
Other	5	5

Source: MAS Research Marketing and Consulting (1989)
Mintel International (2000b)

It has been estimated that in 1999 British citizens took 11.8 million city breaks, of which 9.7 million were in the UK and 2.1 million abroad (Mintel, 2000b). These figures compare with those for 1994 of 10.2, 8.7 and 1.5 million respectively. During the 1990s the number of foreign city breaks doubled. Recent growth has been stimulated by the introduction of no frills low-cost airlines. Paris and Amsterdam have long been the favourites for British people, but recently Dublin and Barcelona have overtaken other European cities to become the next most popular. Foreign short breaks are more likely to be arranged by a tour operator, use serviced accommodation and be by air (Beioley, 1999).

Day Trips

The usual definition of a tourist is of a person who stays away overnight and for 24 hours, which would exclude the day tripper. However, as has been shown, day trips are very important in terms of the numbers made, and it is clear that for many tourist centres of all types a significant part of their business comes from day trips. Most studies of tourism therefore include them. While the expenditure of a day tripper will be less than that of a visitor who stays overnight in serviced accommodation, the large numbers involved ensure that the total income injected into the local economy can be significant. One problem, however, is how to define the day tripper. Should it be solely on the basis of distance travelled or should motivation be taken into account as well? Should the long-distance shopper, for instance, be included?

The leisure day trip market is enormous, although, as just indicated, its scale will depend on how a trip is defined. OPCS (1991) used the liberal definition of a trip of more than 3 hours duration and involving a round journey of over 20 miles. A more recent survey defined the tourism leisure day trip as one lasting at least 3 hours, by people travelling outside their usual environment and one not taken on a regular basis (Countryside Agency, 1999). On this basis nearly 1.3 billion trips were made in Britain in 1998, an increase of 8 per cent over a similar survey made in 1996. About 72 per cent of trips were made to towns and cities, compared to 22 per cent to the countryside and 6 per cent to the seaside. The main reasons for going to a town or city were to eat and drink (23 per cent), to go shopping (21 per cent), for entertainment (15 per cent), to visit friends and relatives (15 per cent) and to sightsee and visit attractions (7 per cent).

Most day trips will take place within a radius of 100 miles (162 km) with an average distance travelled of 31 miles (50 kilometres). The widespread availability of the car and the construction of motorways have opened up many areas that were previously considered remote. It is much easier to get to cities now by car, although in the past and still today they are often well served by train. Given that the vast majority do travel only this distance, the effective day trip hinterland can be determined.

However, some people are prepared to travel further, as evidenced by the day trips made to London from up to 300 miles away. With air travel, much longer distance day trips are possible and it is common in Britain to see air day trips to places such as Rome and Vienna. Given the large population of cities, it is likely that the origin of most day trips is cities, but that cities may and do attract visitors from other cities. The most recent surveys lack information about seasonality, but the results for an earlier one are shown in Table 4.4. Perhaps not surprisingly, leisure day trips to towns and cities show very little seasonality, particularly when compared to those to the countryside and seaside.

Table 4.4 British leisure day trips, 1988–89: destination type

		Quarter of the year			
	All	1	2	3	4
(a) Destination and share (%)					
Inland town/city	54	60	50	48	64
Inland village	13	13	14	13	12
Seaside	16	14	18	22	11
Countryside	15	11	16	17	11
Other	2	2	2	2	2
(b) Destination and trip numbers (millions)					
All	630	129	177	178	147
Inland town/city	340	77	89	82	94
Seaside	101	18	32	39	16

Source: OPCS (1991)

Visits to Friends and Relatives

Vast numbers of trips, whether long holidays, short break or day, are made to friends and relatives, but they have frequently been discounted in studies of tourism. This is because they are largely invisible in the statistics and partly because it was thought that the expenditure was slight. While it is true that most visits to friend and relatives do not involve the use of serviced accommodation, those that last more than a few hours often include either a visit to an attraction or eating and drinking out of the home and therefore involve expenditure (British Tourist Authority and English Tourist Board, 1988b). They were also the main reason for 21 per cent of visits to Britain by foreigners. In fact, many of the visits to friends and relatives have an important secondary motivation of having a holiday or leisure time away from the home. Given the large numbers involved, and the resulting expenditure, this is clearly a market to be encouraged (Denman, 1988).

In theory, the location of the visitor and friends market is the same as that of the population, but in fact that the BTA/ETB survey did not find an exact correlation. It may be that people who live in attractive areas or near particular amenities will find that they have more visitors. With their large populations, cities will always have a large number of visits to friends and relatives, but this could be affected both positively and negatively by the public perception in terms of their appeal or attractiveness. This presents a challenge to the promoters of city tourism to change the image of the city, to provide plenty of things to do and to create civic pride so that residents do want to invite their friends and are proud to show off their city when they do come.

Business Travel

With the possible exception of travel to conferences, business trips take place mainly to cities. Cities are where head offices, sales offices, factories, business services and convention centres are usually found. The amount of business travel to a particular city cannot neatly be equated with its population size. Each city performs a slightly different function in the world of business. World cities such as London and New York attract huge numbers of business people because of the functions they perform as the headquarters of national and international organizations and as the world's largest financial and business services centres. Other cities with large populations may attract relatively few business travellers because they have few head offices and few business services which serve more than the local region and they can be described as predominantly branch plant economies. Particular forms of business organization may develop which encourage travel. In the USA a system of marts is in operation in which retailers travel to a few major cities to examine permament displays of consumer goods. With easier travel the number of major mart centres has been reduced to a few, which include New York, Chicago, Dallas, Atlanta and San Francisco. Travel to conference and exhibitions is a special type of business travel which will be dealt with in a later chapter.

FUNDING URBAN TOURISM

As mentioned earlier, success in obtaining finance is critical to the development of the tourist industry in cities, both for capital development and operational costs. It is a test of the leadership and organization of the industry whether these funds can be obtained. In a situation of scarce resources the tourism industry is inevitably in competition with other activities, whether in the public or private sectors, for funding.

Finance can be obtained from several sources. Many cities look to higher levels of government. In Western Europe the European Union provide grants from various of its programmes for tourist projects. In Britain grants from the Regional Development Fund have contributed to many new tourist facilites from Birmingham's International Convention Centre to Manchester's Bridgewater Concert Hall. These funds have been particular important for general infrastructure such as airports which are vital for the development of the industry. Funding from national governments is naturally extremely important. Apart from general revenue funding, there are often grants for particular programmes. Thus in both the USA and Britain there are grants for urban regeneration which can be used for general infrastructure, the preparation of sites and towards the construction costs of a building. In the USA the establishment of a national historic park in a city will bring capital and recurrent resources. St Louis benefited when its riverfront was designated as the Jefferson National Expansion Memorial Park and later when the Gateway Arch was built. National governments also provide funds when cities host an international event, whether for sport, culture or a world expo. One strategy therefore of the entrepreneurial city is to put itself forward for one of these events. National government organizations can also help cities through their programmes. In Britain national museums, hitherto predominantly located solely in London, have began to open branches in provincial cities and these have been competed for by a few enterprising cities. National tourist boards are also sometimes able to assist cities with either grants for capital projects or funding for promotion for a special event. In the USA, Germany and many other nation–states there is also a strong regional tier of government which can provide grants in the ways just described. Thus, in the city of Cologne in Germany the museums have benefited from grants from the *Land* (regional) government. In the USA many of the states have taken direct responsibility for the construction and operation of tourist facilities. In Atlanta, the State of Georgia established the Georgia World Congress Center Authority to build and operate the convention centre and later also the Georgia Dome. In Baltimore the State of Maryland built the new Oriole Park baseball stadium. In addition to such funding, national and regional/state governments may help cities by granting tax exemptions as in enterprise zones and with bond issues (see below).

In many countries national lotteries exist to provide funds for good causes which include assisting with the capital costs of facilities such as museums, concert halls, theatres and stadiums. In Britain a National Lottery was established in 1994 with good causes in the arts, heritage, sports, charity and the Millennium Fund. Projects bidding for money must provide matching funding, a clause which discriminates in favour of the capital city where it has been easier to obtain donations from firms and individuals. In some other parts of the country where unemployment is high, matching funds have been obtained from regional and urban regeneration grants. The availability of these funds is another challenge to the entrepreneurial city to come up with schemes.

With the decline of population and economic activity, central cities often find it difficult to fund tourist, cultural and leisure facilities. Most of these amenities are used regularly by residents from the entire metropolitan area as well as tourists and therefore one possible solution is to find a way of cross-funding from the suburban municipalities. This can be done on a voluntary basis as when suburban areas contribute to the running of the region's main orchestra. Alternatively there can be some form of metropolitan government with either limited or wide-ranging powers. In Pittsburgh there was a proposal for a regional organization to fund the area's museums.

Cities themselves are usually the funders of both capital and running costs of some of the main facilities used by tourists, as well as sometimes offering either grants or tax rebates to the private sector to encourage development. In the past when the population and economic activity of the central city may have been larger, this was bearable, but with the decline in activity it may become more difficult to fund these amenities. National governments are often cutting back their subventions to local authorities so that the maintenance of basic welfare services is put at risk. In this situation it may be difficult for the city leaders to justify expenditure on facilities that are not considered by many to be essential, and are used by non-residents, notwithstanding the fact that they may bring income into the area. In Britain borrowing finance to pay for facilities is strictly controlled by the central government and has been restricted in recent years. In the USA a popular way of raising finance has been through tax-exempt bonds, with the national government foregoing income. Bond issues require voter approval and in the case of some projects, such as convention centres, this has not always been given at the first time of asking (Sanders, 1992). Finding capital for new projects is critical for the success of a pro-active local government seeking to expand the tourist industry.

One method used by many cities in the USA, France, Austria and elsewhere is to raise finance through a tax on tourists. In the USA this is variously described as a hotel, lodging, bed or room tax, as it is charged only on those staying in hotels. Usually it is in the form of a percentage addition to the room bill. The funds generated in this way can be used to fund both capital projects and the operational costs of organizations such as convention and visitor bureaux (see below). Power to raise finance in this way may reside either with the city or the state, depending on constitutional arrangements. In either case the government body concerned has the right to take a share of the proceeds, treating it as a form of general taxation, although often the distribution of proceeds to organizations and projects is specified. Over time the rate of these taxes has tended to rise as the costs of running promotional organizations have risen and there are more capital projects. The tax rates for cities in the USA are shown in Figure 4.2 and vary from 8 per cent in Las Vegas to 21 per cent in New York.

In recent years additional taxes which mainly fall on tourists have been levied, such as airport taxes, car rental taxes, sales taxes and restaurant taxes (Sanders, 1992). In the case of Atlanta, hotel and motel guests pay 13 per cent, broken down into a 6 per cent sales tax and a 7 per cent bed tax. This has increased from 8 per cent in 1986, to 12 per cent in April 1989, to 13 per cent in September 1989 and is one way that the city funded the holding of the Olympic Games in 1996. The distribution of the tax is shown in Table 4.5, where it is seen that only the bed tax comes back directly to the tourism industry.

The great advantage of this type of tax is that it is a user tax, generally paid by tourists and not residents. Politicians can be shielded from attack by residents claiming that they are paying for the facilities used by visitors. The major disadvantage of the tax

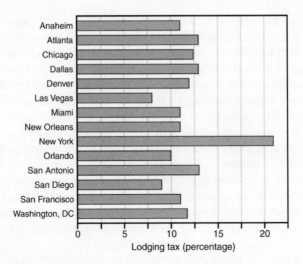

Figure 4.2 US hotel/lodging taxes, 1991
Source: Chicago Convention and Tourism Bureau

Table 4.5 The distribution of Atlanta's sales and hotel/motel tax

Type	Destination	Share (%)
6% Sales Tax	State	4
	Local option	1
	MARTA (Transport)	1
7% Bed Tax	ACVB	1.575
	City of Atlanta	2
	Georgia Dome	2.75
	GWCC (Convention Centre)	0.675

Notes: Payable within the City of Atlanta and Fulton County
ACVB = Atlanta Convention and Visitors Bureau.

is that it raises the cost of visiting a city, and thus could deter tourists. For group visits and sometimes conventions, cost comparisons are made between cities and overall high costs could be a deterrent. It is likely then that strong tourist cities and those with low costs will be able to have relatively high tourist taxes, while cities with high cost and a weak attractiveness will be able to charge only a low rate of tax. Those cities which want to develop the industry, but have only a weak base may find it difficult to raise significant funds from this source. Tourist taxes could deter visitors. In Europe cities such as Florence and Venice are being overwhelmed by tourists and it is alleged that visitor numbers have surpassed the city's carrying capacity. High tourist taxes could not only deter visitors but be used to restore the numerous historic buildings and art treasures. However, such taxation could be regarded as socially regressive as it would prevent poorer people from viewing a heritage which should be avaialble to all. In Britain there are no tourist taxes although organizations within the industry have begun to campaign for such taxes. In 1992 hoteliers in Harrogate agreed to put a levy on guests to pay for the necessary renovations to the town's conference and exhibition facilities.

The private profit-making sector is extremely important in the funding and organization of tourist facilities. It can be expected to finance hotels, shops, restaurants, clubs and sometimes visitor attractions. It will do so, of course, only if profits can be earned. This will happen if tourists are already coming in large numbers and so, to a certain extent, those cities that are already large and successful will generate further investment, while those that have yet to achieve success will find it more difficult to attract private finance. For these cities that are starting out to create a tourism sector, some form of subsidy to the private sector is likely to be necessary to lever investment.

Finally, investment may come from philanthropic motivations or from non-profit institutions. Large corporations may develop facilities in their home city, such as a company museum or give donations for the development of facilities such as art galleries. Local or perhaps non-local charitable foundations may provide funds for a museum or other attraction. Many attractions, at least initially, have been the idea and work of voluntary groups. Enthusiasts may gather artefacts to establish a museum and also raise money for its construction. In many cases these have later been taken over and run wholly or partly by the public sector. Finally, independent institutions like universities have often been responsible for the development of museums, and Oxford, Cambridge and Trinity College, Dublin, have buildings which are part of the attraction of visiting the city.

ORGANIZING THE PROMOTION OF THE CITY

In the past the marketing of cities was often left to the individual firm in the private sector and to whatever role the local authority decided to play. In some cities the local authority decided to take the lead in both developing and promoting the industry with or without the co-operation of the private sector. This is the case in many German cities such as Cologne and also in Britain (Queenan, 1992). However, in recent years an attempt has been made in many cities to create a form of public–private partnership in which the two sectors come together to promote the city (Bramwell and Rawding, 1994). The premise on which these organizations are based is that the promotion of cities to potential visitors is more effective when co-ordinated through large-scale programmes than numerous small independent ones. In the USA the widely found convention and visitor bureaux are an example of a promotional organization. The first convention bureau was established in Detroit in 1896 (Rutherford, 1990; Gartrell, 1994). In Britain examples include the Greater Glasgow Tourist Board and the short-lived Greater Manchester Visitor and Convention Bureau (of which more, see below). Most of these organizations cover the entire metropolitan area rather than just the central city. This makes sense, since boundaries are irrelevant to the tourist, and it is often beneficial to market products jointly wherever they are found within the urban area. However, in a politically fragmented area where there is competition and conflict between local governments, it can be a delicate task keeping all partners on board, since the local authorities in the outer areas may, quite rightly, feel that the focus of marketing is on the downtown area. In all cases it is critical that the marketing organizations are sensitive to this issue and keep a balance between the core and the periphery.

In Britain in recent years there has been a merging of the organizations concerned with marketing the city to businesses to attract inward investment and those marketing the city to tourists. As discussed in the last chapter, with the rise of the entrepreneurial city, local authorities have become more pro-active in selling the city and this has involved various types of marketing. As there is clearly some overlap between these marketing organizations, it has appeared appropriate in some cities to merge these bodies. In both Birmingham and Manchester organizations with the titles Marketing Birmingham and Marketing Manchester have been created, and in the case of Manchester the former tourism visitor and convention bureau was subsumed into the new organization.

These bodies are primarily marketing organizations, undertaking advertising, familiarization tours for the media, and the provision of visitor services. In connection with the latter, many cities have arranged for a card to be sold which gives either free access or discounted access to the main visitor attractions and/or local public transport. They usually have little power to plan or initiate projects, but they can often make an important input into planning and strategy documents. These bodies usually have an independent legal status and are usually not-for-profit companies. The financing of these bodies is clearly a critical element in achieving success in raising the profile of the area. In Britain and Europe, local authorities have made the largest contributions by far (Bramwell and Rawding, 1994; Queenan, 1992; Touche Ross: Greene Belfield-Smith Division, 1991), while in the USA the hotel tax is the main source of income, although many cities pay a subvention to the bureaux. In the late 1980s the national average for the hotel tax was 5.5 per cent. The third source of finance is membership subscriptions. These are usually based on the type of organization and its size. Income is generated also through commissions from bookings and other sales.

In the United States the system of convention and visitor bureaux (CVBs) appears to work well. The number of CVBs increased from 100 in 1980 to 250 in 1989 (Rutherford, 1990). In 1991 CVBs had incomes which varied from $6 million in Washington, DC, to $67 million in Las Vegas (see Figure 4.3). Bureaux may have up to 1,500 members whose subscriptions may contribute up to 40 per cent of the budget. The work of these bureaux is shown by their departmental structure, which normally includes convention and tourism (leisure) sections as well as visitor services and administration.

In contrast, in Britain this type of organization is relatively new and has not always had a good track record; financial failure is not uncommon. It has been difficult to persuade private sector firms to contribute, although some have been willing to give support via advertising in brochures or gifts in kind as when hotels provide free accommodation for visiting travel writers. Consequently these organizations have relied very greatly on the public sector, which itself may be under severe financial restraint. Even though the local authority or local authorities may be making by far the largest contribution, the membership of the ruling executive is usually divided equally between the two sectors. Budgets are much smaller than in the USA. Glasgow has one of the largest budgets at £2.2 million, followed by Birmingham with £1.4 million. In Manchester the former VCB only had a budget of £0.5 million, of which over half came from local government. Obviously the size of the budget will determine how much can be spent on advertising, market research, visitor services and staff (Touche Ross: Greene Belfield-Smith Division, 1991). In France the position is very similar to Britain. The Office of Tourism in Lyons receives over 70 per cent of its funds from the public sector (Renucci, 1992).

Promotional organizations often undertake research on the type of visitors to the city and their satisfaction with the product. Such research can obviously be very useful in

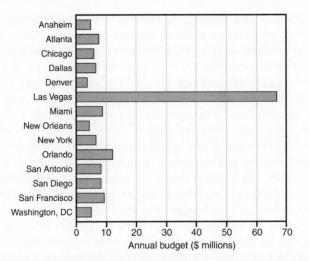

Figure 4.3 US convention bureaux budgets, 1991
Source: Chicago Convention and Tourism Bureau

understanding the market and using this information to improve the product and target particular markets. Research may also assess the impact of tourism on the city, the income generated and the jobs created and this may be used to campaign for more resources for the tourism sector.

A critical issue for these organizations is to demonstrate how effective they are, how many extra visitors have travelled to the city as a result of their promotional activities? The bureaux usually collect statistics on the number of enquiries handled and the number of bookings made, but these might have gone directly to the companies concerned had they not been there. Without a counterfactual position it is always going to be difficult to prove their effectiveness.

SELLING THE CITY

There is clearly a relationship between the ideas used to develop the urban product or products and the way that the city will be sold. However, the former may be informed by how the existing city is sold. One key idea that marketeers have used is that of the *unique selling point*. There is a great danger in a globalizing world that all cities will become alike, that they will become 'anywhereville'. With the same companies operating in most major cities there is a very real danger of serial reproduction or clone cities. In the recent past when cities constructed new buildings there was a tendency for the architecture to be similar, which is one reason why there is now a desire for the landmark building. Again, with cities tending to follow similar paths, each city tended to construct the same type of buildings: convention centres, museums, arenas, stadiums, etc. The use of best practice will again often result in a similarity between cities.

But if all cities are alike, the potential tourist will not want to go there, so it is important to find the unique selling point, the distinctive features which can be sold to stimulate the desire to travel, to differentiate one place from another so that they are not substitutable. History and heritage are always important starting points in this quest. What important and famous role has the city played in history and what associated buildings and artefacts remain? Historic cities like Florence, Rome and Venice are easily able to exploit these atributes, but many other cities can find important and fairly unique historical survivals; witness Dublin displaying the ancient hand-written manuscript of the Book of Kells. National identity is another selling point. Tourists like to visit a city with some 'foreign' character, where they allegedly do things differently; have special foods and drink, have different customs and festivals, other religious traditions, vernacular architecture and where the character of the people has been shaped by a different history and struggle. For Americans even going to a Canadian city has that different air. The Scottish and the Irish play upon this national identity to woo the tourist, particularly so in Edinburgh and Dublin. Another uniqueness that can be exploited concerns famous people who have lived in and been associated with the city. Whether statesmen, politicians, writers, artists, sportsmen or entertainers, a museum can be opened with them as the theme, possibly in their their original house. Liverpool has exploited the link with the Beatles via a visitor attraction, public sculptures, Beatles festival weekends and the opening of Paul McCartney's childhood home. Atlanta builds on its connections with the famous film *Gone with the Wind*, and also Martin Luther King. Glasgow uses the architect and craftsman Charles Rennie Mackintosh, internationally known for his art nouveau work, to sell the city. Laurier (1993) has pointed out that Mackintosh lived in the late Victorian period, when Glasgow was a great city, albeit known for industry, and that Mackintosh was only one member of the Glasgow school, but in spite of this he has become the representative figure of this time and style. Very special buildings also have the power to draw visitors. There are usually historic buildings which have featured in the media until they have obtained iconic status and come to represent the city, as with the Eiffel Tower and Paris. The construction of landmark buildings, it is hoped, will create a new unique feature in the city which will draw visitors, The recent example of the Guggenheim Museum in Bilbao, Spain, illustrates the power of such buildings.

Notwithstanding the attempt to discover unique selling points, there is a great deal of similarity in the way large cities sell themselves. Bramwell and Rawding (1996) describe the 'big city imagery' widely used to present the city as exciting, lively, cosmopolitan, with lots to see and do. Because they all are appealing to particular markets they tend to give prominence to arts and culture and to heritage and heritage attractions.

The use of slogans or the branding of cities is another way of selling cities. Slogans may work on the basis of constant repetition so often used that there is an association with the city. In the USA the phrases used do not immediately conjure up the city but they have become identified; the Big Apple and New York, and Peach with Atlanta. Elsewhere there is an attempt to link the city with some of its attributes. Atlanta later adopted the slogan 'Come celebrate our dreams' which combined various ideas from the Olympic Games being held in the city in 1996 to the famous words of Martin Luther King ('I have a dream') (Ward, 1998). Birmingham's Europe's Meeting Place linked the city with its role as a location for conferences and exhibitions. The pottery industry city of Stoke has adopted the following slogans successively: 'Do China in a day' and 'the city that fires the imagination', while a textile town used the slogan 'cotton on to Burnley'. Other slogans are simply more descriptive and perhaps less likely to stimulate a visit, such as Liverpool: Maritime City, and Sheffield: Sports City. It can be difficult to find a slogan which is acceptable to all concerned with the promotion of the city. In the case of Manchester the marketing agency spent a significant sum of money with an agency before ariving at the slogan 'We're up and going' which was quickly attacked by some of the leaders associated with the music and club scene, resulting in it being dropped and senior figures in the marketing agency losing their jobs (Ward, 2000a, 2000b). Many cities which are not well known hint that the attractions of the city are a well-kept secret which will surprise the visitor (Ward, 1998). Another popular line is to emphasize the liveliness, vibrancy and animation of the city. The use of a slogan is also used in the general marketing of the city, and there may be some confusion if more than one is used; does this dilute the message or is it possible to target different audiences?

Associated with slogans is the use of a logo. This should reinforce the slogan and the image that the city is trying to convey. In December 2000 a new logo for London was announced but was quickly attacked by critics as not conveying the image of London as a 'vibrant and sophisticated city' (*Financial Times*, 1 December 2000).

The appropriation of the past can be fraught with problems, for whose past is it that is being sold? Only parts of the past are selected and usually these are aspects which are not controversial and will have appeal to the markets being targeted. Frequently this is a past which does not involve working-class people or ethnic minorities and the issues which they faced (for Atlanta, see Whitelegg, 2000). In so far as their identity is linked to the city, these slogans can be seen as changing their own identity. This is why the creators of images and slogans need to test them on the inhabitants as well as outsiders.

SUSTAINABLE URBAN TOURISM

The idea of sustainable urban tourism has received relatively little attention (see Allwinkle and Speed, 1996; Hinch, 1996). There are at least three aspects to this topic. The concept of the 'carrying capacity' of an area has received much attention in various other types of destination. It involves a number of components; the physical capacity of a building or built environment to carry a finite number of people, the eroding effect (wear and tear) of large numbers on the built environment, the increasing costs of large numbers which might outweigh the economic benefits, the degrading of the tourist experience as numbers increase and the degrading of the residents' experience of their locality as tourist numbers increase. For any one of these it might be possible to calculate a point, a threshold of tourist flows above which the benefits are exceeded by the costs, and by combining them to calculate the carrying capacity of a city. The level would vary from city to city depending on the capacity of buildings and scale of the urban area affected. Once the carrying capacity had been reached, it could be argued that flows should not be allowed to increase in order to keep tourism sustainable. Many have suggested that in cities such as Florence and Venice, where the historic core is relatively small, the carrying capacity has already been reached and why proposals, so far unrealized, have been put forward to limit numbers.

A second aspect of urban sustainability concerns the maintenance, rehabilitation and re-use of old buildings. Tourism has played an important role in finding new uses for these buildings, uses which generate an income and so enable the buildings to be kept in good order. Examples include using old warehouses, railway stations and goods buildings, or stock exchanges for hotels, museums, theatres, shopping centres and exhibition centres. If well restored, these buildings can add character and quality to the built environment and help make the city a more attractive place to visit.

A third aspect of urban sustainability concerns the reduction of motor vehicle movements and thus the amount of air pollution. Visitors should not be encouraged to bring their vehicles into the core area for tourism and so create congestion and pollution. It should be possible to arrive and move around the area without the need for a car. The ideal is a compact tourism zone, with the clustering of resources, so that visitors can walk around. When, as is the case in cities such as London, New York and Paris, the tourist area is very extensive and this is not possible, then there should be suitable forms of public transport (see below). These aspects of urban sustainability should be borne in mind when a tourism strategy is being prepared.

LINKING THE CORE AND THE PERIPHERY

The main city attractions are usually located in the city centre and core area. This is partly a consequence of history, with historic buildings and long-established museums being found here. It is also, as discussed above, a consequence of recent policies which sought to place new attractions in the core area to reinforce its central role and to regenerate decaying zones. Nevertheless there are frequently important attractions in the suburbs and just outside the built-up zone. In the case of London, important historic buildings such as Hampton Court Palace and Greeenwich are examples and in the case of Paris, the Palace of Versailles. Sometimes large visitor attractions needing much space and a greenfield site have been constructed on the periphery, albeit later engulfed by the expanding urban area. Independent suburban local authorities also often attempt to develop visitor attractions such as a local museum and over time these can become quite important. Without doubt all these tourism attractions away from the core area are a significant resource for the city developing tourism, but the problem is how to incorporate them into the urban product and how to get visitors to move from the core to periphery, which is only partly a matter of transport. Visitor attractions add to the mass of attractions which a city has to offer. For those places with limited resources, albeit one or two of high quality, but which might not persuade a visitor to stay long, the availability of further attractions close by would be important in building up a sufficient mass. For those cities already well endowed with attractions, extra resources can still be helpful. They can persuade visitors to stay longer, to turn a short break into a long break. They can be used to develop the portfolios of specialized or themed attractions, thus appealing to different and special interest markets. In capital cities a fuller package of 'royal heritage' sites could be developed while in older industrial cities the package might include a series of industrial heritage sites.

THE ROLE OF TRANSPORT

The importance of good transport has often been underestimated in discussions of the development of urban tourism. It plays a vital role both in bringing visitors to the city and then in transporting them around. Improvements in transport have had a dramatic effect on tourism flows to all types of destination and this is no less true for cities. For distances up to 300 kilometres, the car, coach and train are very important while for longer distances air travel is essential. Improvements in these transport media by reducing travel time and cost greatly extend the distance tourists are prepared to travel and it extends the range or market area from which cities can draw visitors. The organization of transport, including package tours, is also very important. Through these means travel is made easier and cheaper.

Improvements continue to be made in long-established forms of transport such as roads and railways. New motorways, bridges and tunnels can cut travel times and increase flows to cities; the only problem that can occur is where to park in cities. New fixed road links such as bridges across estuaries and straits have opened up new markets for city tourism and the links between Denmark and Sweden are but a recent example. The advent of high speed trains has had a similar effect. The combination of a high speed link and the Channel Tunnel has had a dramatic effect on tourism flows between London, Paris and Brussels, particularly on the outward movement from London. Further developments of the system can be expected to have a similar impact, and aspiring tourist cities will seek links to the network.

The great impact of air travel on tourism flows is not surprising. Journeys which on land (and sometimes by sea) would have taken two days can now be accomplished in two hours, no longer than many road journeys within regions and countries. This opens up the possibility of a short break in a distant city which would have been inconceivable in the past because of the long duration of travel time. Within Europe the city break market has developed rapidly since the early 1980s with tour companies making good savings for the tourist on travel and accommodation. Once again the leisure tourist travelling at the weekends, when business travel on aircraft and in hotels is low, can make great savings. The main growth has been in the short-haul and short break market where flight times are up to 3 hours. For long haul, where the flight times are much greater, 7 hours in the case of the Atlantic crossing, and the cost is higher, the short break market has not surprisingly been slower to develop. But it is growing and a 4-night break in New York or other East Coast cities is becoming increasing popular for Europeans. Long-haul international flights tend to be concentrated in a few hub airports, often where the national carrier is based. This gives advantage to the cities at the hub but disadvantages other cities where a further air link is required. In Germany and Italy, Frankfurt and Milan gain but Berlin and Rome, albeit capitals, lose out.

The recent development of cheap, no frills airlines, stimulated by the deregulation of travel in the European Union in 1997, has resulted in the further growth of city breaks (Mintel, 1999a). In Britain it is reported that short country hotel breaks have been hit as visitors switch to more exotic foreign locations using the new services. In cities such as Amsterdam, Athens, Dublin, Florence, Madrid, Rome and Venice which have benefited from the new low-cost services there has been a surge in demand with hotels full to 'bursting point', visitors finding it difficult to find hotel rooms at short notice and a rise in hotel room rates (*The Observer*, 2 October 2000). Possessing a large airport, not too distant from the city, with scheduled services to a wide range of destinations and also with budget-priced airlines is now essential for the aspiring tourist city. It should also have good means of communication between the airport and the city centre, at least an express coach service and preferably a rail link. The absence of such facilities, as with the city of Florence, can be a deterrent to potential visitors.

Good internal transport is equally important, both to enable the visitor to move around the core area and to travel to attractions in the outlying areas. This topic will be discussed more fully in Chapter 8.

CONCLUSION

In the past 20 years the strategy of urban tourism has moved from the very simple idea of advertising a few attractions to a much more comprehensive approach which seeks to develop a product, understand the visitor markets for the product, make the city user-friendly for the tourist and create organizations which can promote and sell the city. The following chapters will examine different aspects of the urban product.

Chapter 5

Visitor attractions

There are many reasons why people are drawn to cities, but one of the most important is the visitor attraction. This might be a historical building, a museum, a view from a high structure or even a theme park. The importance of visitor attractions versus any other reason for visiting the city will vary from one place to another as does the role of any one visitor attraction versus all the others. Until recently few tourists visited Bilbao, but the opening of the Guggenheim Museum gave the city global recognition with the resulting upsurge in the number of visitors. Although the city is not without other appeals, it is this one facility which acts as a tourist magnet (see later). In contrast, the cities of London and Paris have some of the world's best visitor attractions, but except for a few enthusiasts it is unlikely that most tourists would say that any one of them was the specific reason for their visit. More likely they would say that there was so much to see and do from the cityscapes, the visitor attractions, the entertainment, shopping and the general atmosphere.

Although there are differences between one city and another, the study of tourism strategy documents (see Chapter 4) suggests that most cities regard the visitor attraction sector as a critical factor in their survival, prosperity and growth as tourist destinations. Visitor attractions are perceived as being able to stimulate the development of destinations and form the core of the destination product. According to Richards (1992):

> Every visitor attraction is an element of a tourist destination and can be a vital element which provides the major activity at the destination and the primary reason for visiting the destination. A small attraction in a place with a strong image as a destination will not attract visitors in its own right, but will benefit from the ready-made flow of visitors.

For many years, and particularly since the opening of the Guggenheim Museum in Bilbao in 1997, the aspiring tourist city has sought to expand the number of visitor attractions and to improve the quality of the existing ones. Many facilities, such as museums, are in the public sector and public funds can be used for development. For private sector and independent (voluntary) ones, grants may be given or obtained for their development. The encouragement of the visitor attraction sector for its role as a motivator of travel is congruent with the other objectives of urban governance. Visitor attractions exist for local people as well as tourists, and the older attractions were established for this purpose alone. New visitor attractions can be sited in, and assist with, urban regeneration. These zones and the architecture of the new buildings, as the example of the Guggenheim illustrates, can help change the image and visibility of the city. They can also be sold to the mobile executives as lifestyle opportunities.

The aim of this chapter is to understand more fully the role which visitor attractions can play in the urban tourism economy, how they can be developed, the critical factors for their success, how they relate to each other and the other tourism resources of the city, who uses them and who they attract, and their contribution to urban regeneration. As a prelude to discussing these topics, the next section examines the characteristics of visitor attractions before moving on to discuss the supply of and demand for visitor attractions.

DEFINITION AND TYPES OF VISITOR ATTRACTION

There are various definitions of a visitor attraction, but the one that is perhaps the most comprehensive is that by the Scottish Tourist Board (1991):

> A permanently established excursion destination, a primary purpose of which is to allow public access for entertainment, interest or education, rather than being principally a retail outlet or a venue for sporting, theatrical or film performances. It must be open to the public without prior booking, for published periods of the year, and should be capable of attracting tourists and day visitors as well as local residents.

Middleton's (1988) statement adds a futher dimension: 'A designated permanent resource which is controlled and managed for the enjoyment, amusement, entertainment and education of the visiting public.' This management and marketing aspect is also emphasized by Walsh-Heron and Stevens (1990) who state that a visitor attraction is 'managed to provide satisfaction for its customers' and will also 'provide an appropriate level of facilities and services to meet and cater to the demands, needs and interests of visitors'.

Swarbrooke (1995) has classified visitor attractions into two types: those which were purpose-built to attract visitors and those which were not designed for this purpose but have subsequently become so. The former include museums and art galleries, heritage centres and theme parks, and the latter include cathedrals and churches, historic buildings, archaelogical sites and gardens.

Another important distinction already referred to concerns ownership, whether by the public sector, the private sector or the voluntary (non-profit-making) sector, each of which will have different objectives and modes of operation. The public sector is an extremely important provider of visitor attractions, most prominently seen in museums and art galleries. Museums date back to the seventeenth century when a few states, then usually monarchies, began to provide access to national collections of paintings, sculptures, decorative arts and archaelogical remains. In Europe the core of many national collections remains the original royal collections. Subsequently the donation of collections by the aristocracy was another means by which national museums were established. The British Museum was established in 1753 and interestingly its building was later funded by a national lottery. By the nineteenth century the modern state was in the business of establishing national collections, whether of the arts, science or natural history. The aims of these national collections can be illustrated by those of Britain's Royal Armouries:

- to care for and preserve objects;
- to arrange these objects for exhibition;
- to maintain records;
- to promote the public's enjoyment and understanding of arms and armour.

National museums have traditionally tended to see their role in terms of conservation, research and education. They have been usually relatively well funded which has enabled them to offer either free entry or at a price which is greatly subsidized. In the past free entry was justified on educational grounds, but today an added reason may be the stimulus which this gives to tourism. For understandable reasons, they have been mostly located in capital cities, which gives these cities a tremendous resource for their tourism industries. To house these collections, grand, inspiring buildings were erected in the nineteenth century, usually in the classical architectural style. Apart from the objectives stated above, national museums have often been expected to generate nationalistic feeling, particularly important where new states were coming into being. This is illustrated particularly in the case of military and war museums.

Over time these national museums have steadily increased their collections, both as a result of purchase and donations. This has put pressure on space and financial resources. Many museums have sought to build extensions, but this has not always been possible on cramped sites. Alternatives involve either a second museum in the capital city or a museum/exhibition space in another city. In London, the Tate art gallery split into two in the late 1990s and opened a second gallery, the Tate Modern, in a converted disused power station on the river front in the centre of London. At the same time the museum has opened branches in Liverpool (where the original donor, Tate, came from) and St Ives and has entered into an agreement with Sheffield for the short-term loaning of paintings. The establishment of branches in other cities by national museums has been a source of controversy with national elites claiming that these collections should be kept in the capital where they are allegedly more accessible (to them at least!). In Britain the creation of the National Railway Museum in York and the relocation of the Royal Armouries collection to Leeds created such protests. However, provincial cities have been pleased at the prospect of a branch of a national collection to add to their visitor attractions and have competed to obtain them, outbidding each other in the funds they have been prepared to contribute to the construction of a new facility.

National museums located in capital cities arouse much envy from provincial museums because they appear generously funded and receive many donations. It is relatively easy for them to raise funds for an extension either from rich individuals (whose name may appear on the extension) or from large corporations. They are also more likely to have their special exhibitions reviewed in the national press, thus increasing attendance. However, in recent years they have been under various pressures to demonstrate their worth, by increasing visitor numbers and to generate income via sales of goods, catering, corporate hospitality and sponsorship (Kay, 1996). Notwithstanding their generous basic funding, they have to operate in a more commercial way and use marketing to attract visitors and income. One aspect of this is the special event, such as the art blockbuster, discussed in a later chapter. Museums have had to become more visitor friendly, more interactive, more participative, more hands-on and use advanced technology to create exciting displays. Critics such as Hewison (1991) argue that by being forced into the market-place museums have lost the values on which they were based and that to attract sponsorship they have to be more contemporary, less critical and align exhibitions with consumerist products.

Local authority museums developed in the nineteenth century and were one consequence of rapid urbanization, As large cities evolved they aspired to have a museum and art gallery, mainly to provide education and culture to the population, or at least the emerging middle classes, but no doubt also to demonstrate that they were a place of significance. In Europe and later in North America, wealthy local people assisted with the creation of collections and construction of buildings, which once again were meant to be impressive. By the late twentieth century many of these local sources of wealth had disappeared as companies were floated on the stock exchange and individuals took their wealth elsewhere. These museums have always relied overwhelmingly on funding from the local authority and this has limited the scale of finance and periodically been a reason for cut-backs, as in times of difficulty other more basic welfare services have always been able to claim priority. Notwithstanding these problems, local authorities have been keen to expand their museums and other attractions, for general education reasons and also as a tourism resource. Once again, the collections of local authority museums have been growing larger and there has been a need to find extra space. By splitting up the collection and establishing a new building a separate museum could be created. The width of municipal collections has also been increasing. Deindustrialization in the second half of the twentieth century focused attention on old industries and also old ways of living which resulted in the creation of industrial and folk museums, often in the original premises. In 1991 Birmingham opened The Discovery Centre in the Jewellery Quarter by turning the original, unaltered workshops of a firm that had closed into a museum. Local authority museums have not been immune to the commercial pressures described above which have confronted the national museums. In some cases a long tradition of free entry has been overturned, and particularly for new museums, entry charges have been imposed. In order to improve existing museums and create new ones, local authorities have had to be pro-active, innovative and entrepreneurial. This has meant seeking grants and donations wherever they can be found, including lottery and EU funds. Persistent resource constraints have meant that museums have to be justified by demonstrating the contribution they make to the community. In this respect, visitor numbers have become very significant as has their value to tourism. New museums are expected to contribute to the attraction of tourists and also to urban regeneration. In the case of the Greater Manchester Museum of Science and Industry, these aims are included among its 15 objectives, as follows:

- to act as catalyst in the regeneration of Castlefield (a fringe area of the city centre) and inner Manchester generally;
- to contribute to Manchester's growing role in tourism;
- to act as an economic stimulus not only through the spending power of visitors, but also in the ordering of goods and services in the locality;
- to engage in marketing and publicity to enhance the public awareness not only of the museum and Castlefield, but also the region generally.

This museum was deliberately located in a redundant railway goods yard which includes within its site the world's first passenger station, the terminus of the 1830 Manchester to Liverpool railway, thus making a contribution to preservation, renewal and regeneration in the area.

Visitor attractions in the private sector operate to make a profit. While occasionally they involve historic buildings and sites and their conservation, as at Warwick Castle in Britain, they are run on a purely commercial basis. A private sector visitor attraction must cover all its running costs, pay off debts incurred in its construction and return a profit to its shareholders, and most of this will be achieved via the entry charge. The most characteristic visitor attractions in the private sector tend to be large in scale, to have high visitor numbers and to have an important entertainment or pleasure dimension (Deloitte and Touche, 1997). However, smaller attractions can be profitable where the scale is optimum, the overheads low and there is a steady if not large flow of visitors. Many of the most successful private visitor attractions cater for family entertainment and include zoos, aquariums, theme parks and entertainment complexes. This sector was transformed in the second half of the twentieth century by the creation of the Disney theme parks, the first one being at Anaheim in California in 1955. Built on a large scale, enough to keep a family occupied for a day, they involve fantasy, entertainment and rides. This was an innovation that was quickly followed by other operators around the world and both Disney, Universal and Six Flags have developed or taken over parks outside the United States. The high quality of the visitor experience at the Disney theme parks has proved to be a benchmark for all other visitor attractions, influencing them to include more fun and entertainment (Deloitte and Touche, 1997). Because of their physical scale, they need a great deal of space, thus, theme parks are not generally perceived as distinctly urban attractions. Many are located in the countryside while others have been sited on the edge of cities. Disney World in Florida was located in an undeveloped area but as a result of its growth and the other theme parks it has attracted to the area, the population has grown to one million, making it a significant urban location (Foglesong, 1999). While, in theory, all these attractions rely on private capital, there are numerous instances where the grants have been given to entice them to an area and perhaps to assist with urban regeneration, where the general infrastructure has been paid for by the community and where other concessions have been obtained, as with the modification of planning laws.

Many private sector visitor attractions are associated with other activities and have as their aim the enhancement of corporate profitability, although in most cases they will still have to pay their way. Such establishments include factory tours and visitor centres where it is hoped the demonstrations will raise the image, visibility and sales of a product. These are usually located at the factory, as the example of Cadbury World in Birmingham illustrates (see Swarbrooke,1995, case study), but in some cases the visitor attraction may be located elsewhere, as with the World of Coca Cola, sited in Atlanta's downtown area. In the Potteries area of Britain, there are many such visitor centres associated with the industry and it is sold to tourists under the slogan 'Do China in a Day' (Ball and Metcalfe, 1992). This idea of associated visitor attractions has been spreading more widely as witnessed by sports museums and fun parks at shopping centres (Stevens, 2000). In the countryside many farms have developed visitor attractions as a means of diversification.

The voluntary sector is very diverse and often involves trusts which have been established to preserve something, whether this is a collection (in a museum), a steam railway or an historic property. The purpose of opening up the site as a visitor attraction is in part to generate income to achieve the aims of the trust, although clearly there will also be an aim to provide public access. In recent years a few hard-pressed local authorities have handed their museums over to trusts in the hope that they can become self-supporting. Included in this sector may be churches and cathedrals which in the past would have been open free to the public. As the cost of maintaining these old buildings is high and the incomes of churches are falling, they are often turning themselves into entry-charging attractions with the usual array of visitor facilities. Many of these voluntary sector attractions have received grants from the public sector to support the preservation that they are doing and also to support the role they have as a visitor attraction for tourists. In Britain in the late 1980s these 'independent museums' received 53 per cent of their income from public funds (quoted by Hewison, 1991).

The visitor attractions in both the private and voluntary sectors are highly dependent on customer income and thereby visitor numbers, and cannot fall back on a public subsidy should these not reach a breakeven point. Failure to reach this point may quickly result in closure. This has been seen among the spate of openings in Britain in the late 1990s, many aided by Lottery money. Based on over-optimistic forecasts of visitor numbers, lower than expected attendance figures quickly revealed them to be unviable. The National Centre for Popular Music in Sheffield was premised on attracting 400,000 visitors a year, but never achieved more than 130,000 a year and closed within two years.

When visitor attractions are classified by type, this generally refers to whether they are a museum or art gallery, historic building, garden, wildlife centre, theme park, etc. In recent years there has been an increasing variety of visitor attractions and it is not possible to devise one typology which neatly and in a watertight way enables every attraction to be classified in an entirely satisfactory manner (Robinson, 1994). Very often old buildings are used as museums and could be classified in either category. In the 1980s new heritage attractions came to be described as 'experience attractions' distinguishable from museums because they were not centred on collections, although some element of this may have been present (Johnson, 1991).

VISITOR NUMBERS

Annual attendance is the primary performance indicator for visitor attractions, including those in the public sector, and has had the effect of shifting their aims towards market-driven approaches (Koster, 1996). From the point of view of the tourism industry, the success of an attraction is measured not only by the number of visitors it receives, but also by the proportion who come from a distance (that is from outside the local area) and the extent to which it persuades visitors to stay overnight and thus make a greater economic impact. In recent years statistics on the number of visits made to attractions have been collected, and although they are not always reliable or completely comprehensive, it is possible to compare facilities and their appeal and to examine the trends in visitation over many years. In general with more leisure time, easier travel and greater affluence, visitation is increasing, but at the same time, as will be discussed later, there is a greater supply, and also there is competition from many other parts of the leisure sector, so success is not assured. To a certain extent every visitor attraction has to depend on its own merits, how well presented it is and how it meets customer needs. However, comparing visitor numbers across different sectors, it is apparent that some attractions in some sectors, noticeably theme parks, because of their theme element and because of their scale are able to attract visitors in their millions, while the average number to a country house might only be about 40,000, although there may be far more country houses than theme parks. Within each sector there will be variations reflecting many factors, including the scale and capacity of the facility, the length of opening, the cost of entry, the scale of marketing and the likelihood of repeat visits. Attractions located in populous areas have a large potential market on their doorstep, but although people may come once, they may never come again. Attractions located in tourist areas have a potential population of visitors which is much larger than the local population. Further, if there is a turnover of visitors, i.e. different people come each year, then the number of potential visitors may be very large. Again, holiday-makers with plenty of leisure time may be more inclined to use a visitor attraction than local people as they are looking for something to do.

All these factors are important in understanding the number of visitors to an attraction, but there is a further factor which is difficult to pinpoint but which explains the success of certain visitor attractions in both the numbers they attract and the distance from which visitors come. Attractions are described as being in the top rank, world class, the premier league, five star, unique, special, as being a must-see or unmissable. This in part relates to the qualities of the attraction; a large collection of paintings including many by the most famous artists in the world, a view from one of the highest structures in the world over one of the world's most beautiful cities, the largest and most decorated churches in the world, or a museum containing some of the world's most important archaeological artefacts. However, this quality of excellence may be only part of the appeal. These attractions have wide appeal in terms of their theme and also because they are very widely known because of the media attention. As with cities, this may be organic, mention and pictures just naturally appear, as with Paris's Eiffel Tower, but there may also have been an element of marketing, as with the Disney theme parks. In MacCannell's (1976) and Leiper's (1990) terminology, these visitor attractions have very strong 'generating markers' or information. But in whatever way, these are attractions which have the ability to draw visitors from a long distance away, which will in part explain the large attendance figures. In general, the average person will not travel a distance to see an attraction which is similar to one they have in their home region or country. Accordingly, zoos and science/industry museums do not have the appeal described above. Some types of attractions, such as theme parks and aquariums, which were once fairly rare, have been copied in large numbers and ceased to be as effective as tourist magnets.

Two examples of this impact can be illustrated. The Louvre art gallery and museum in Paris is in the top handful of such institutions in the world. In recent years there has been considerable investment in extending and improving the museum, including the construction of a pyramid in the courtyard where some of the visitor services are concentrated. Visitor numbers have increased from around 3.5 million to 5 million and Figure 5.1 shows the origin of visitors. Only 22 per cent come from Paris and its region with a further 16 per cent from the rest of France, leaving 62 per cent from the rest of the world. In the case of the British Museum in London, where there is free entry, unlike the Louvre, visitor numbers have also nearly doubled in recent years to reach 6

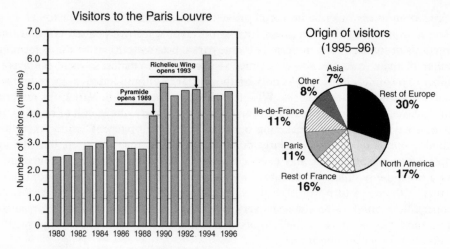

Figure 5.1 The growth of visitor numbers and their origin at the Louvre, Paris

million in 1997 and a similar proportion come from outside the country (see Figure 5.2). Both these museums have outstanding collections, but they are also situated in two of the world's most popular tourist cities which provide a ready market.

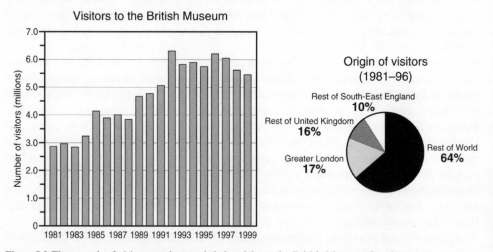

Figure 5.2 The growth of visitor numbers and their origin at the British Museum, London

On the basis of the proportion of visitors who come from different catchment areas, visitor attractions can be classified as local, regional, national or international, although some facilities may attract a high proportion of non-locals because they are situated in a popular destination which draws visitors from a wide area. Swarbrooke (1995) also classifies visitor attractions into those which are 'primary' and have a quality on their own to motivate tourists to travel a distance, and those which are 'secondary' which lack this quality. Leiper (1990) suggested a threefold classification: primary being those attractions which are known in advance and influential in the decision to travel; secondary being those known in advance but not influential in the decision to travel; and tertiary being those not known before travelling to a place.

The number of visitor attractions in this top level is relatively small. They are well known and have the ability to draw people from a distance even when they are sited in what at first sight appears to be a most unpromising area. For most attractions this is not the case. Tourists want to visit a city because of its image and general qualities and only when they arrive do they learn about the attractions that are there (Middleton, 1994). Of course, there are some visitors with specialist knowledge and a strong interest who will go to places because they are drawn to a particular attraction, but they are the minority.

THE VISITOR ATTRACTION LIFECYCLE

The product lifecycle model has been developed by marketeers to illustrate the demand for new products. Initially, demand is low as the product is expensive and may still be undergoing technological development. Many firms may enter the industry believing that they have a product of the future. As the product becomes known, and there is more confidence in it, demand begins to increase. This enables economies of scale to be gained and the price to fall, which in turn encourages more sales. However, only a few firms gain the economies of scale and these become the survivors from the original entrants. After a period of rapid increase in sales, demand begins to slacken as market penetration is reached and there may be a fall in sales to reflect replacement demand. After this mature stage, there may be fall in demand as other new products come along to replace the original product. However, either this may not happen and demand will remain strong, or with further product development there will be a rejuvenation of demand. This model can be applied both to an industry and to a particular product. The timespan for any product lifecycle will vary; for some products it will be decades while for others in areas of rapidly changing technology, it may be only a few years.

Swarbrooke (1995) and others have attempted to apply this model to new visitor attractions (see Figure 5.3). It is suggested that rather than a slow increase in demand there will be a rapid growth of demand brought about by publicity and the novelty of the new attraction. A peak demand will be reached quickly followed by a slow decline in visitor numbers. This will reflect the fact that most of the people in the immediate area will have seen the attraction and not make a repeat visit. In the past, repeat visits were probably more common, but today with so much choice of things to do this is less likely. The modern visitor is looking for something different, for novelty (Richards, 1996). Accordingly, they may also be drawn to other new visitor attractions in the area or other alternative uses for their time. This scenario appears to suggest that the facility is dependent on the population in the local region. However, it might be that the quality of the attraction is such that it can draw visitors in from a larger area and thus maintain visitor numbers. This will happen if the visitor attraction is fairly unique and there are no competitors. Alternatively, with further product development, rotating displays and special events (see later chapter), it may be able to encourage repeat visits and so maintain visitor numbers. As mentioned above, an attraction in a well-developed tourism area may well be able to survive as there is a continuous flow of potential visitors arriving in the area. Unlike the product lifecycle cycle for manufactured goods, there are few economies of scale and thus no reductions in price with time, unless after the capital costs have been paid off, the firm decides to lower entry charges.

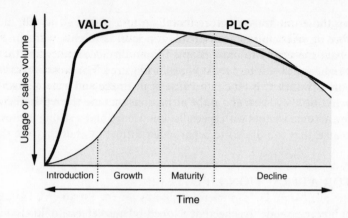

PLC   Product life cycle
VALC   Visitor attraction life cycle (after Swarbrooke, 1995)

Figure 5.3 The product lifecycle and visitor attraction lifecycle models
Source: After Swarbrooke (1995)

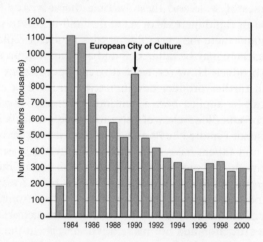

Figure 5.4 Visitor trends at the Burrell Collection, Glasgow, 1984–2000

Evidence to support these ideas can be found. Glasgow opened the Burrell Collection in a brand-new building in 1983. Visitor numbers quickly reached 1 million but have since been in steady decline except for 1990 when the city was European City of Culture with numerous events which attracted many tourists (see Figure 5.4). This example is unique in one respect in that under the terms of the bequest of William Burrell it was stated that the collection should only be shown on its own. This has prevented the use of special events using materials outside the collection as a means of boosting repeat visits. Not surprisingly, the city council has been trying to have this clause declared invalid. Although Glasgow has been developing its tourism industry (see Chapter 7), visitor numbers are clearly not enough to sustain visitor levels at this attraction. Many other new visitor attractions show a similar decline, although usually not so severe. Continued falls in visitor numbers may call for a radical rethink, with either a wholesale revamp or even closure. Granada Studios Tours, a TV theme park in Manchester centred on the *Coronation Street* set, opened in 1988 and for several years attracted over 600,000 visitors. However, by the late 1990s visitor numbers were declining rapidly. It became uneconomical to run and no ideas for rejuvenation were forthcoming so the attraction was closed.

THE SUPPLY OF VISITOR ATTRACTIONS

There are few reliable and comprehensive figures for the number of visitor attractions, but what evidence there is suggests that there has been an explosive growth in the late twentieth century. In 1999 in Britain no less than 65 per cent of visitor attractions had been opened since 1970 (ETC, 2000). The growth of museums also illustrates this point. In 1860 there were about 90 museums in Britain. By 1887 the number had grown to 217, by 1963 to 876 and by 1984 to 2,131. The Museums and Galleries Commission estimated that in 1989 there were 2,500 museums and art galleries, and that a new one was opening every two weeks (but some were closing as well). In the USA in the 1960s a new museum opened every 3.3 days and by the early 1980s there were 6,000 museums, of which 2,000 were funded by some level of government (Glaser, 1986). A 1989 survey by the American Association of Museums recorded over 8,000 organizations using its broad definition, of which nearly two-thirds had been opened since 1960 (American Association of Museums, 1992). There has also been an increase in the number of museums in Western Europe in countries such as Germany, the Netherlands and Switzerland (Schouten, 1998). In a survey of cultural attractions in Western Europe, G. Richards (1996) found that between 1970 and 1991 the number had increased by 113 per cent. World-wide, it is estimated that there are over 25,000 museums.

The growth in the number of visitor attractions reflects various factors. There has undoubtedly been a desire to preserve the best of the past and to display more of our culture. The growth of income and the ease of travel have made commercial attractions viable. At the same time communities ambitious to develop their tourist industries have been encouraging the development of new attractions. Frequently this motive has been linked with the need to find anchors for regenerated areas. In Britain the advent of the National Lottery in 1994 and its policy of concentrating on capital grants (at least for the first five years) encouraged many new museum projects with at least 25 major facilities in the period 1994–2002 (Waycott, 1999). But a crucial question to be asked is whether there are enough visitors to go round. Is there market saturation? Will visitors be diluted over too many sites with the result that many are unviable? Will there be Lottery 'white elephants'? Will the visitor attraction lifecycle be speeded up as new attractions syphon off visitors from existing ones? One estimate has suggested that in Britain the Lottery-funded projects are based on attracting 24 million visitors or 6 per cent of visits to all attractions in a market which at best is growing by only 1.3 per cent a year. A study of industrial heritage attractions found that although the number of visits was increasing, this was entirely due to new sites and that the average number of visitors per site was falling in what was described as a mature product (Woodward, 2000). The increased competition in the industry has certainly stimulated quality and innovation, most notably in the way that entertainment has been introduced into many attractions. Museums sometimes describe themselves as being in 'edutainment' or 'infotainment' and providing 'opportunities for learning with fun'.

THE DEMAND FOR VISITOR ATTRACTIONS

There are three aspects of demand which are relevant to an understanding of the role of visitor attractions in city tourism. The first concerns the actual demand for attractions as shown by visitor figures and surveys taken at these places. The second concerns the general demand for visitor attractions as shown by surveys of recreational behaviour, and the third concerns surveys of tourists' actual behaviour in cities. Unfortunately the data on all these aspects are neither comprehensive nor reliable, but what is available can shed some light on the situation.

In Britain the number of visits to attractions is published and the figures are analysed (BTA/ETB annual). They are not completely comprehensive as a number of privately run attractions refuse to divulge their admissions. In the case of free attractions, estimates are given and these may not be completely reliable. Over the years the reports have become more comprehensive and so comparisons over time may again not be valid. The figures suggest that during the 1980s there was significant growth in numbers at all types of visitor attractions, but that during the 1990s, particularly the late 1990s, entries to traditional visitor attractions such as historic properties and museums, have been static. This accords with the survey by G. Richards (1994a, 1996) who found that between 1970 and 1991 entries to cultural attractions in Western Europe increased by 100 per cent, with the rate of growth varying according to the economic cycle. One partial explanation for these trends is that during the 1990s several national museums were forced to introduce charges with a resulting fall in entries. Any growth that has occurred has tended to be at non-urban attractions such as the new farm attractions. As a consequence, facilities have had to fight for both new visitors and repeat visits by updating their exhibitions and laying on special events. Those that have done this have kept their numbers up, while the others have seen them fall. Another explanation for the situation in Britain is the impact of the introduction of Sunday shopping which diverted demand away from visitor attractions.

While there are a very large number of visitor attractions, there is only a small group of attractions which draw their visitors in hundreds of thousands. In the United Kingdom, the 43 museums and art galleries which attracted more than 250,000 visits in 1999 were responsible for 43.2 per cent of all visits to this type of attraction, although they represented only 2.4 per cent of sites for which there was information. There was also geographical concentration with the 11 museums in London in the above list responsible for 26.2 per cent of all visits within this category. This is likely to be the situation across the visitor attraction industry. In reality, there are only a small number of facilities which either have the quality to draw large numbers and/or are situated in the right place.

Information on the number of visits to the visitor attractions in Britain's major cities outside London are shown in Table 5.1. During the 1980s the number of visits was increasing and many cities gained new visitor attractions. However, during the 1990s many cities saw visitor numbers decline as visits to both old and some new visitor

Table 5.1 Visits to attractions in British cities outside London

Rank	City	1981	1991	1999
			Visits in 000s	
1	Edinburgh	3781	4139	5916
2	Glasgow	1394	2743	3634
3	York	2412	2432	1954
4	Liverpool	998	1751	1549
5	Birmingham	859	1786	1543
6	Bristol	1363	1235	1543
7	Manchester	534	1699	1487
8	Portsmouth	713	1401	1192
9	Cardiff	837	851	1056
10	Nottingham	1330	1647	860
11	Leeds	350	385	851
12	Bradford	224	988	824
13	Sheffield	538	675	NA

Notes: Excludes churches and gardens. Includes visitor attractions in the urban core and other major ones in the urban area.
Source: ETB Research Services

attractions fell, possibly in line with the product lifecycle model. This was a period when there were increasing leisure opportunities and thus more competition. In some cases, as in Nottingham, the decline was possibly caused by the introduction of entry charges. In Edinburgh and Glasgow there was a continuing flow of new attractions, or refurbishments of old ones, which offset any decline in the surviving facilities. Leeds also gained three new attractions in the 1990s. Many cities are in the process of adding to their visitor attractions, a process aided by grants from the National Lottery in the late 1990s, but at the time of writing it is not possible to assess their success.

Surveys of visitors to these attractions reveal different profiles. As might be expected, families (young adults and children) are mainly drawn to zoos and wildlife parks including aquariums, theme parks and certain children-friendly museums such as natural history, science, industry and railways. These attractions draw visitors across the social class spectrum. Museums and art galleries attract visitors from a wider age range, from 18 to 55 particularly and from social classes ABC1. Studies of museum visitors suggest that the length of education is a critical factor in determining whether people visit museums and art galleries. Bourdieu (1984) has argued that education gives the individual the necessary cultural capital to appreciate museums. G. Richards (1996) has suggested that the increase in museum attendance in recent years reflects the lengthening of education for many in society. Because the well-educated and higher socio-economic groups have the ability to travel and spend more than other groups in society, it is perhaps inevitable that visitor attractions will be geared to attract them.

A crucial question for urban tourism is how many of these visitors come from outside the local area and thus bring income into the economy. Many surveys ask patrons for their home area so that they can be classified into locals (those within 10–20 miles), day trippers and tourists (i.e. those staying overnight). Table 5.2 shows the results of some of these enquiries. Within Britain, London has the highest proportion of tourists, with all other centres having a much lower share. Edinburgh and Glasgow do well, but most cities only have a small share. However, if day trippers are taken into account, it can be seen that many cities have up to about 25 per cent of visitors coming from outside the immediate local area, and thus making a significant contribution to visitor numbers. As

Table 5.2 Museum visitors by origin: selected British cities

Area	Percentage of the total		
	Local resident	*Day tripper*	*Tourist*
London	29	27	44
Glasgow (1985)	56	19	25
Merseyside	65	20	15
Ipswich	36	34	30
Glasgow (1990)	50	23	27

Source: Myerscough (1988a, 1991)

a general summary of this point it can be suggested that the larger the attraction in terms of attendance, the greater its share of tourists is likely to be. Perhaps this is obvious, since to attract large numbers an attraction will have to draw people from well outside its local area.

Some surveys of visitors at attractions also ask whether the main reason for coming to the city was the attraction. Replies can be classified into: (a) sole reason; (b) one among a mixture of reasons; and (c) of no importance. This enables an estimate to be made of the importance of attractions in winning visitors to the city. The results for a survey in Glasgow are shown in Table 5.3, where it can be seen that the visitor attraction is very important for people travelling from home, but not very important for the tourist.

Table 5.3 Glasgow museum and art gallery attendances, 1986: main reason for visiting area or city (%)

Reason	Resident	Day visitor	Tourist
To visit this venue	48	56	11
To visit the arts in general	14	10	5
General sightseeing	11	11	16
Work	8	6	8
Shopping	4	3	–
Visiting friends and relatives	3	11	59
Personal business	8	3	1
Other	3	–	–

Source: Myerscough (1988a)

Another type of survey has inquired into the motives of visitors to attractions. In a study of heritage attractions it was found that most visitors did not have specialist interest in the topic but were merely looking for a day out (Prentice, 1989, 1993). G. Richards (1996) in his study of cultural attractions in Western Europe similarly found that only 9 per cent could be described as 'specific cultural tourists'. A survey of visitors to the British Museum in London found that many did not have a clear idea of what they had come to see and some had come because they were with a group (Capstick, 1985). The visitors in these surveys were already in the area on holiday but it is unlikely that they would have been attracted to the area because of the attractions. In another study of an art museum it was found that the underlying motives for the visit were 'to be given food for thought', 'to learn something' and 'to enrich your life' (Jansen-Verbeke and Rekom, 1996). No doubt the reasons for visiting a theme park would be very different.

There are surveys of recreational behaviour which ask whether the respondent has visited a museum or art gallery in the past 12 months. In the United States the National Endowment for the Arts has undertaken regular surveys which are summarized in the Statistical Abstract of the United States. One question concerns visits to art galleries where the incidence of positive responses has increased from 22 per cent in 1983 to 35 per cent in 1997. At all dates the likelihood of visiting art museums is correlated very closely with the length of education, having a higher income and being between 18 and 54. In Britain different surveys give different results which may reflect the definitions used (Hooper-Greenhill, 1994). A 1998 Mori poll for the Museums and Galleries Commission showed that in the previous 12 months 35 per cent of the respondents had visited a museum and 33 per cent had visited a zoo or wildlife park. However, another survey showed that only about 22 per cent of the population have visited a museum in the last twelve months, a figure that does not appear to have changed much over the years (Social Trends). In the Netherlands a similar result was found with 34 per cent having visited a museum in the past 12 months (Schouten, 1998). As these surveys ask repondents to recall events which may be up to a year previously, there could be an underestimate of the actual situation.

Table 5.4 Frequency of visiting museums

Type of visitor	Percentage of sample
Frequent: visit three or more times a year	17
Regular: visit once or twice a year	37
Occasional: last visited between one and four years ago	14
Rare: last visited five or more years ago	14
Non-visitor: never visited a museum	18

Source: Merriman (1991)

In addition to the likelihood of visiting an attraction, there is also the question of frequency. Some surveys also suggest that among certain groups the frequency of visiting museums has gone up, and one conclusion is that there is a group of heavy users, who may constitute a significant proportion of museum visitors (Hooper-Greenhill, 1994). In a 1985 postal survey Merriman (1991) asked respondents whether they had visited a museum or art gallery in the last year. On this basis he was able to classify them into five groups (Table 5.4) with the 'frequent' group, defined as those who visited three or more times a year, accounting for 17 per cent of the total. In a similar survey in Toledo, USA, Hood (quoted in Greenhill, 1988) divided respondents into three categories on the basis of frequency: frequent, occasional and non-participants. The frequent visitors formed only 14 per cent of the total but were responsible for 40–50 per cent of all visits. They were motivated to do something worthwhile, having the challenge of a new experience and having the opportunity to learn. G. Richards (1996) came to similar conclusions from his surveys of cultural tourists in Western Europe.

Surveys which ask repondents about their behaviour while on holiday during this period are likely to be more reliable and perhaps show a higher percentage going to visitor attractions. In London up to 60 per cent of overseas visitors report that they will visit at least one attraction (LTB annual) while for domestic visitors the equivalent figure is only 16–17 per cent for staying and day trippers. In Liverpool surveys of visitors at the Albert Dock, where there are four attractions, found that 28 per cent were going to the attractions, a higher figure than for surveys in the city centre. In these surveys the other and equally important activities were shopping and general sightseeing (TMP, 2000). Overall, these surveys should make commentators cautious about suggesting that visitor attractions are by far the most important reason for visiting cities, and that the only way to attract more visitors is to develop more attractions. They are clearly important for some people but not everyone.

Unfortunately, there are few surveys which measure the pattern of visiting in cities, i.e. whether according to Fodness (1990), there is 'customer interchange'. For instance, it would appear natural that a visitor to one art gallery in a city would also visit another one if present and that there would be a high customer interchange between them. Likewise, between science and industry museums and also between historic buildings. This would enable an assessment to be made on the extent to which the visitor attraction market was unified, segmented or discrete.

VISITOR ATTRACTIONS AND THE DEVELOPMENT OF DESTINATIONS

The relationship between visitor attractions and the growth of a tourist destination is a difficult one to untangle and is likely to vary from one city to another so making precise generalizations impossible. The appeal of many cities is far wider than just visitor attractions and so how these other aspects of the city are developed is just as important as the visitor attraction sector. The aim of aspiring destinations is to persuade tourists to come to the city and then stay for some time. To achieve this there must be many things to do, and undoubtedly one of the most important of these is provided by visitor attractions. So whether as the initial draw or as a means of encouraging the tourist to stay longer, the visitor attraction sector is very important.

Small places may be dominated by a single visitor attraction. If that facility is of a very high quality, then it may draw very large numbers and Swarbrooke (1995) has suggested that because of this, other attractions, as well as other amenities, may be drawn to the location. As more attractions come to the site, its appeal is increased and more visitors arrive, with the result that there may be a virtuous circle of growth and with it an ever broadening array of visitor attractions. Orlando in Florida illustrates this process. The Disney organization picked the undeveloped area in the mid-1960s as a site for a theme park. It was well located with respect to motorways and because it was undeveloped the land could be bought cheaply and the community was prepared to give concessions (Foglesong, 1999). Disney World, the Magic Kingdom, opened in 1971, has attracted over 10 million visitors a year. Since then the corporation has continued to create further theme parks including Epcot (1982), Disney-MGM Studios (1989) and the Animal Kingdom (1998), and Disney sites now have over 41 million visits a year. As a consequence of the success of Disney, numerous other theme parks have been attracted to the area including Sea World (1973), Universal Studios (1990), Splendid China (1993) and Discovery Cove (2000). The area has also become important for conventions and the number of hotel bedrooms is over 92,000. As a destination it receives over 36 million visitors a year, of whom nearly 8 per cent are foreign. In 30 years the population of the area has grown to over 1 million.

In this case one major visitor attraction has caused a place to develop and been the reason for other attractions coming to the area. In the case of major capital cities, there

Table 5.5 New visitor attractions in London, 1993–2000

Year	New visitor attraction
1993	Buckingham Palace
	Lloyds of London Visitor Centre
	Winston Churchill's Britain at War Experience
	Spitting Image Rubberworks (later closed)
1994	Shakespeare's Globe Theatre and Exhibition
1995	Albert Memorial Visitor Centre
1997	London Aquarium
	BBC Experience
1998	Sega World
	Magic Circle Museum
	Estorick Collection (art gallery)
1999	Vinopolis
	Premier League Hall of Fame
	Guildhall Art Gallery
2000	London Eye (Ferris Wheel)
	Dali Universe
	Tate Modern
	Gilbert Collection (Somerset House)
	Hermitage Collection (Somerset House)

are many reasons for visiting the city and visitor numbers are already large. There are already many visitor attractions, but the success of the destination will stimulate the creation of many more. These in turn will further increase the appeal of the city, so many things to do and worth another visit, with the consequence of increasing visitor numbers. So there becomes another virtuous circle of growth, success begetting growth. The example of London illustrates this case. Hardly a year goes by when there have not been new attractions (Table 5.5). Some are in the public sector, but even here success in obtaining grants is easier than in smaller places because success in obtaining visitors appears much more assured, thereby justifying the giving of a grant. There are also many private sector attractions, which see the opportunities of the market.

Second-tier cities provide a third case where the role of visitor attractions can be examined. Here there are a limited number of attractions, many good but not of the highest class to win a large number of visitors from a distance and maybe not good enough on their own to warrant too many people staying for a short break. These types of destinations have placed much significance on gaining further visitor attractions, but can they pull in the visitors? Without a major magnet it is unlikely that visitors will be drawn solely because of visitor attractions. The fact that there are many will contribute to the general appeal and image of the place. Encouraging more visitor attractions could be risky in that without extra tourists, visitors could be spread more thinly, making each attraction less viable (Middleton, 1994). In this case the facilities would be in competition with each other. However, on the other hand, if the city is being sold in a particular way, as a city of art, of heritage, etc., then having a group of allied but complementary attractions could strengthen the marketing of the city. In this case the attractions could be seen to be working collaboratively rather than competitively. The example of Glasgow's Burrell Collection in a city which is selling itself as a city of culture, suggests that it is difficult. Glasgow has been attempting to create a group of art/cultural attractions in the hope that there will be a critical mass which will make the breakthrough, but this has not happened yet.

URBAN REGENERATION AND SPECIAL DISTRICTS

The creation of visitor attractions by cities is not merely a policy to attract tourists and provide better amenities for local residents but one that can be used to facilitate urban renewal. The spatial problems and policies of cities have already been discussed in Chapters 3 and 4. Decay is affecting the fringe areas of the city centre and the surrounding inner city. Policies are aimed at regenerating these areas with the city centre as the initial focus for new and growing economic activities, in the hope that the positive impacts will spill over and trickle down to the inner city. One method of starting this process is to locate the new or expanded visitor attractions in the city centre fringe area, in some cases as flagship projects. A large project, built with architectural distinction, will boost confidence in the area. In many parts of the world, visitor attractions have been the anchor for regenerated dockland zones. In the well-publicized Baltimore case, the Inner Harbor was planned with three such attractions; an aquarium, a science museum and a viewing platform at the top of the World Trade Center. Since its opening in 1980 there have been attempts to get further visitor attractions, but in some cases these have failed. There are also benefits of clustering visitor attractions. It will enable visitors to move easily from one attraction to another, and, if this is known in advance, may encourage more visitors to come to the city. With a critical mass of visitor attractions there will be some additional visiting as visitors may learn of another attraction that they did not know previously and make a visit. In 2000 at Somerset House in London two additional attractions were added, namely the Gilbert Collection and the Hermitage Collection, which drew many visitors and benefited the existing Courtaulds Institute An attractions quarter will have an identity within the city in a way that one attraction would not. A complex of museums enables the city to project a clear image of itself and obtain a high profile, even though most tourists may only visit a few

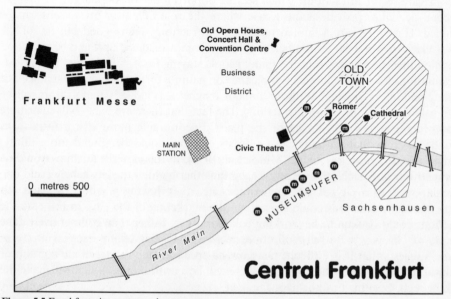

Figure 5.5 Frankfurt city centre and museums

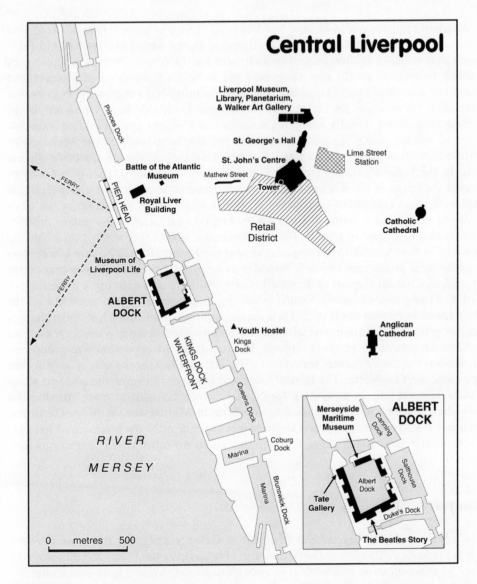

Figure 5.6 Liverpool city centre

of the total number of attractions. Co-ordinated events and special exhibitions within the attractions can be used to boost attendance with greater effect than for any one organization. Clustering will also accelerate external impacts in the form of souvenir and craft shops, and restaurants as the necessary thresholds will be reached sooner (Couch and Farr, 2000). However, Jansen-Verbeke and Rekom (1996) have questioned some of the advantages, arguing that each museum will have a different target group with no necessary overlap and that few tourists will wish to visit more than one or two museums in a day.

Many cities have therefore adopted policies of grouping attractions, although clearly there are limits to this policy and many older facilities, such as museums, may be scattered around the city in historic buildings and cannot be moved. One of the earliest examples of museum grouping is to be found in Berlin where Museum Island (Museuminsel) consists of five museums built between 1830 and 1900 as a flagship of cultural federalism for the new German state. In South Kensington in London four museums were developed in the late nineteenth century but perhaps the best known example is Washington, DC, where the Smithsonian Institution has 13 museums in the central area. More recently cities in Germany like Cologne and Frankfurt have followed a similar policy. Frankfurt has used the southern bank of the Main as the location for seven of its 24 museums, 11 of which were established in the 1980s (Figure 5.5). In the 1980s eight new museum buildings were constructed, part of a policy to change the image of the city using architecture. These museums attract about 2 million visitors a year. This policy of creating new museums has arisen because of the city's desire to prove that it is one of Europe's leading cultural cities with a mix of facilities providing a high quality lifestyle for its inhabitants, and that it is not just a banking centre. The South Bank (Museumsufer) is near the historic Romer Square where there are also some attractions and so it provides a compact tourist area. In preparation for its role of Cultural Capital of Europe in 2001, Rotterdam is creating a museumpark with five museums. Currently Vienna is seeking to extend its area of museums on the Ringstrasse northwestwards to create a museum quarter, and Munich is undertaking a similar process. In Britain several cities have considered creating such quarters, but their realization has been more difficult. Liverpool has the opportunity to group new attractions on the reclaimed waterfront. The Albert Dock is the site of a Maritime Museum, the Tate North, The Beatles Story and Liverpool Life and the adjacent Kings Dock site, used only as a car park for 20 years, could be used for more attractions if only they could be found (Figure 5.6). Similarly in Manchester the fringe Castlefield area was conceived as tourist and leisure zone, but except for the Science and Industry Museum and Granada Studios Tours (now closed) no other visitor attractions have been created.

Case Study: Bilbao

The opening of the Guggenheim Museum in October 1997 had the most dramatic impact on a city's tourism industry that arguably has ever been seen and although this may be a one-off case, it is significant enough to be worthy of a brief case study.

Bilbao is a northern Spanish city, the capital of the province of Vizcaya, one of the three provinces that form the Basque Region. From the middle of the nineteenth century iron ore was mined there, giving rise to an iron and steel industry and also shipbuilding, other heavy engineering industries and chemicals. These lined the riverside below the city, which also acted as a port, to the nearby estuary. By the 1980s, metropolitan Bilbao had a population of just over 900,000, of which 400,000 were found within the city boundaries. Until 1975 when Franco died, Spanish industry was heavily protected, but subsequent exposure to competition caused many firms to close. Within about ten years 100,000 manufacturing jobs had been lost in the Basque Region, or about 25 per cent of the sector total. Unemployment rose to 25 per cent, and in Bilbao many industrial sites lay derelict, including some close to the city centre.

The response by the local authorities in the Bilbao region was to prepare a strategic plan for the metropolitan region and to seek to restructure the economy to a service-based one and also to transform Bilbao's image (Henry and Paramio-Salcines, 1998). The example of other cities including Glasgow, Baltimore and Pittsburgh was studied and followed (Gomez, 1998; Gonzalez, 1993). The city was fortunate in that significant funds were available, enough to establish a development corporation and pay for infrastructure improvements including a new airport and metro. It was also hoped to enhance the status and image of the city through a major cultural project, but the city lacked any renowned collections of art. The project would also act as a visitor attraction, enhance the quality of life, create jobs and symbolize the renewed dynamism of the city.

At the time that Bilbao was looking for a partner for its major cultural project, the New York-based Guggenheim Museum, specializing in modern art, was seeking to establish a third European museum (after Venice and Berlin). Other cities were considered, but only Bilbao was able to offer both a building and an endowment to buy works of art. Although works of art would be purchased, the main exhibitions would be those that had been exhibited at its other sites, and they would have little connection with the local culture. Some Basque nationalists saw this as evidence of cultural imperialism, while others thought that the culture should be indigenous and democratic, but local political leaders justified their action by saying that it would put them on the circuit of global tourism (McNeill, 2000). Barcelona, Madrid and Seville had all staged international events in 1992 and Bilbao's leaders were keen to make a similar claim for the city. In 1991 the director of the Guggenheim travelled to Bilbao with a view to establishing a museum in a disused wine storage warehouse. Its image was to be enhanced through the construction of a large cube on its roof. The architect Frank Gehry was invited to attend as he had experience of similar conversions (van Bruggen, 1997). Both agreed that the building was unsuitable and suggested as an alternative an industrial site besides the river that was being cleared for regeneration and this idea was accepted (Figure 5.7). Following a limited architectural competition, Frank Gehry was contracted to design the $100 million building which has been described as a 'monumental cubist sculpture of a ship'. The schimmering titanium clad structure also includes a 165-ft atrium. It was opened to acclaim in October 1997 and travel brochures often describe it as the 'architectural masterpiece of the twentieth century'. Its image was very quickly diffused around the world, no doubt helped by its American connections.

Hitherto, Bilbao, as one might expect of an industrial place, had not been noted as a tourist city. About 60 per cent of its visitors before 1997 were business people, including attenders at its trade fairs, and there were few leisure tourists. While it was hoped that the Guggenheim would have an effect, the visitor forecast numbers for this entry charging attraction, were put at only 500,000. This total was exceeded in the first six months, and the figure for the first three years was 3,457,000. There was a small drop after the first year but entries as of the third anniversary were still running at the rate of 1 million a year. Overall, 18 per cent of the visitors have come from the local region, 36 per cent from the rest of Spain and 46 per cent from outside the country (Guggenheim, 1999, 2000). This local component has tended to fall while the foreign share has increased, perhaps an indication of the success of packaged short breaks. Plaza (1999, 2000a, 2000b) has attempted to evaluate the impact of the museum on the tourism industry of the region, taking into account other developments which might attract

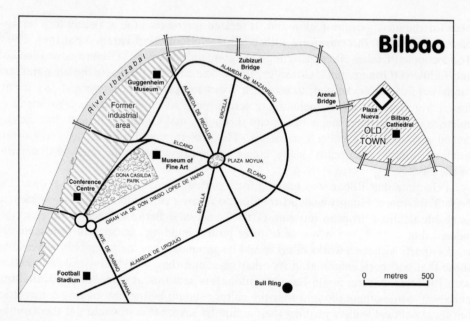

Figure 5.7 Bilbao city centre

tourists. She estimates that about 50 per cent of the increase in visitors to the region, or over 200,000 people, is due to the museum. Other surveys have suggested that the Guggenheim is the overwhelming reason why foreign visitors come to Bilbao and that it is the architecture that attracts them rather than the art inside. This has led to the comment that the best marketing ploy for an art gallery is to have a spectacular building.

It is not unknown for new visitor attractions to have a large initial effect, but the discussion above of the visitor attraction lifecycle suggests the possibility of a declining pull. This can only be seen to apply to the Guggenheim in time. It may also depend on whether the city can expand its other attractions. Bilbao city centre is attractive and it has two small museums, but this is unlikely to be enough. Certainly, the initial impact of the Guggenheim has been very impressive, only theme parks have done better among entry-charging attractions. However, local critics argue that the money spent on the Guggenheim has displaced funds that would or could have been spent on local cultural projects.

Since its opening, the importance of stunning architecture and its impact on image and visitor numbers have been discussed even more than previously and many cities are seeking to emulate its example. Just as cities like Amsterdam have described themselves as the 'Venice of the North' in the hope that Venice's fame will benefit them, so new visitor attractions such as the Lowry centre in Salford, Manchester, are describing themselves as the Guggenheim of the North. At least 60 cities have contacted the Guggenheim to seek a branch hoping that the magic can be worked again. The Guggenheim have decided to site their next museum in Rio de Janeiro. Other architects who have the ability to design impressive must-see buildings are in great demand, and nearly every new museum that is opened is compared to the Guggenheim to assess how far it measures up. Architecture has now become an element in the competition between places. Apart from the new project in Rio, and a museum in Las Vegas, the Guggenheim is having another new Gehry-designed museum in Manhattan, New York, aided by generous donations, and has also linked up with St Petersburg's Hermitage Museum and the Kuntshistorisches Museum in Vienna to enable the exchange of paintings and curatorial staff to boost their collective 'marketing and picture power' (Honigsbaum, 2001). Many see this as an attempt to create a global museum brand, the 'McGuggenheim'.

THE IMPACT OF VISITOR ATTRACTIONS

The direct impact of most visitor attractions is fairly small. Employment in museums is not large. Glasgow, which has one of the largest municipal museum services in the country, employed only 367 people in 1986. Of these, 11 per cent were in management, 26 per cent in curatorial services and education, 56 per cent in technical and security and the rest not classified. Since 1996 over 100 jobs have been lost because of the municipal financial crisis. Many visitor attractions employ part-time labour, and where visitor flows are uneven, this may be seasonal. Small independent museums often rely on unpaid volunteers without whom they could not function. Visitor attractions may have an additional impact if they are responsible for drawing tourists to the city who stay overnight and spend money elsewhere, from shops to restaurants. This may happen if there is a cluster of attractions which collectively acts as a magnet.

CONCLUSION

The aim of this chapter has been to assess the role of visitor attractions in the development of urban destinations. As a motivator for travel they can be very important at the regional, day-tripper scale, providing the main reason for the visit. By encouraging the development of visitor attractions, cities have been able to strengthen their regional roles. However, such travel may not have a great impact on the local economy as these visitors may not spend much outside the attraction and if it is free, there may be greater costs than benefits. Furthermore, without continuing or repeat visits, even these benefits may reduce over time. Accordingly, it is necessary for these attractions periodically either to update their offering or to put on special events.

In the case of the tourist or overnight stayer, visitor attractions seldom act on their own to draw visitors to the city. The example of the Guggenheim Museum in Bilbao, often described as an 'icon attraction' is exceptional, and may not persist after the novelty has worn off. In general, it would appear that tourists are attracted to a place by its general image and the range of things to do, of which one type will be visitor attractions. It is therefore sensible to develop a range of visitor attractions to offer the potential tourist, even though any one visitor may only go to one or two of them. One of the outcomes of a successful city break is that the visitor leaves with the feeling that there was so much to do, but so little time, and that they would like to return – a message that they may pass on to their friends.

The average tourist is unlikely to be drawn to a city because of its visitor attractions if he or she does not have any specialist interests. However, niche markets are growing, a product of rising education and wider experience. Surveys have revealed that among a small but growing group of patrons there is increased visiting frequency. These visitors are choosing to travel to places to pursue their specialist interests. Art museums are able to tap this market as there is no substitute for seeing original works. A cluster of high quality art museums or other visitor attractions between which there is some synergy, could act as a magnet for this growing segment of the city break market.

One of the problems of cities attempting to develop visitor attractions is that there is the danger of serial reproduction. A city develops a new type of attraction which is successful in gaining visitors from a wide area and immediately other cities follow suit, until every city has a similar facility and tourists no longer have to travel to have this experience. The example of aquariums in American cities illustrates this scenario. Currently a new breed of high tech attractions are being developed and there could be a similar scramble by cities to obtain them. The dangers of serial reproduction will be enhanced if global corporations emerge in the visitor attraction industry. Already Disney and other theme park operators are becoming multinational. Another possibility is for museums to join together in consortiums and share artefacts and special exhibitions, again, reducing the need to travel. The ambitions of New York's Guggenheim Museum, described above, could be a foretaste of what is to come.

The expansion and development of visitor attractions have played a major role in urban regeneration. Through using redundant buildings, derelict sites and the construction of stunning new buildings, they have assisted the rejuvenation of run-down zones and the creation of exciting new quarters. This impact may be almost as important as the role they play in winning tourists.

Chapter 6

Conferences and exhibitions

Conferences and exhibitions are activities that are often regarded as one of the staples of city tourism, particularly in North America. In some cities up to 40 per cent of those staying overnight in serviced accommodation have come for this type of business tourism. Conferences and exhibitions are perceived to be strong growth sectors in which the visitor spends an above average amount and which operate for most of the year. As a consequence they are considered to be a very desirable basic activity for tourism in cities. In the post-war period there has been a proliferation of new conference and exhibition facilities. Critics have suggested that they have been built as 'symbols of civic virility', and that perhaps as a consequence there is a considerable over-provision of such facilities. Cities compete to attract this business not only with other cities but with other types of places such as resorts and rural areas in the case of small conferences. So, as Listokin (1985) has pointed out, 'the economic prize is great, but so is the competition'. This should make cities think deeply before investing in the construction of facilities.

Conferences and exhibitions can be considered as two distinct types of activity, but there are increasing links between them. Many conferences include an exhibition so that the would-be conference centre has to provide space for this purpose. Similarly, conferences are often held in association with exhibitions, and once again exhibition centres are providing conferences facilities within the site. In 1983, 26 per cent of exhibitions held in Britain had an associated conference (Lawson, 1985a), while a survey of US conventions found that 24 per cent had exhibitions (Petersen, 1989). It is the large conference or convention which is most likely to have an associated exhibition. The American convention centre illustrates these tendencies. It consists of a series of large halls which can be used either for exhibitions or with seating installed for conferences. The US model of a convention centre in a downtown area with hotels and other complementary facilities adjacent is being adopted by many cities throughout the world. In the 1980s the Japanese designated 25 cities as international convention venues and between 1986 and 1991, 16 centres and associated facilities were built. Such is the congruence between these two activities that they are usually considered to be one industry, using the acronym of either in Europe, MICE – meetings, incentives, conferences and exhibitions – or in the United States, CEMI – conventions, expositions and meetings industry. The scale of the industry is indicated by the fact that several textbooks have been written for those who intend to make a career in it (Rutherford, 1990; Davidson, 1994; Gartrell, 1994; Astroff and Abbey, 1998; Rogers, 1998).

While some might think that the conference and exhibition industry is a somewhat specialized activity for cities, it has frequently been pointed out that down the centuries cities have been the place where people came together to meet and discuss and that meetings are the quintessential function of cities.

The aim of this chapter is to explore the dynamics of the development and location of the conference and exhibition industry. How do conference and exhibition organizers choose places for their events? Does the location of the event influence whether potential participants attend? What is the role of the public and private sectors in the provision of facilities and on what basis are their investment decisions made? How is increasing globalization influencing the development and location of these activities? What is the relationship of these activities to the rest of urban tourism, with hotels, with leisure activities? What are the impacts of these activities on the urban economy and urban regeneration? Finally, statistical evidence will be presented to evaluate the scale and location of the industry.

CONFERENCES, CONVENTIONS, CONGRESSES AND MEETINGS

These terms are used in different countries to describe what Zelinsky (1994) called 'a temporary assemblage of human beings' and will be assumed to be synonymous. Conferences are convened for a number of different purposes, for policy-making, for the exchange of information and ideas, for training and for group bonding and networking. The social purpose of conferences are always important and may not be connected with the explicit purpose of the meeting. Delegates use the event to meet old friends and maybe to do private deals. There is also often a recreational purpose so that participants can have a short holiday, either during or after the conference. Companies sometimes deliberately locate their conferences in exotic locations to facilitate this aspect, either as reward for past efforts or as a way of motivating staff; this is usually referred to as 'incentive travel'. Because of this recreational aspect many conference organizers make arrangements for partners to be able to come and lay on special programmes for them during the conference sessions.

Conferences are organized by and on behalf of a wide range of bodies which can generally be classified as either corporate or association. Corporate meetings are arranged by companies and other profit-making organizations to achieve operational efficiency. For the purpose of the conference industry, corporate conferences are only defined as such when they take place away from work premises although the nature of the activity could be very similar to that undertaken on work premises. The association conference may involve educational, scientific, professional, political, religious or social organizations. Apart from achieving the objectives of the association, they are also a means of generating income which is easier and less painful than raising subscriptions. Conferences vary from an intergovernmental summit, the annual conference of a political party, a church synod, a symposium for scientists, a regional conference of a trade union, a company strategy meeting, or a world meeting of Rotarians.

Some conferences take place on a regular basis, such as the annual conference and quarterly or half-yearly meetings, while others are one-off and may involve a unique set of circumstances. The latter might involve a political summit to solve a crisis or a conference to commemorate the anniversary of a past event. Meetings may last from one day to a week or more. Conferences occur throughout the year, although there is a lull in the holiday periods: July and August for the summer holidays and late December–early January for Christmas and the New Year. The peak periods tend to be from March to June and September to November, a timing which makes the conference business attractive to seaside resorts.

Table 6.1 Types of meetings and exhibitions in Chicago, 1998

Type	Number	Delegates	Share (%)	Average size	Spend per person ($)
Convention	1,431	1,012,920	23	708	1220
Corporate	33,364	1,101,000	25	33	366
Trade shows	156	2,290,080	52	14,680	1597
Total	34,951	4,404,000	100	126	1202
1990 Total	28,355	3,173,118	–	112	752

Source: Chicago Convention and Tourism Bureau

Conferences vary in size from ten people to more than 20,000 participants. The term convention is usually reserved for the larger meetings. Figures for Chicago show the breakdown between the different types of meeting and their various impacts (Table 6.1). The vast majority are small and have fewer than 100 attendees. Most of these small meetings are corporate ones arranged by companies for policy-making, training, new product launches, technical exchanges, or sales (Rutherford, 1990, p. 113). The lead time for these meetings is relatively short. It is in the association market, including political parties and trade unions, where the conference may be large and could have up to several thousand delegates. The lead times for these conferences is relatively long, usually at least two years. As national and international organizations evolve, so organizations with large membership are likely to come into being and there is the possibility of mammoth-sized conferences. Within these organizations there is likely to be a hierarchy of meetings from the global to the regional level. While the importance, publicity and impact of large conferences are great, there are relatively few such meetings and if every facility was built to accommodate this kind of meeting, they would be under-used most of the time and be a waste of scarce resources.

The larger the organization and the wider the area from which it draws its membership, and the longer the conference, the more likely it is that delegates will have to stay overnight, a factor of greater importance when measuring the impact of conferences. In contrast to these large association conventions, many corporate meetings are small in size, last only one day and often require no overnight accommodation for many of the delegates. Of the 44,300 conferences held in Frankfurt in 1990, only 8,100 required delegates to stay overnight. These day meetings are not necessarily for local and regional delegates. Nodal cities with good motorway, high speed train and scheduled air links can draw participants from a wide area, and sometimes to facilitate this type of business, conference centres, often in hotels, are built near airports. Although local 'away day' conferences are probably counted in any statistics, it is questionable whether they should be counted as tourism.

While it is widely believed that the number of conferences and the number of participants are increasing, it is difficult to demonstrate this state of affairs with comprehensive and reliable statistics. Conferences do not have to be registered, so that numerous small ones can go undetected and unrecorded by a tourist board attempting to count them. Many hotels are unwilling to release details of conferences they have hosted because of commercial confidentiality. Figures collected by the organizations affiliated to the International Association of Convention and Visitor Bureaus (mainly North American) suggest a doubling of the size of the industry during the 1980s, but in no way can they be regarded as an exact estimate. The buoyancy of the conference business argues against those forecasters who, years ago, predicted the demise of meetings because of the wider use of the telephone, teleconferencing and fax machines. There does appear to be a need for face-to-face contact for which modern technology cannot act as a substitute. The information explosion may be another reason why there is greater need for more conferences. What is certain is that there are more and more special interest groups who are scattered world-wide and whose interdependence and desire for interaction require them to come together from time to time, a situation made possible by improvements in transport (Zelinsky, 1994).

Conference planners have a choice not only of the type of venue but also of location. For some meetings, particularly if they last only a day, a central location which is easily accessible to all delegates is important. For longer meetings delegates will be prepared to travel further. Nevertheless, many associations move their conference around the country so that over a number of years travel time is equalized among delegates. In the USA conventions might rotate on a regular basis around the west coast, the centre and the east coast, and possibly from north to south. In Britain the political conferences rotate between the north and the south, particularly between Blackpool and Brighton.

Table 6.2 US meeting planners' evaluation of destination choice factors, 1991

	Percentage agreeing very important	
	Corporate	Association
Availability of hotels and facilities	69	68
Ease of transport	66	57
Transport costs	56	47
Travel distance	46	50
Climate	31	19
Recreation	27	11
Glamour	10	8
Sights/culture	12	11

Source: Meetings and Conventions, March 1992, 91–161

Surveys of how decisions are made as to where to locate a conference suggest that there are four main factors (Coopers and Lybrand Deloitte Tourism Leisure Consultancy Services, 1990; *Meetings and Conventions*, March 1992, 91–161) (see Table 6.2). First, organizers must be convinced that there is a high standard of conference and accommodation facilities available. For a few very large conferences the choice may be limited, as there may be only a few conference centres that have sufficient capacity to accommodate the required numbers. However, for smaller conferences there may be a very wide choice. Second, there is the question of the cost of the hire of the facilities.

Third, there is accessibility or location, which becomes more important, the wider the area from which the participants are drawn. Cities with a major airport have a better chance of attracting international conferences, and within large countries such as the USA, cities with hub airports again have an advantage in winning trade. Fourth, there is the attractiveness of the area to delegates. Attendance at the conference may be greater if it is located in an area which is recognized as a tourist centre. The attractiveness of an area may be as much a question of perception and image as it is of reality, and is likely to be an influence on both the conference planner and delegate (Oppermann, 1996a, 1996b; Oppermann and Chon, 1996). Oppermann considers that attractiveness and image will be more important factors either when the delegates are paying their own fares, or when the conference is organized as incentive travel. This factor will also influence whether partners accompany the delegate. Popular locations might be capital cities, historic cities, seaside resorts and scenic rural areas. Unpopular locations might be industrial cities and places which have a reputation for being unsafe. Oppermann mentions that in the USA Los Angeles and Miami are often considered dangerous. Although the conference market is growing, there is great competition between venues to attract the business, and having the right ambience might be the key factor in the decision if other factors are equal. Judd and Collins (1979) write:

> It would seem that tourist appeal is a prime consideration in convention site selection. Although many small and medium-sized cities are competing for a share in the business, large cities with their multitude of entertainment, cultural and commercial attractions remain the primary cards for conventions.

Corporate meetings, with the exception of incentive travel, are less likely to be affected by the attractiveness of the location.

The basic physical requirement for a conference is a large room or hall of sufficient size to accommodate the expected attendance, a facility which in simple form is widely found. However, increasingly, extra resources are needed such as special lighting, microphones and loudspeakers, projection equipment, the possibility of simultaneous translation, break-out rooms for when the conference divides into smaller groups and catering, including banquets. Overnight accommodation does not usually need to be in the same building. As elsewhere, there are rising expectations and many conference organizers are seeking a venue of a very high standard.

Conference venues include the following:

1. Multi-purpose large halls, arenas, civic centres, concert halls and theatres, all of which are found in large cities.
2. Large purpose-built conference/convention/congress centres which have been constructed in recent years, usually by the public sector, but occasionally by private companies. These have not only large halls for the main conference sessions, which can seat from 1,000 to 5,000 delegates, but also smaller 'break-out' or function rooms when the conference divides into sub-groups.
3. Most hotels have at least one large room, usually built either as a ballroom or for banquets which can be used for conferences. Of course, hotels can also provide catering and sleeping facilities. In recent years new large hotels have been built with the conference trade in mind and they have a very high standard of facilities. In addition, starting in the USA and now spreading to Europe, special 'convention hotels' have been constructed, which have very large halls, seating up to 1,600,

smaller meeting rooms and up to 2,000 bedrooms. Such hotels can provide for all the requirements of a conference with no need for delegates to leave the building. In the USA these types of hotels have been pioneered by companies such as Hyatt and Westin and in Europe by Maritim. Large hotel companies often develop links with major organizations and companies and can influence the location of their conferences.

4. University and other educational establishments where there are lecture rooms and possibly sleeping accommodation. Usually these are only available outside term time.
5. Small conference centres catering for up to 300 delegates. Some of these were originally created for companies, trade unions or other organizations for training puposes, but are now being offered to a wider market. In Britain these centres are often found in the countryside and were frequently in a former large house.
6. Miscellaneous or unusual venues. In recent years a number of organizations have offered their facilities as conference centres. In Britain sports clubs, football, cricket and racing, have entered the conference market as a way of generating income from under-used resources. When new stands have been built, high grade conference facilities have been included. Delegates may gain some excitement by being able to see a famous ground. Other organizations from churches to museums often have dedicated rooms for training and education which are under-used and in recent years these bodies have also entered the conference venue market. Most of these facilities are in cities and towns.

The importance of each of these types of venue will vary from city to city, depending on the characteristics and scale of its conference business, including the breakdown between corporate and association and between large and small meetings. In Atlanta about one-third of all delegates coming to the city pass through the convention centre.

Table 6.3 Pros and cons of convention centre development

Pro	Con
High levels of delegate spending	High development costs
Increased employment	High carrying costs
Enhanced urban image	High operating cost
New facilities for use by city residents	Losses on operations
Redevelopment of blighted area	Infrastructure costs
Secondary economic activity	Opportunity costs
Spin-off development in centre's locale	Loss of property taxes
Improved fiscal health for municipality	Continuing costs for police, firemen, etc.
	High debt charges

Source: Fenich (1992)

Some of the planning for conference facilities is controlled by the private or independent sectors. As has been seen, hotels have become very important providers of conference facilities and where there are conference centres, hotels provide the sleeping accommodation. Some facilities have been built and operated by the private sector, such as the Wembley Conference Centre in London. Universities and educational establishments also provide conference facilities, and in recent years they have been upgrading these and in some cases constructing all-year round purpose-built centres.

However, increasingly it is the public sector which finances the main dedicated venues (Petersen, 1989). Rutherford (1990) found that in 1989, 95 per cent of convention facilities in the United States were publicly owned. The public sector has traditionally provided large halls for meetings, but in many cases they are no longer regarded as being of an acceptable standard. This has raised the question as to whether public authorities should construct conference or convention centres. The experience of many such facilities is that they lose money, as the facilities must be let at a low rent in order to attract business because of the competitive nature of the industry. They are 'loss leaders', and/or it is not used for sufficient days in the year for overheads to be covered (Safavi, 1971; Fenich, 1992). In spite of this situation, many conference centres have been justified on the grounds that they bring business to the community and that jobs are created elsewhere, as in hotels. As Petersen (1989) has noted, most convention centres have been built to make something else happen, to be a catalyst for urban regeneration, part of a vision for economic renewal and to be a stimulus to the construction of hotels. Fenich (1992) has summarized the pros and cons of the arguments for convention centres, as shown in Table 6.3 Notwithstanding these positive arguments, the public in the USA have been wary of this proposition, as shown by bond issue referendums which have sometimes been lost (Sanders, 1992). In recent years capital subsidies have become available to projects in inner city areas from local, regional, national and supranational institutions. Birmingham's International Convention Centre received a £41 million grant from the European Union.

The public sector may also have a role in planning the complex of facilities, namely the location of the conference centre, the hotels and other facilities. An example of this process is to be seen in Boston in the USA (Law, 1985). The Boston Redevelopment Authority wished to improve the convention business. An existing building, the Hynes Auditorium, opened in 1965 with 14,000 square metres of space and a capacity of 5,000 seats in the main hall, needed upgrading and extending, but there was also a need to provide hotel accommodation nearby. To achieve these ends, a deck was constructed over an urban motorway and railway, and several hotels, including two convention hotels (Marriott and Westin) were built (see Figure 6.1). These were linked by pedestrian walkways to the convention centre. In all, 5,000 bedrooms were provided within half a kilometre of the Hynes Auditorium, as well as an upmarket shopping mall, Copley Place, for delegates. The whole complex is within walking distance of the historic core of Boston should delegates wish to explore the city. Boston illustrates how convention districts are being created in many American cities, and how these ideas have been exported to Europe, where cities like Birmingham are attempting to do the same. As well as subsidizing the cost of the conference centre, grants may be available for the construction of hotels to serve the industry.

There is of course a need for the public and private sectors to come together to market the facilities, a topic already discussed in Chapter 4. Usually within the tourism promotion organization there is a section dedicated to the attraction of conferences, sometimes given semi-independent status, called a conference bureau. These organizations not only publicize venues and destinations but can also assist in the booking of facilities. Within Britain there were 104 such bureaux in 1999. These bodies usually make claims as to the amount of conference business that they have attracted to a destination, but it is difficult to assess how influential they have been. It is probably true to say that an area without a promotional body could easily lose business, but when

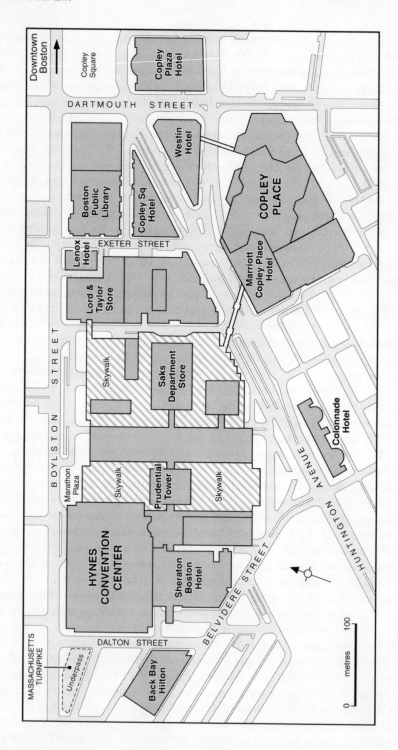

Figure 6.1 Boston's convention district around Copley Square

every area has a similar body, the influence of any one is likely to be slight.

Impact studies of the conference business are often crude and perhaps not too reliable. It has already been mentioned that there are few comprehensive figures for the conference business. The best estimates relate to conventions, where it is possible to obtain statistics on the number of delegates, and using surveys of their expenditure, derive an estimate of the income created. From these figures and using national ratios, an estimate of the number of resulting jobs can be obtained (for Orlando, see Brawn, 1992). Regular surveys of delegate expenditure are undertaken for American conventions. Results for 1973 and 1988 show the breakdown of expenditure (see Table 6.4).

Table 6.4 Convention delegate expenditure

Type of expenditure	*Percentage of total*	
	1973	*1988*
Hotels (room service)	37.7	51.0
Hotel restaurants	16.0	11.0
Other restaurants	16.8	11.4
Shopping	10.3	8.2
Entertainment	9.5	5.0
Local transport		4.3
Other		9.1

Note: This latter figure is similar to the 1990s' figures quoted in Astroff and Abbey (1998 p. 6).
Source: International Association of Convention and Visitor Bureaus, Delegate Expenditure Survey 1973 (quoted in Judd and Lollins, 1979) and 1988

One of the principal physical impacts of conference centres is the stimulus to the construction of hotels. A successful convention centre, as the example of Baltimore illustrates, quickly results in the construction of several hotels.

INTERNATIONAL CONFERENCES

The growth in the number of international conferences is not surprising given the process of globalization in which the world becomes ever more interconnected. There are more international organizations now, either governmental, political, scientific, religious, recreational or corporate as with the rise of transnational companies. In addition, many national bodies are choosing to go off-shore for their conferences and the national conferences of organizations are attracting increasing numbers of foreign delegates. This trend for more international conferences and for the greater internationalization of national conferences can be expected to continue. Figures for international conferences are available from the Union of International Associations based in Brussels. This organization collects statistics from its members on the number of conferences held which have at least 300 participants, a minimum of 40 per cent foreigners, at least five nationalities, and a duration of at least three days. This definition excludes many smaller events. Its statistics show a steady growth in the number of international conferences: an average of 194 a year in the 1930s, 1,272 in the 1950s, 1,934 in the 1960s and 3,931 in the 1970s (Labasse, 1984). In 1979 there were 4,345 conferences and by 1989 this had risen to 8,207, with 9,400 recorded for 1999.

Europe was by far the leading continent, with over 5,350 meetings in 1999 or 57 per cent of the total, a proportion which has been slowly decreasing in recent years. It was followed by North America (16.2 per cent) and Asia (13.4 per cent) with over 1,500 and 1,250 conferences each. However in terms of countries, the USA was the most important with over 1,200 meetings, followed by France (634) and Britain (609). Other important countries were Germany (602), Italy (384), the Netherlands (367), Australia (310), Spain (306) and Belgium (294).

Table 6.5 International conference cities

City	Number of conferences		
	1983	*1990*	*1999*
Paris	252	361	247
Brussels	145	194	187
Vienna	142	177	165
London	235	268	161
Singapore	77	136	140
Berlin	62	166	136
Amsterdam	44	108	125
Copenhagen	72	85	113
Sydney			106
Washington	17	101	103

Source: Union of International Associations, Brussels

In terms of the leading cities for international conferences, Paris has been the most important for many years (see Table 6.5). In the second tier are London, whose importance has fallen, and Brussels and Vienna. Singapore, Berlin, Amsterdam and Copenhagen have improved their position in recent years. The number of conferences and the ranking of Sydney have risen dramatically in the 1990s and its exposure in the Olympic Games should ensure a continuation of this high ranking. Some previously important cities, notably Geneva, Madrid and Rome have experienced a fall in the number of conferences and their ranking. Other important cities include New York, Helsinki, Budapest, Hong Kong, Strasbourg and Prague. The top twenty cities account for 24.3 per cent of the total number of conferences. As other capital cities improve their conference facilities it is likely that there will be a wider spread of international conferences within a growing total.

The explanation of the pattern shown by these figures is connected with the role of these cities in the world and in the national systems of organizations. Many world organizations have their headquarters in cities like Paris, London, Geneva, Vienna and New York. Other cities, such as Brussels and Strasbourg, are the headquarters for important supranational bodies like the European Union. National capital cities may also be the headquarters of large organizations which arrange international conferences. However, the quality of the experience available in these cities may also affect the number of conferences they attract, which might be one explanation why Paris tops the list.

In many countries, other than federal states, the capital city completely dominates the pattern of international conferences (Go, 1991). For the UK in 1999 there were 609 meetings, of which 161 were in London, with the next city, Edinburgh, having only 69. However, London's importance has decreased in recent years, perhaps either because of high costs or poor facilities. Other cities having international conferences included

Brighton, Cambridge, Birmingham and Manchester. The mention of Cambridge in this list illustrates the fact that scientific conferences may be attracted to important university centres. Another reason why capital cities dominate the pattern is that hitherto they have had the best international air links. As second-tier cities attract more scheduled flights to more locations, this dominance may diminish.

The Conference Industry in the USA

With a population of 250 million spread over a large territory and a well-developed economic structure, it is not surprising that there is a very large conference industry in the USA. In the 1990s it was estimated that there were over 20,000 regional, national and international associations of which 80 per cent held an annual general meeting (Astroff and Abbey, 1998). In addition, subgroups within these associations, including regional bodies, might hold meetings. Many of these associations are very large and it has been estimated that 6,000 to 7,000 have an attendance over 500 and thus require special facilities. The group holding large conventions can be divided between those which have very large meetings, 10,000 to 15,000, the medium-sized, 5,000 to 10,000 and the small 500 to 5,000. As mentioned above, national associations are likely to move around the country, but a few which are strongly based in particular regions may be less mobile. Thus the organizations connected with the automobile industry usually stay in the Mid-West. In addition to these associations there is a large corporate market with many of the world's major companies based in the USA.

Statistics on the convention market are collected by various organizations such as the International Association of Convention and Visitor Bureaus (IACVB) and the magazine *Meetings and Conventions*, but unfortunately because of different sources and definitions used, the figures do not always agree. *Meetings and Conventions* relies on a survey of meeting planners and because only about 70 per cent reply, the figures are generally considered an underestimate; however, unlike in the IACVB statistics, the corporate sector is identified (*Meetings and Conventions*, February 1986, April 1988, May 1990, March 1992). The total number of meetings increased from 752,000 in 1979 to 1,031,400 in 1991, and attendance increased from 64.0 million to 80.8 million. The main areas of growth were in the corporate and association meetings.

These figures provide further evidence of the growth of the industry, albeit at a slower rate than suggested by the IACVB statistics. They also show the effect of the recession, evident in the decline between 1989 and 1991. The relative importance of the different sectors can also be observed. The corporate sector was responsible for 78 per cent of the meetings and 61 per cent of the attendance in 1991, but the average number of delegates was only 62. The major association meetings (conventions) had 1 per cent of the meetings and 11 per cent of the attendance, with a mean size of 843, while the other association meetings formed 21 per cent of the total, with 28 per cent of the attendance and an average size of 105. The attendance figures for delegates were supplemented by their partners, to give total visitor numbers of 79 million. The proportion of delegates taking partners with them was highest at conventions.

To supply this market numerous convention centres and hotels have been built. At the end of World War II there were only a handful of convention centres in cities such as New York and Chicago (Graveline, 1984). According to Listokin (1985), between

1970 and 1985 over 100 convention centres were built. Var *et al.* (1985) also state, 'Before 1960 only about two dozen North American cities bid for the convention trade, but now the number is over one hundred.' By 1989 there were 331 convention centres and the number was predicted to increase to 434 by 1995 (quoted in Fenich, 1992). Another indication of the scale of the growth is that convention exhibit space increased from 6.7 million sq ft in 1970 to nearly 18 million sq ft in 1990 (Sanders, 1992). Nearly every major city which lacked such a facility sought to provide a purpose-built centre, nearly always at public expense (Safavi, 1971). Examples are Atlanta (1976), St Louis (1977), Baltimore (1979), Pittsburgh (1981), Washington (1983) and Philadelphia (1993). In those cities where an old facility already existed, a new and more modern one was often added or built as a replacement; examples are San Francisco (1981) and New York (1986). Many successful convention centres have been extended, often more then once.

As mentioned above, the convention centre is a building which can be used for both conferences and exhibitions, having large halls where seating can be installed, and many ancillary 'break-out' rooms for smaller meetings. In the major cities most convention centres were built as part of downtown renewal schemes, usually on the edge of the core area. Small cities and suburban communities are now beginning to construct convention centres, as at Valley Forge near Philadelphia and Gwinnett near Atlanta. A favourite suburban location for a convention centre is near a major airport. One of the most successful of these is found at Rosemont near Chicago's O'Hare Airport. Many convention centres have been built in resorts, which begin with the big advantage of having many hotels. Examples include Las Vegas and Atlantic City where gambling is (or was) the main attraction and Anaheim and Orlando which have grown around Disney theme parks. There has been a massive expansion of convention hotels which may have up to 2,000 bedrooms. The major chains include Hyatt, Sheraton, Marriott, Westin and Omni. Such hotels can host large conferences without the use of a convention centre although they usually serve these as well.

Table 6.6 US convention cities, late 1990s

Rank	City	Delegates
1	Las Vegas	3,900,000
2	Dallas	3,800,000
3	Atlanta	3,500,000
4	Chicago	2,000,000
5	San Francisco	1,450,000
6	New Orleans	1,302,900
7	New York City	1,200,000
8	Orlando	998,000
9	Anaheim	767,689

Table 6.6 shows the distribution of delegates to conventions and trade shows for the top nine cities. The list consists of the main cities and resorts. However, even for the major cities there is no simple correlation between population size and the number of delegates. Many large cities in the north-east are missing from the list. It is perhaps not surprising that rustbelt cities such as Cleveland, Buffalo and Pittsburgh do not figure prominently in the list. In a similar way, there does not appear to be any simple correlation between importance and the amount of exhibit space or hotel rooms, al-

though Petersen (1992) has suggested that the supply of hotel rooms is crucial and is determined by the strength of office activity, which is presumably a proxy for business travel. This underlines earlier statements that a number of variables contribute to whether a city has been able to successfully develop a conference industry.

Table 6.7 Types of location used by US meeting planners

Location	Percentage using						
	1979	*1981*	*1983*	*1985*	*1987*	*1989*	*1991*
1 Corporate							
Downtown	59	54	64	58	57	64	61
Resort	59	61	47	44	47	55	52
Suburban	52	55	47	45	44	44	50
Airport	37	37	24	27	28	29	29
2 Association							
Downtown	61	56	68	70	70	61	64
Resort	35	38	39	40	36	42	42
Suburban	52	52	34	39	34	34	36
Airport	47	46	24	31	29	24	25

Note: Other locations mentioned included private conference centre, suite hotels, condo resorts and university centres.
Source: *Meetings and Conventions*, May 1990, March 1992

Comparing attendance statistics for the beginning and end of the 1980s, it is apparent that there is both stability and change. Inter-regionally the convention industry is shifting to the sunbelt (Price Waterhouse, 1991). New York and Chicago remain very important, but are less dominant. The most notable change is the rise of the resorts, Las Vegas and Anaheim raising their rank, and Orlando having a spectacular period of growth. Some cities well established at the beginning of the period, like Houston, Detroit and Kansas City, have stagnated, while a few cities such as St Louis have been able to increase their ranking. In 1981 the top twenty convention cities received 18 million delegates, nearly 42 per cent of the IACVB total. By 1989 the top twenty received 23 million delegates, only 31 per cent of the IACVB total, suggesting that although there was an overall increase in the number of delegates, these were spread more widely, allowing new places to participate in the market. Surveys of meeting planners reveal that the downtown area remains the favourite location for conferences in spite of the fact that the suburban centres and resorts can often offer lower prices and in the latter case recreational facilities (Table 6.7).

Case Study: Atlanta

In order to understand the spatial dynamics of the convention business in the United States it is useful to examine the growth of one successful city. From the mid-1970s the convention trade began to grow rapidly in Atlanta. Convention attendance doubled from 1.8 million in 1989 to over 3.5 million in 1999. This gave it third rank in the USA which compares with its twelfth rank for the population of its metropolitan area. Atlanta has been one of the most rapidly growing metropolitan areas in the country, increasing in population from 1.7 million in 1970 to 2.8 million in 1990 and to an estimated 3.1 million in 1998. Unlike other top convention centres, it is neither a world-class business metropolitan area like New York nor a resort. Environmentally, its city centre would not be ranked as highly attractive, and although it has been attempting to change the situation, the city would not rate highly for either visitor attractions or night life. So how has Atlanta become so important for conventions?

Atlanta is a good example of the American urban tradition of boosterism (Rice, 1983). Ever since its foundation, its leaders have looked for ways to make the city more important. In recent years this has involved using slogans such as 'Atlanta: Gateway to the South' and 'Atlanta: The World's Next Great City'. Its mayors have usually given strong leadership in this area and since 1941 there has been a pro-active private sector organization, Central Atlanta Progress, pushing for improvements in the downtown area. Good communications have played a significant role in the city's rise from its beginnings as a railway junction in 1836 to possessing one of America's main hub airports in the post-war period. In 1999 Hartsfield Airport handled 78 million passengers. This nodality has enabled the city to become the dominant metropolis in the South-East of the USA.

One consequence of this position has been the maintenance and enlargement of its marts, permament exhibition centres for consumer and other goods. Progress in this field is illustrated by the construction of new buildings in the downtown area: the Merchandise Mart in 1961 (extended in 1968), the Apparel Mart in 1979, Inforum (for computers) in 1989 and the Gift Mart in 1992 (see Figure 6.2). These buildings, designed by the architect developer John Portman, drew traders from the South-East and created a demand for hotel accommodation. In 1967 John Portman designed the first atrium hotel, the Hyatt Regency, and later as the convention business expanded, more spectacular hotels were built.

Running parallel with the development of the mart industry, the city has also sought to create a convention industry. A civic centre was opened in 1965, but this was clearly inadequate for the growing business. Therefore, the city and business leaders persuaded the state to establish the Georgia World Congress Center Authority in order to build and operate a convention centre, which was opened in 1976. This was the first modern convention facility to be owned and operated by a state (Graveline, 1984). In 1984 the exhibit space was increased from 350,000 to 640,000 sq ft and a further extension in 1992 increased it to 920,000 sq ft, making it one of the largest facilities in the USA. By 1990 out-of-town attenders alone numbered 650,000 a year.

A third strand of Atlanta's tourism industry has been the development of sports facilities and the gaining of sports teams. Following the construction of the Atlanta-Fulton County stadium in 1965, the city attracted the Braves (baseball) team from Milwaukee. The Omni Coliseum, now Philips Arena, was opened in 1976 for use by the Hawkes (basketball) team, which had been attracted to the city in 1968. In 1990 Atlanta competed for and won the right to stage the 1996 Olympic Games and also in separate bidding, the Super Bowl (American football). To host these events, several new facilities were constructed, including the Georgia Dome, opened in 1992, which can also be used for conventions and exhibitions. A new stadium was built for the main Olympic events and after the event was reduced in size to become the Turner Field, the new home of the Atlanta Braves. Other new facilities for the Olympics became a legacy for the local universities. At the same time the general infrastructure was improved and there were many initiatives to 'beautify' the city centre including the creation of the 'Centennial Park'. The funding for most of the convention and sports facilities has come from state

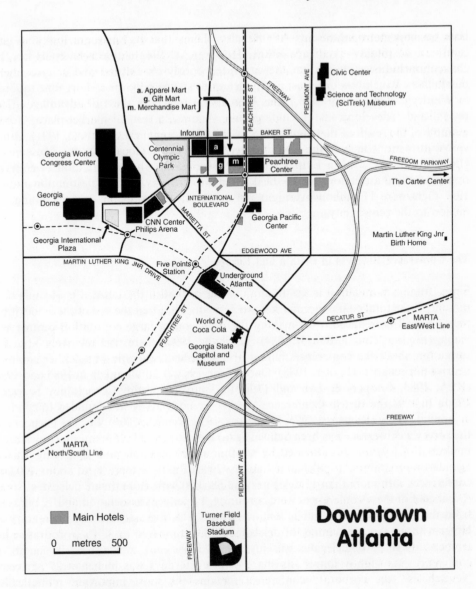

Figure 6.2 Downtown Atlanta

bond issues to be repaid from hotel taxes and the profitable operation of the activities. This latter feature of the Atlanta convention industry has so far distinguished the city from many other places where centres are run at a loss.

Atlanta's success in the convention industry owes much to its early development of facilities and hotels and to its dominance in the South-East of the country. For many years it was the obvious choice for meetings in that part of the country, although now it is being challenged by centres such as Orlando and other cities in Florida. There are even two convention centres in Atlanta suburbs, including one at its highly successful airport. Early success and profitability meant that Atlanta's facilities could be expanded and more hotel accommodation provided. City leadership and state backing have also been an important ingredient. Atlanta also claims that its costs are low and that 'southern hospitality' is an advantage. However, in 1982 a research report on the convention industry stated that the city rated poorly on cultural and entertainment possibilities, which was one reason why delegates stayed only for a short time (quoted in Whitlegg, 2000). Since then it has been trying to rectify these disadvantages. The revival and redevelopment of Underground Atlanta, a festival market-place, is one example of the result of these policies (Sawicki, 1989; Kent and Chestnutt, 1991). Other visitor attractions include the CNN Center, the World of Coca-Cola, the Museum of High Art and the Martin Luther King Jr Historic Site. The combination of conventions, sport and attractions has enabled Atlanta to grow as a tourist destination and by 1997 there were 17 million overnight visitors to the metropolitan area including 7.7 million to the central city.

The Conference Business in Britain and Europe

Since Britain's population is less than a quarter of that of the USA, it is obvious that not only is the total conference market much smaller, but that the size of the association meetings will be reduced, thus making the provision of large convention centres less viable (English Tourist Board, 1984). Until the 1990s there was relatively little information about the conference market and what was available was neither comprehensive nor reliable (Hughes, 1988). One-off surveys were undertaken in 1985 and 1990 (RPA, 1985; Coopers & Lybrand Deloitte Tourism Leisure Consultancy Services, 1990). In 1994 the British Conference Market Trends Survey was founded to conduct an annual survey (Richards, 1996; Shallcross, 1998; Costley, 2000). For the purposes of the survey a conference has been defined as (a) a meeting in hired premises; (b) lasting a minimum of 6 hours; (c) attended by a minimum of 8 people and (d) having a fixed agenda or programme (Spiller and Ladkin, 2000). In 1998 there were about 470,000 conferences with more than 15 delegates and 686,000 with more than 8 delegates. Some 73 per cent of these conferences were corporate, 14 per cent association and 12 per cent from the government and public sector. However, as the association conference was larger with an average number of delegates of 83, compared to 38 for corporate conferences, its share of delegates was just over 25 per cent, and also as its length of conference was slightly longer, its share of delegate days was higher at 27 per cent. Nevertheless, the corporate conference remains the most important numerically. Whereas association and public sector conferences tend to be held in purpose-built or university conference facilities, the corporate conference is usually held in a hotel and particularly an urban hotel (including an airport one). In Britain most conferences were held in the Midlands and southern England, including London. This presumably reflects the accessibility of these areas and to a lesser extent the supply of facilities. The annual surveys suggest that the conference market was fairly flat with little growth during the mid- to late 1990s.

In the popular mind the main providers of conference facilities are the seaside and inland resorts. This is because the high profile political parties and trade unions have traditionally held their conferences here. Resorts began to develop the conference business in the inter-war period in an attempt to extend their short summer season. They had a large quantity of accommodation at a wide range of prices and of different quality and could use their theatres and halls as conference venues. All these facilities were close together with catering and entertainment on hand. The main resorts where the conference trade is important are Blackpool, Brighton, Bournemouth, Torquay, Eastbourne, Scarborough, Llandudno and the inland resort of Harrogate. With the continued evolution of the industry, many resorts found that their old venues were inadequate and have had to construct purpose-built facilities. This has happened at Brighton (1977), Harrogate (1982), Llandudno (1982), Bournemouth (1984) and Torquay (1987), while Eastbourne has been extending or upgrading its facilities since 1934. All of the centres are publicly owned and often subsidized by local councils. Only those in Blackpool have been privately owned, but here the lack of investment has resulted in a decline of the trade.

Major cities have been an important location for conferences in Britain, and it is a role that has grown and is likely to continue expanding. Their advantages include good communications, good road, rail and air links, venues and hotels, and a range of visitor attractions and entertainments which may draw delegates. Cities have a good supply of hotels and one which is expanding, as will be discussed in a later chapter. These are very important for corporate conferences as was mentioned above. Traditionally, large conferences held in cities have taken place in multi-purpose public halls, concert halls and theatres. An example would be the Royal Albert Hall in London. But many of these older buildings are old-fashioned and lack the amenities required to hold conferences such as good catering facilities and 'break-out' rooms. Not surprisingly large cities found it difficult to attract the association conference market, and yet as they began to develop a strategy for the expansion of tourism, the conference market was perceived as an obvious component. This raised the issue as to whether cities should invest in purpose-built conference centres and, if so, of what size. The 1984 ETB report had estimated that there were only 150 large conferences a year with an attendance of over 1,000 and that building a centre to hold much more than this could be a risky venture. Some cities such as Cardiff and Nottingham have built modern multi-purpose halls which can be used for conferences. Birmingham, as will be discussed later, decided to build an American-style convention centre, which was opened in 1991. Subsequently Edinburgh has opened a 1,200-seat conference centre in 1995, Glasgow a 3,000-seat facility in 1997 and Manchester a small 800-seat convention centre in 2001. In London the prestigious but small Queen Elizabeth II conference centre was opened in 1986, but otherwise London has lacked large good modern facilities, although this may change in the near future. This may be one reason why its ranking for international conferences has fallen. It has certainly prompted tourism planners and civic leaders to seriously consider how conference centres can be built.

Major cities nearly always have large and important universities and higher educational institutions which in recent years have become important providers of conference accommodation (Paine, 1993). In an effort to boost their income universities began to market their facilities, halls, lecture rooms and accommodation, for use during the vacation. Where these facilities are all together on one site, as with campus universities, this can be very convenient. Universities have been successful in gaining academic and scientific conferences, and also have an advantage in terms of cost. However, in many cases their facilities are now regarded as inferior to what can be found elsewhere, particularly the halls of residence, and there is a need to upgrade them. Some universities have built conference centres for all-year-round use, which can meet the expectations of the industrial and business markets. There are no published figures to show which universities and which locations are the most successful, but it is known that places like York, Warwick, Durham and the Cambridge and Oxford colleges do well, suggesting that good facilities plus the ambience of the locality are important. However, many of the universities in large cities, such as Manchester, also attract a great deal of business.

The number of conference centres in Britain has been steadily increasing since the 1960s (Spiller and Ladkin, 2000). Spiller and Ladkin's survey showed that in earlier years these centres were mainly provided by the public sector, but in the 1990s the private sector was becoming an important provider of centres.

A similar picture emerges of the conference scene in Europe, although there are few comprehensive statistics (Smith, 1989). The earlier account of international conferences revealed how important capital cities were, particularly Paris, Vienna, Brussels and Geneva. In Germany the congress business is linked to the exhibition trade with large centres found within the *Messe* (exhibition centre). Munich hosts over 8,700 congresses a year with more than 700,000 delegates. In France conferences are divided between Paris, the major provincial cities and the resorts. Major new conference centres have been built, often replacing obsolete facilities, in the cities at Nantes (1987), Lille (1994) and Lyons (1998) and on the coast at La Baule, Deauville, Nice (1984) and Monaco (1999).

The Conference Business World-Wide

There is not space to record the development of conference and convention centres around the world. Information can be obtained from trade journals such as the British *Conference and Incentive Travel*. In recent years there has been a very large number of new conference centres opened world-wide. Young countries aspire to have this facility in their capital city as a symbol of modernity, so that they can host political summits even if it remains empty for most of the year, just as in the past they wanted an oil refinery. In the rapidly developing parts of the world, the conference business is also growing and cities desirous of playing a regional role, such as Hong Kong and Singapore, have been expanding the industry. Singapore established a convention bureau in 1974, initially to promote conferences in hotels. During the 1980s and 1990s several facilities for conferences and exhibitions were constructed and by 1996 (just before the Asian economic crisis), there were over 426,000 foreign delegates to the city (MacLaurin and Leong, 2000).

EXHIBITIONS, EXPOSITIONS, TRADE SHOWS AND FAIRS

The word exhibition is normally used to describe an organized public display of manufactured goods and works of art. Here the word is used to describe the temporary display of sample goods in a specialized exhibition. This chapter will not discuss world fairs and expos which, while including goods, have other elements and will be discussed in Chapter 7 under special events. Nor will this chapter discuss US marts, permanent displays of consumer goods for retailers, which, as observed earlier, are important in regional centres and therefore attract business visitors.

The advantage of an exhibition is that sellers and and buyers are brought together and business can be easily transacted. Firms selling goods can send representatives to potential buyers, but it is not always possible to take the goods with them, particularly if they are large or there is a wide range. Buyers can visit manufacturers, but may be disinclined to do so because of the need to visit several to compare products. Printed materials such as brochures can be sent, but the purchaser may wish to see the product before purchasing. The exhibition thus serves a very useful purpose for both sellers and purchasers, particularly in the area of materials, machinery and goods which firms buy from each other. Contacts made at exhibitions can be followed up by agents. All industries will use a mix of selling techniques, and in some industries and some countries exhibitions may be more important than in others. In 1990, industry in Germany spent 25 per cent of its advertising budget on exhibitions, in France and the USA the comparable figure was 14 per cent and in Britain the figure was only 8 per cent (*The Observer*, 14 April 1991). Figures showing the floorspace leased by exhibitors reveal steady increases in recent years, after a decline in the early 1990s, and suggest that exhibitions are becoming a more popular way of selling goods (and services) to other firms and the general public.

Exhibitions can be classified into trade only, trade and public, and public. Trade shows are for goods sold to other firms and cover articles such as machinery. Consumer goods may also be displayed for the retail trade. The modern trade show has developed from the trade fairs of the past. These displayed a wide range of goods. In the post-war period these general fairs evolved into specialist exhibitions covering a particular industry. Some trade fairs showing consumer goods may be open to the public, often the first few days are trade only, followed by public days. An example of this type is the Motor Show. Public exhibitions are concerned with consumer goods and services, an example being the Ideal Home Exhibition. Public shows can have very large attendances, while trade-only shows will have smaller numbers, although this will depend on the size of the industry and the extent of the area from which participants are drawn. A very specialist exhibition which is the only one of its type attracts exhibitors and visitors from all over the world, and may have a very large attendance.

Exhibitions generally last from three to five days, but their duration can be anywhere from one day to a month. Many exhibitions are held every year, but some of the more specialist ones may occur in a cycle of every two, three, four or five years. In general, the specialist exhibitions will occur on the same site on every occasion, but some rotate between sites, often with different organizers. Exhibitions are held throughout the year but, as with conferences, there are few over the major holiday seasons.

Exhibitions may be organized by a trade association, by a company associated with an exhibition centre, or by a company which specializes in organizing shows. Frequently the trade association works with both types of companies. Firms linked with exhibition centres have been deliberately established to fill the space available and seek out industries and services which are not yet adequately catered for by the existing calendar of exhibitions. In Germany 80 per cent of the shows are organized by the *Messe* (Lawson, 1985). New industries and services are clear targets for these exhibition organizers.

Exhibitions are held in large halls, and an exhibition centre usually consists of a series of linked halls which can be used either independently or in combination. Very large exhibition centres may host more than one event at the same time. Today most exhibition centres are purpose-built, but a few have been converted from other uses, such as Manchester's G-Mex, which was a railway terminus. Many exhibition centres also have space outside. A specialist type of showground is the agricultural fair ground, which is mainly outdoor display space. Exhibition centres also require catering facilities and perhaps office space. In recent years exhibition centres have begun to provide rooms for meetings, since conferences often take place in association with shows. Sometimes these conferences take place in hotels which have been built nearby. To be viable, an exhibition centre should be used as much as possible, but as has been seen, this is difficult during the summer and Christmas–New Year holiday periods, and because of the inevitable gaps between shows. To overcome these seasonal lulls, halls may be let out for other events such as product launches. Even so, it may be difficult to achieve a level of use above the 200 days a year figure.

Many exhibition centres are publicly owned, although usually operated by an autonomous company. Such companies may have several shareholders. In Germany, the *Messe* is usually owned jointly by the city and the provincial (*Land*) government, perhaps with a small shareholding by the trade unions and the Chamber of Commerce. A similar situation occurs in France, while in Britain, Birmingham's National Exhibition Centre is 99 per cent owned by the city and 1 per cent by the Chamber of Commerce. A few exhibition centres, such as Earls Court and Olympia in London, are privately owned. Manchester's G-Mex is jointly owned by the local authorities and a private company.

While the aim of all exhibition centres is to be profitable, there is widespread public support. Those that are publicly owned have obviously benefited from initial funding for the capital cost, and this type of support may continue for extensions and renovations. Even privately owned facilities, such as Earls Court and Olympia in London have received grants towards extensions and upgrading. A few facilities may also require an operational subsidy, at least during their early years. There are several reasons why this subsidy may be given. The most obvious one is that the facility will bring income into the area and thus help create jobs, even though most will be outside the centre, in hotels, shops and restaurants. This will be important where unemployment is high. The German government has helped Berlin and Leipzig for these reasons. In Britain, inner city funds have been used to assist exhibition centres. Another reason for subsidizing exhibition centres is the prestige they bring to an area. Governments may provide funds in order to create a national 'shop window' and thus assist exports, as has happened in Britain and the Netherlands. Even where there are no direct subsidies to the centre itself, the local authority may support the venture through improvements to the surrounding infrastructure.

Like the conference business, the exhibition industry appears to be growing. In the 1980s Lawson (1985b) estimated a rate of growth for Europe of 4 per cent a year. More recently Ladkin and Spiller (2000) have suggested that between 1994 and 1998 the European industry, as indicated by exhibitor participation, was growing by over 4 per cent a year. There are no statistics on the international geography of the industry, but the information on the industry reported below suggests that it is very important in Europe and particularly in Germany. The modern *Messe* of Germany evolved at the beginning of the century from the centuries-old trade fairs. The Germans have maintained their lead through the development of specialist trade fairs as well as the con-

Many tourist attractions have been developed in redundant docklands. In Manchester, Salford's 'The Lowry' (right) lies on one side of the Ship Canal while on the other side is the Imperial War Museum of the North (below).

London has the greatest supply of world-class visitor attractions in Britain and every year new attractions are opened, increasing the pull of the city. The National Gallery in Trafalgar Square (below) was established in 1824 while the London Eye (the ferris wheel) was only opened in 2000 (opposite).

Liverpool's historic listed Albert Dock has been recycled as a tourism resource with three visitor attractions, a festival market-type shopping area and a hotel. The majestic and monumental Anglican Cathedral is seen in the background.

GUGGENHEIM BILBAO

Bilbao's Frank Gehry Guggenheim Museum illustrates the power of architecture to attract tourists. Before it was opened in 1997 few foreign tourists would have thought of visiting the city. (Reproduced with permission of the Guggenheim Museum).

Birmingham has developed a tourist quarter on former wasteland just to the west of the city centre. The International Convention Centre (including Symphony Hall) was opened in 1991 (above), while behind it is the National Indoor Arena and the leisure area of Brindley Place (left).

Glasgow has been developing its tourism resources since the early 1980s. The Scottish Exhibition and Conference Centre was opened in 1985 on the north bank of the Clyde and extended in 1997 with a 3,000 seat auditorium, nicknamed the 'Armadillo' (top). In 2001 the Scottish National Science Centre was opened on the opposite bank of the river (bottom).

tinued development of their facilities. Their strength is not in the number of shows, but in their large size and international character. Germany is, of course, an important industrial country and it could be expected that there would be some correlation between exhibitions and industrial development. Frequently, as in Detroit in the USA, there is a link between trade fairs and the industries which are important in the local region. Unlike the case with conferences, there does not appear to be an 'attractiveness' factor affecting attendance at exhibitions. It is primarily the quality of the show which determines attendance.

At the level of the urban region there is is often a debate as to best location for an exhibition centre. A central site near the city centre provides the facility with good accessibility by public transport, and access to the varied amenities of the downtown zone, including hotels and night life, and assists with the revitalization of the inner city. Early twentieth-century *Messe*, such as those of Cologne and Frankfurt are in fact centrally located, but later centres are likely to have found inner city sites either already developed or too expensive. Only where the innner city is in decay, such as in Glasgow, has it been possible to build an exhibition centre in the central area. Inner city sites may have problems with insufficient car parking and congested road access, Frequently it has been necessary to choose a site on the periphery where undeveloped land was available with good communications and at low cost. The case of Birmingham's NEC, which is in just such a location, will be discussed below. The disadvantage of such a position, is that initially at least, it is too far away from hotels and other facilities which the visitor may want.

Trends in the exhibition industry can be measured in various ways: the number of shows, the number of exhibitors, the amount of space rented (gross or net), the number of visitors, the foreign component, and figures relating to income and expenditure. Unfortunately, while there has been an increasingly good collection of statistics for the industry, the figures are not always comparable, some relating to all shows and others just to trade shows, and some covering only exhibitions over a minimum size.

The impact of an exhibition centre can be measured in terms of different components. First, there are the number of jobs in the centre itself. Typically these are not large. In the early 1990s Cologne *Messe* employed 450, while Manchester's G-Mex employed only 40. These comparisons are not as straightforward as they appear since some centres contract out most of the services they require. Second, there are the jobs in ancillary activities, such as display construction and exhibition organization. These may or may not be near the exhibition centre. Third, there are the jobs created by the visitor, both the exhibitors and the attenders. These people can be divided between those who visit for one day and those who stay overnight. Such impact studies have been undertaken for a number of centres and those for Birmingham will be discussed later.

Exhibitions in Europe

There is a long tradition of fairs in Europe going back to the Middle Ages, but these general festive events have long been transformed into specialized trade exhibitions. However, because of this long evolution it was possible for Cuadrado-Roura and Rubalcaba-Bermejo (1998) to postulate a wide range of factors which have affected the growth and location of exhibition centres: tradition and history, population and economic standing, accessibility, infrastructure and communications, geographic location, tourism and environmental conditions, public investment and local government support policies, the city's international prestige, ground capacity and conditions, and the industrial composition of the locality. In recent years more comparative statistics have become available, but care is needed when comparing the different indicators. Figures are available for the rented space, number of exhibitions, number of exhibitors, and number of visitors and these can be broken down between domestic and foreign. Some statistics only include trade fairs and not public fairs. Further, since some exhibitions run on a two- or three-year cycle, it can be misleading to take only one year's figures (Rubalcaba-Bermejo and Cuadrado-Roura, 1995; Ladkin and Spiller, 2000).

Germany is the most important European country for trade fairs and also the one which has the most international exhibitions, whether measured by origin of exhibitors or visitors. But as the industry is divided among many places it does not have the largest centres. Paris and Milan are the two most important centres followed by Hanover, Cologne, Munich, Düsseldorf, Frankfurt and Bologne. Birmingham and London are important, and more so if public shows are included.

Germany: the *Messe*

With the largest exhibition centres and the most well-developed programme of trade fairs, Germany can be considered to be the leader in the field. Although there is a long tradition of fairs, the industry has been greatly affected by two world wars and the division of the country, but its resilience is shown by the fact that it has been able to recover and restore its position. With a strong industrial base, it has been able to develop trade fairs of international importance with a significant proportion of participants from outside the country. Statistics show that during the 1980s and 1990s rented floorspace continued to show an upward trend but attendances levelled off during the 1990s (Table 6.8). Within the country there are 24 exhibition centres with the industry distributed as shown in Figure 6.3. Table 6.9 shows the key statistics for the 11 major

Table 6.8 Trade show trends in Germany

	1983	1990	1995	1999
Space rented (sq metres)	3.8	5.1	6.3	6.6
Exhibitors	83,600	110,966	141,721	161,158
Foreign (%)	34.5	42.0	43.3	47.9
Visitors (m)	7.7	8.2	10.4	10.1
Foreign (%)	6.5	14.0(1989)	17.9	18.1
No. of trade fairs				131
Hall capacities (sq metres)			2.1	2.4

Source: AUMA (20001)

centres. The high attendance figures for centres such as Frankfurt reflect the presence of shows with a large public element.

The figures reveal that there are a 'big six' in the industry, namely, Berlin, Düsseldorf, Frankfurt, Hanover, Cologne and Munich. Other important centres are Essen, Hamburg, Nuremberg and Stuttgart. The principal ancient centres of the industry were Frankfurt, Cologne and Leipzig. For Frankfurt and Cologne, modern exhibition

Table 6.9 The major German exhibition centres, 1989 and 1999

City	Hall Floorspace (m sq m)		Attendance	
	1989	1999	1989	1999
Berlin	83,500	160,000	1,195,509	986,758
Düsseldorf	171,300	233,000	1,368,421	1,483,158
Essen	90,000	90,000	734,704	466,668
Frankfurt	263,005	289,931	1,153,930	2,012,242
Hamburg	62,500	64,200	231,945	241,215
Hanover	461,240	469,655	1,512,763	1,457,158
Cologne	250,000	286,000	829,190	862,048
Leipzig	222,174	101,000	545,300*	485,689
Munich	105,000	140,000	1,056,112	934,087
Nuremberg	86,000	133,000	156,846	372,099
Stuttgart	59,500	59,500	188,318	71,036
Total			7,973,038	9,372,158

Notes: Includes figures for combined trade and public shows. Covers 11 of 24 centres. *(1990) figures.
Source: AUMA (2001)

grounds were built on the edge of the city centre in 1907 and 1926 respectively. Leipzig's fortunes suffered as a result of its situation in East Germany within the communist bloc, although it was given a role as a showcase for COMECON. However, since reunification in 1990 the federal government has pledged to restore its fortunes and a new *Messe* has been built on a site on the city's periphery at a cost of DM 1 billion with a grant of DM 300 million. Leipzig is likely to keep its ties with former COMECON members (*The Financial Times*, 19 November 1991). Munich has also built itself a new *Messe* on the urban periphery. Frankfurt, Düsseldorf, Hanover and Munich have all developed their trade fairs very successfully in recent years.

Britain: exhibition centres

The British industry is small compared to the German one, partly, as noted, because British firms have not chosen to use this method and spend a smaller proportion of their advertising budgets on exhibitions, although this has been increasing in recent years. British exhibition costs have been high, partly because of the lack of government support, and this may have acted as a further deterrent (Lawson, 1985b). By the end of the nineteenth century many of Britain's large cities had developed halls which could be used for exhibitions, mostly public shows. Examples are Bingley Hall in Birmingham, the Kelvin Hall in Glasgow, and Belle Vue in Manchester. By the 1950s and 1960s it was apparent that many of these halls had become obsolete. At the same time British industry was looking for exhibition space where it could display its goods to home and overseas buyers. In 1959 the Federation of British Industry's Pollitzer Report suggested that there should be a national exhibition centre, an idea that was later accepted by the government who offered a small sum of money. In competitive bidding Birmingham won the right to build the centre and the NEC was opened in 1976 (see below). Subsequently Glasgow obtained the Scottish Exhibition and Conference Centre (1985), and Manchester found a new use for an old railway terminus when it opened G-Mex in 1986. London's need for a large modern exhibition centre has recently been achieved with the opening of ExCel in the London Docklands.

Figure 6.3 German exhibition cities

Tables 6.10, 6.11 and 6.12 indicate the trends for the industry and also the location, scale and importance of the different centres and regions. The industry expanded rapidly during the late 1970s and 1980s, then suffered during the recession of the early 1990s before growing again to reach a peak in 1997. The decline in the period 1997–99 mainly affected industrial trade shows. While there are many exhibition centres in Britain, most are small, and with the exception of Birmingham and London, they are not able to compete in the market for the large international trade shows. As the figures show, public exhibitions are very important within the industry, particularly for the

Table 6.10 Exhibition trends in the UK

Category	1983	1990	1992	1997	1999
No. of shows					
All	393	779	672	841	817
Trade			351*	491	447
Trade and public			115*	40	28
Public			225*	310	342
Net rented space (million sq m)	1.3		3.1	3.3	3.1
Attendance (millions)					
All	6.7	9.2	9.2	10.8	10.1
Trade	2.4		2.2	2.6	2.3
Trade and public			3.5	1.0	0.7
Public			3.5	7.2	7.1

Note: *(1994) figures.
Sources: Lawson (1985a), Lawson and Wilkie (1985), Exhibition Venues Association (2000)

Table 6.11 Exhibition centres in the UK in 2000

City (date of opening)	Area (square metres)
Aberdeen	10,300
Belfast Kings Hall	10,000
Birmingham NEC (1976)	190,000
Brighton Metropole	8,125
Edinburgh (Ingliston)	7,500
Esher (Surrey)	15,820
Glasgow (1985)	18,830
Harrogate (1959)	15,000
Kenilworth NAC	20,703
London	
Alexander Palace	13,070
Barbican (1982)	8,000
Earls Court (1887)	59,000
ExCel (2000)	65,000
Kensington (1980)	6,595
London Arena (1989)	8,000
Olympia (1886)	39,000
Wembley (1987)	17,000
Malvern	10,568
Manchester G-Mex (1986)	10,000
Telford	10,008

Note: There are at least 12 smaller centres. Figures in brackets indicate the date of establishment.

smaller centres. These generally attract visitors mainly from local and regional markets, and therefore have less economic impact.

The USA: convention centres

In the USA, as mentioned above, the convention centre has a series of large halls and can take trade shows. With the exception of Cleveland and Houston, all the largest exhibit halls are convention centres. In recent years there has been a great expansion in specialized exhibition centres. One example is the Bayside Exposition Hall in Boston, opened in 1982 with an area of 180,000 sq ft. The largest exhibition centre is McCormick Place in Chicago with 2.2 million sq ft. The number of trade shows increased from 4,500 in 1972 to 9,000 in 1982 (*British Business*, September, 1984), and the industry grew by 72 per cent between 1981 and 1990 (*Meetings News*, 1992, 44–45).

Table 6.12 Location of exhibitions in the UK (%)

Region	1984	1997	1999
London	44	29	36
Rest of South East	10	6	5
South West	9	7	6
West Midlands	10	25	25
North West	7	6	6
Yorkshire	14	8	8
Scotland	4	8	8
Other	2	5	7

Source: Exhibition Industries Federation (1989), Exhibition Venues Association (2000)

Case Study: Birmingham

Located centrally within England, Birmingham is one of Britain's major provincial cities, with a population of over 1 million and lying within a conurbation of over 2.5 million. Its rise to prominence began in the eighteenth century when it was known as the town of a thousand trades, but they were mainly connected with metal working. At the beginning of the twentieth century, its engineering skills enabled it to become a major player in the newly developing motor vehicle industry, and this trade was to be a mainstay until the late 1970s when the city experienced severe deindustrialization. The city has had strong civic leadership for many decades and has always been regarded as a progressive city. In some respects this has had its downside. From 1919 its chief engineers argued for an inner ring road around the city centre to keep traffic out. This was eventually achieved by the early 1970s but proved to be too tight a collar with unfortunate effects on the appearance of the environment.

In the post-war period Midland industrialists were concerned about the lack of exhibition facilities, the two existing centres having become obsolete. The Pollitzer Report had argued the case for a national exhibition centre, but its sponsor, the Federation of British Industry, had proposed that the obvious location for it was in London at the Crystal Palace site. When the government invited bids in the late 1960s many assumed it would automatically go to London. Even when in 1970 it was announced that the National Exhibition Centre would be built in Birmingham, many predicted that it would be a 'white elephant'. Birmingham's bid had been made by the city in partnership with the Chamber of Commerce. The site chosen was on the edge of the built-up area, adjacent to motorways, the main Birmingham to London railway and the airport. It was opened in 1976 with an area of 89,000 square metres, and has proved very successful and profitable, so much so that it has undergone several expansions and now has an area of 190,00 square metres. Within the site there is also an arena and two hotels. For the year 1992–93 when there were 183 events it was estimated that the total employment impact of the centre in the region was 12,200 (KPMG Peat Marwick, 1993). The only disappointments have concerned the problems arising from the peripheral site. So good are the train services to London that some visitors commute from there while others complain of the distance to the city centre.

Birmingham's success encouraged it to consider developing the conference industry. Plans were drawn up for an American-style convention centre on a decaying zone just west of the city centre, where in fact the old Bingley Hall exhibition centre had been located. The centre would also include a concert hall and the site was adjacent to a

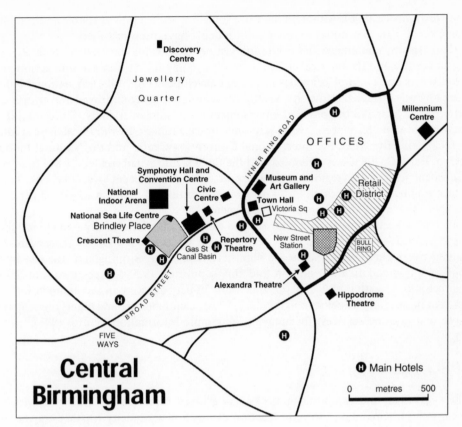

Figure 6.4 Central Birmingham

repertory theatre. A pre-build impact study suggested that about 125 jobs would be created in the centre while the total impact was estimated at 1,959 jobs (JURUE, 1983). Financing the project was a problem, but by the late 1980s Birmingham's economic position had so deteriorated that it had become an assisted area, with the consequence that it was also eligible for grants from the European Union. A £41 million grant plus loans enabled the project to go ahead and the International Convention Centre, which can seat up to 5,000, was opened in 1991. Since then it has attracted about 100–110,000 delegates a year (not including the 400,000 a year who attend Symphony Hall) and some of the high profile events, such as European Union and G-8 summits, have put the spotlight on the city. A study of people's perception before and after one of the summits showed that they had a more positive view of the city. It is situated next to the 13,000-seat National Indoor Arena, also opened in 1991, with which it could be used for very large events. One knock-on effect has been the construction of hotels round about, and its development has certainly contributed to the regeneration of the area, notably around Brindley Place (Figure 6.4). A post-build impact study estimated the number of jobs created inside and outside the centre at 2,700 (KPMG Peat Marwick, 1993). However, there are criticisms. The centre runs at a loss (£2.4 million in 2000) and the losses are even greater when debt payments are included. These are borne by the city and it has been argued that other council services have suffered as a result (Loftman and Nevin, 1995, 1996). Although there are some low-skilled jobs available and training was offered, very few adjacent inner city residents have been recruited.

Criticisms by conference and exhibition visitors concerning the range of amenities in the city centre and the physical environment have stung the city council into action and parallel arts and cultural strategies have been developed (Lim, 1993). A national ballet company was attracted to the city, visitor attractions are being improved and efforts are being made to make the physical environment more human friendly. Since the NEC was opened there have been several economic impact studies. By the 1990s these studies were covering the NEC, the International Convention Centre and the National Indoor Arena. For 1998–99 it was estimated that the three facilities had created 21,844 full-time equivalent jobs in the region, an increase of 5,200, 30 per cent over 1992–93. Total visitor numbers had increased by 24 per cent and of the £711 million spend, 53 per cent was personal spend and the rest business spend.

In 1997 an economic impact study of the tourism sector in the city (which excludes the NEC) was undertaken and it was found that for the year 1996–97 there were 2.1 million overnight stayers and 19.7 million day trippers to Birmingham. Income from tourists amounted to £760 million and this supported 19,550 direct jobs and 7,800 indirect jobs or a total of 27,350. Of this total, 20 per cent were in accommodation, 39 per cent in catering, 24 per cent in retailing, 12 per cent in leisure and entertainment and 5 per cent in other services (Birmingham Economic Information Centre, 1998).

CONCLUSION

The conference and exhibition industry has evolved rapidly since the 1960s with an expansion of demand and the construction of much new capacity whether convention centres or hotels. When all types of activity are considered, including corporate meetings, the industry is widely dispersed, but most attention has focused on the large convention and exhibition which takes place in a specially constructed facility or purpose-built hotel. It is useful to recap the features which explain why particular cities have become important before examining the prospects for new entrants.

One critical factor in the success of cities has been the supply of facilities and accommodation. While the capacity of the hotel industry is important, and it may be high in business centres and resorts, a key requirement has often been the provision of a dedicated convention centre (or conference centre, exhibition centre, etc.). This is where the contribution of the public sector has been important as these facilities frequently run at a loss. By taking a broad view of the benefits to the community, the public sector has usually been able to justify its investment. The perceived benefits are employment gains (inside and outside the facility), publicity and image improvement, and urban regeneration. Convention facilities have often been deliberately located in decaying fringe areas of the city centre where a convention quarter could be established including the attracted hotels and other amenities. Critics have argued that the benefits have often been greatly exaggerated, that the poor and unemployed have not found jobs, and that funds are often displaced from basic welfare functions such as education.

The conference industry cannot be isolated from the rest of the tourism industry. Its participants, particularly those attending large association conferences, are usually seeking urban amenities preferably in an exciting environment. This is why cities such as Las Vegas have become among the largest convention destinations, and why places like Barcelona, Bilbao and Sydney have risen rapidly in popularity in recent years. It is also why cities such as Atlanta and Birmingham have learned that they need to broaden their appeal and that convention facilities alone are not enough. The conference and exhibition industry can thus be seen to be part of the complex of tourism industries with linkages to hotels, visitor attractions, shops, catering and entertainment. The hotel stock that has been brought into being by the convention industry can of course, when not needed for this purpose, be used to attract the leisure, short-break visitor.

There are several factors which have been seen to be important in the rise of convention cities. An early interest in the industry, as was the case with Atlanta, gives the city the benefit of initial advantage. Trade can be built up before too many other cities become involved and the competition stiffer, and the profits used to improve the facilities. A location in a part of the country where there are not too many rivals is another advantage, since as has been seen, conferences tend to rotate around a country. Some cities in the North-East of the USA may find it difficult to compete because there are too many rivals nearby. Other advantages include having an attractive physical environment, having a range of visitor attractions, having good evening amenities and having good accessibility, particularly via an airport. Not all of these may be necessary, but being strong in at least some of these is important. Image is also important. Many older industrial cities have a poor image which may make the attraction of delegates difficult. Finally, not to be forgotten when assessing the success of particular cities, is the quality of management which is necessary if a centre is to be successfully sold (Petersen, 1989).

These points are relevant when considering the possiblity of new cities attempting to enter the market. As in other areas of the economy, there are barriers to entry. Existing cities have a well-developed product. It is risky to invest in the necessary infrastructure when there is no certainty of a return on the investment and success in the endeavour. In the case of trade shows, some cities have captured a particular market through the organization of specialized industrial exhibitions.

Against these pessimistic forecasts, it can be posited that in a growing market there is usually room for new entrants. New industries are evolving and trade shows can be created for them. The conference organizer or delegate is often looking for something different so that existing centres cannot be assured of maintaining their position. In any case most conferences are not fixed locationally but rotate around a country, and there is always the possibility of a city being selected in the future. A city that wished to enter the industry should be able to capture a share of the market, provided it has a rounded and well-thought-out strategy, and the determination to pursue it over a number of years. Atlanta and Birmingham were selected as case studies because they illustrated how a city could go about creating a conference industry.

Chapter 7

Culture, entertainment, sport and special events

The cultural, entertainment and sporting activities of cities have not traditionally been regarded as part of the tourist industry. Theatres, concert halls, clubs, gaming centres and sports grounds were all built to meet the needs of the resident population, and probably until at least recently a very high percentage of their patrons would have been local. After many years of neglect, a great deal of investment is going into these areas, including a significant amount from the public sector. Among the various reasons for this, three are worth mentioning. First, some of these activities are perceived to bring prestige to a city and raise its profile in the outside world. As cities are desperate to attract inward investment and the first stage in this process is to gain attention, having a high profile in the arts and sports is a good starting point. Second, related to this is the perceived importance of quality of life factors, which are believed to be significant to management when investment location decisions are made. Third, these activities are perceived to have tourism potential. If the events are of a sufficiently high quality, then potential patrons will be prepared to travel some distance to attend. There is clearly some validity in this idea, since places such as Aldeburgh (in Suffolk) and Stratford-upon-Avon have traded on arts tourism for many years. But could this phenomenon become more widespread and be a significant component in the tourism industry of many cities?

The term 'special event' covers many activities, as will be discussed later. However, one important example is the festival, which as with culture, entertainment and sport has usually been created to meet the needs of local people. But as with some of these other topics, the reasons for holding festivals is now being perceived differently, and once again the motives of achieving a high status profile and attracting visitors are coming to the fore. In discussing these topics it is important to be aware of the multi-purpose aims behind the development of these activities, and that it is not always easy to separate out the pure tourism element. The adoption of these policies is, as with other policies discussed in this book, a consequence of the transformation of the approach and operation of local governance towards more pro-growth and pro-active strategies (Henry and Paramio-Salcines, 1999).

CULTURE

The terms 'arts industry' and 'culture industry' are sometimes used interchangeably and in a comprehensive way to include not only the performing arts, but also museums and art galleries (where works of visual and decorative arts may be found), cultural heritage, special events such as arts festivals and the producing arts, as in some studies of the economic importance of the arts (McNulty, 1985; Tighe, 1985; Myerscough, 1988a; Hughes, 2000a). Similarly, the terms 'cultural tourism' and 'cultural cities' are likely to involve all of these activities (Richards, 1994a). Here the use of the terms will be limited to the performing arts and in particular to the role of theatres and concert halls. Because of their size and thus high threshold population, cities have always been important for the location of drama, concerts, ballet, opera and other arts (Blau and Hall, 1986). Patrons living in smaller places have to travel to big cities to experience live performances and in the process become tourists (Hughes, 1986). Some patrons may be prepared to travel from one city to another in order to experience either a piece of the repertoire or performers not available in their local city.

Any understanding of the role of the arts in cities needs to be put in the context of the changing approaches to and trends in the arts in the late twentieth century (Bassett, 1993). There have been three broad thrusts, each with several strands within them. First, there has been a movement to make the arts wider and more inclusive by widening access, developing arts centres in communities, broadening the definition of arts to include new and more technical arts and also popular culture, embracing the production of the arts as well as their consumption, and including the culture of ethnic minorities. Second, the wider impacts of the arts have become more important in the thinking about policy-making, whether this is economic impact (e.g. revenue and jobs), role in urban regeneration and place marketing (and thereby assisting in the attraction of investment), enhancing lifestyle opportunities for mobile executives, the use of public art to improve the appearance of the environment, or the potential to attract tourists. Third, a more commercial approach to the arts has become essential as a consequence of reduced or static public funding. The arts must seek corporate sponsorship and funding and attempt to pay their way. Ironically, in view of the first approach, this may mean that the arts become less innovative and challenging, and more likely to play 'safe' as they seek to appeal to both sponsors and their predominantly middle-class audiences, at the expense of community-based arts programmes (Griffiths, 1993; Lim, 1993).

Any economic impact that the arts can have is constrained by the fact that only a small percentage of the population attend performances. A survey of participation in the USA for 1997 found that only 25 per cent of adults had attended a musical in the previous 12 months, 16 per cent a classical performance, 16 per cent a play and 12 per cent a jazz performance, with much less for ballet and opera (Table 7.1). However, these proportions were higher than the corresponding figures for 12 years earlier, suggesting growing interest. Attendance was greatly affected by the level of income and education, which, as Bourdieu has discussed, provides one with cultural capital to appreciate such performances. It is likely that the position is similar in Britain and Europe (Myerscough, 1988a). Apart from inclination, performance accessibility is probably a major factor affecting participation, with accordingly higher rates in cities.

However, until recently these cultural resources of cities were perceived as purely

Table 7.1 Participation rates for various arts performances in the USA in 1997

| | *Percentage attending at least once a year* | | | | | |
	Jazz	*Classical music*	*Opera*	*Musical*	*Play*	*Ballet*
All	12	16	5	25	16	6
Household income						
Under $10000	5	4	2	12	10	2
10000–19999	6	8	2	12	7	3
20000–29999	8	10	2	17	10	4
30000–39999	11	13	3	21	16	5
40000–49999	11	15	5	23	15	6
50000–74999	16	22	8	32	20	8
75000–99999	23	26	6	41	27	10
Over 100000	27	35	13	51	32	13
Education						
Grade school	2	2	–	6	3	2
Some high school	3	4	2	13	7	2
High school grad	7	8	2	16	9	4
Some college	15	18	5	28	19	7
College grad	21	28	10	44	28	11
Grad school	28	45	14	50	37	14

Source: US National Endowment for the Arts (1997). Survey of Public Participation in the Arts, quoted in *Statistical Abstract of the United States*, Table 446.

local amenities, and not as part of the tourism resource base. Starting in the USA and, increasingly, in Britain, the arts are considered to have economic importance, a tendency which some believe will result in their devaluation, and also result in a focus of providing for the more affluent (Hughes, 1989a). The reasons why the arts are thought to have economic importance is that they have a high profile, a 'quality' label which gives and will give prestige, a positive image and the potential to bring publicity to cities (Whitt, 1988). Their presence suggests that a city has a level of civility and culture and is progressive and resourceful (Shanahan, 1980). In the USA it has been argued that they have become the centrepiece of growth strategies (Whitt, 1987) often developed by public–private partnerships. With sports and special events, they will offer a high quality lifestyle which will attract professionals, who are important in the new industries and services which cities must attract, to live in the city and in turn persuade major companies that the city concerned is a good place in which to locate a facility (Hendon and Shaw, 1987). They may also attract tourists and help bring life back to city centres, thus assisting revitalization (Bianchini *et al.*, 1988; Bianchini, 1991). The arts have traditionally been located in the urban core, and as Perloff (1979) has written, 'The arts serve to increase the element of excitement and variety which is the key to urbanity. Government and the private sector need to recognise the role of the artist as dynamic city builders.' In Britain several cities have adopted cultural policies during the 1980s and 1990s including Birmingham, Bristol (Griffiths, 1995; Griffiths *et al.*, 1999), Coventry, Dundee (McCarthy and Lloyd, 1999), Glasgow (see below), Liverpool, Newcastle (and Gateshead) and Sheffield (Comedia Consultants, 1989; Bianchini, 1991). However, many of these cities are focusing on popular music culture rather than the 'high arts'. In France since the decentralization reforms of 1982, large cities have had more funds and greater freedom to pursue cultural policies (Renucci, 1992).

The physical manifestation of these policies is witnessed in the renovation of old facilities, the construction of new concert halls and theatres, and the evolution of cultural districts (Wyne, 1992, Chapter 2). Cultural quarters give visibility to the arts function and may encourage the additional clustering of ancillary activities. They are often located on the edge of the city centre in order to assist regeneration, but in the USA in some cities they are a little removed in districts that are sometimes referred to as mid-town. In the USA, arts districts are found in cities as diverse as Boston, Dallas, Pittsburgh and St Paul (British American Arts Association, 1989). Two of the most famous cultural quarters are those of the Kennedy Center in Washington and the Lincoln Center in New York, the latter also having its Broadway theatreland. Interestingly, finance for the facilities in these districts often comes from the private sector and private foundations, which partly reflects the role of business elites in growth coalitions and their perception of the arts as having high status and a quality label (Whitt, 1988).

In Britain many theatres have been refurbished since the the early 1980s, often through a mix of finance from the public sector, private donation and commercial investment. The influx of commercial investment reflects the increasing affluence of the local population and the fact that with easier car travel, because of the construction of better roads, the hinterlands of theatres have increased. Concert halls have also been built or are planned, sometimes as single purpose facilities (Glasgow, 1990; Manchester, 1994), sometimes as part of a conference centre (Birmingham, 1991), or sometimes as a multipurpose facility (Cardiff, 1983, and Nottingham, 1982). Once again, cultural or arts quarters have been planned in British cities, notably in Birmingham, Bradford, Newcastle (and Gateshead) and Sheffield. London, of course, has its own established arts zones in the West End theatreland and the South Bank (Hughes, 1998a; Newman and Smith, 2000). In Britain the term cultural quarter has been used also to denote an area of production. Sheffield's zone includes small workshops and recording studios (Oatley, 1996; Brown *et al.*, 2000). Another perceived advantage of developing the arts is that they contribute to the evening economy of the city centre, bring more people into the area and help keep the zone a safer place (Comedia, 1991).

One criticism of these policies is that often they have been property and regeneration motive-led. They are ways of using empty or under-used land rather than being inspired by artistic ambitions or as part of a community education initiative. Another criticism is that a monopoly land use zone of theatres and concert halls can be very dead in the daytime.

As with museums and convention centres, the architecture of new buildings can make a positive contribution to the visibility, prestige and attractiveness of the area. The Sydney Opera House (1973), located on the stunning harbour, is a landmark building which has helped put Sydney on the world map, as well as strengthening the tourism resources around the harbour. The Lowry (centre) in Salford, Manchester, opened in 2000 on a disused pier in the Manchester Ship Canal, has a similar objective of assisting regeneration, changing the image of an area, and raising the profile of the area. Such buildings are also perceived as flagship projects, boosting confidence in an area and attracting other investment. If successful, they create civic pride.

Only a small amount of research on tourism and the arts has been undertaken. Cwi (1980), in a study of the impact of the arts in cities, concluded that it was overwhelmingly through tourists that the performing arts could generate income for the urban region. In most cities probably only a small percentage of patrons at any per-

Table 7.2 Tourism and visits to theatres in Britain in 1984

Place	Residents	Day visitors	Tourists	
			British	Other
London	39	21	5	35
Elsewhere	82	10	8	0

Source: Myerscough (1988a), Table 5.1

Table 7.3 London West End theatre audiences by origin

Performance type	Percentage of respondents in survey		
	London resident	Other UK resident	Foreign
Modern drama	39	28	33
Comedy	37	35	28
Modern musical	20	45	34
Traditional musical	14	26	60
Revue/variety	42	47	11
Opera	59	31	10
Dance	63	24	13
Classical plays	43	32	25
Children's shows	47	44	9
Thrillers	22	18	60

Source: Gardiner (1991)

formance could be classified as tourists, i.e. coming from outside the immediate region. The share will obviously in part be related to the importance of tourism in the local economy and the amount of the performing arts available, and is therefore likely to be high in capital cities. Tighe (1985) suggested that tourists represented 37 per cent of audiences in New York in 1983–84. In Britain the situation has been studied by the Policy Studies Institute which confirms the importance of visitors in London's theatres and concert halls (Myerscough, 1988a; Hughes, 1998a) (Table 7.2). These figures show the combined share, but in fact most visitors attend theatres and only a few go to concerts. The results for the different types of theatrical production are shown in Table 7.3, where it is seen that the visitors prefer musicals, thrillers and to a lesser extent comedy and drama. One would expect the share of visitors to vary from place to place. In a few special places the share of non-residents is very high, as in Aldeburgh (77 per cent), Stratford-upon-Avon (60 per cent) and Bath (53 per cent). Another special case is that of seaside resorts, where in the short summer season the proportion of tourists is very high. However, in most British cities the share of non-residents is likely to be less than 20 per cent, and only in London do they form the majority. In London 60 per cent of theatregoers come from outside the city and of these one-third from outside Britain (Hughes, 1998a, 2000b; Martin, 1998). A survey of theatregoers in Manchester in 1985 found that 70 per cent lived in Greater Manchester, a further 12 per cent lived outside but had travelled from home, and 18 per cent had stayed overnight with just under half using serviced accommodation (Manchester Polytechnic, 1985). This compares with a 1986 survey in Glasgow which found that 85 per cent of the patrons were Greater Glasgow residents, 13 per cent were day visitors, and only 2 per cent were staying overnight (Myerscough, 1988b). For the day visitors attending the theatre or a concert, the overwhelming main reason for coming to Glasgow was the performance, while for the tourist this was not a reason for two-thirds. During the 1990 European Year of Culture, Glasgow greatly increased the number of visitors attending theatres and concerts, although they still only formed 29 per cent of the audiences (Table 7.4). In North America only about 5–10 per cent of theatre patrons stay overnight and so consequently have a low economic impact (Petersen, 1989).

As audience research increases, there is more information about the profile of patrons

Table 7.4 Attendance at Glasgow theatres and concerts, 1986 and 1990

	Numbers (000)		Change	Percentage		Difference
	1986	*1990*	*%*	*1986*	*1990*	
Glasgow City	484	800	+66	41	46	+5
Outer Glasgow	524	420	−19	44	24	−20
Day visitors	149	330	+125	13	19	+6
Tourists	27	188	+596	2	10	+8
All	1184	1738	+47	100	100	−

Source: Myerscough (1991), Tables 45 and 47

including their geographical origin. However, it is still quite difficult to determine the role which the arts play in attracting people to cities. Do they come primarily because of the arts, or with the arts as part of a bundle of attractions, or as mere entertainment when they are there (Hughes, 1989b)? It is likely that the number of people for whom the arts are a prime draw is very small, and that for most visitors the possibility of attending a theatre or concert is a bonus after they have made the decision to visit the city (Hughes, 1997b, 1998a). In most cases the opportunities in the performing arts available in other cities are likely to be very similar to those in the home city and therefore not a reason for making a trip (Richards, 1994b). Language may be another factor which reduces the importance of the arts as a prime motive for travel. Many of the tourists recorded in surveys may in fact be visiting friends and relatives. A third research question concerns the ancillary activities engaged in by the arts tourist and the pattern of expenditure. The arts tourist is likely to be more affluent and therefore a high spender (Whitt, 1988). This should help support the restaurants and perhaps speciality shops. There is not enough space to discuss the wider issue of the role of the arts in influencing economic development, but it is always likely to be difficult to prove that they are a major influence, given the multiplicity of factors involved.

ENTERTAINMENT

The word entertainment can convey several meanings. Used in a very broad way, nearly all the attractions of cities could be said to provide entertainment, whether they are museums, concert halls or sports. However, as Hughes (1989b) points out, in everyday usage it has overtones of undemanding amusement or diversion and is therefore frequently used in a more narrow way to convey mass or popular culture as compared to the 'high' culture discussed in the last section. As such, the term might include 'pop' concerts, comedy and the music hall, theatre musicals, cinemas, dance halls, clubs, various types of gambling from casinos to bingo, and what in the USA is euphemistically called 'adult entertainment' where commercial sexual services are provided. Eating and drinking can also be included within this heading. In many cities these activities are often described as the leisure industries. Once again, the large size of cities has meant that these activities have been well developed to serve the local population, but because of their scale and 'quality' (*sic*) they have the power to attract people from other areas.

The role of entertainment in western societies appears to have been increasing in recent years. Chapter 5 discussed how entertainment is becoming a feature of visitor attractions. Critics of the media, including television and newspapers, argue that there has been a 'dumbing down' as entertainment replaces 'high' culture and serious re-porting, and editors discover that entertainment content raises audience levels. There is a sense in which entertainment becomes addictive. The excitement and hyped-upness of entertainment create a need for a continual supply of stimuli. At the same time en-tertainment and advertising encourage a hedonistic lifestyle in which new and different experiences are sought, producing an inflation in expectations. One example of this phenomena can be witnessed in the pre-wedding hen and stag parties. From a night out in a local pub these have developed in some cases to a weekend drinking in a distant and usually foreign city and even to a week in an exotic coastal resort. Cities such as Amsterdam and Dublin have benefited (?) from a growth of such trips, but it is likely as these become 'old hat' other and more novel destinations will be sought out.

The growth of the entertainment/leisure economy is having a significant impact on the economy of city centres. There has been a symbiotic relationship between the increase in the number of people living in the city centre and the growth of leisure activities. People are attracted to come and live in the area because of its good resources of leisure activites and at the same time the presence of a strong local market stimulates further expansion. At the same time the critical mass of facilities encourages consumers not only from the wider urban area but also from the region and possibly further afield, so that these activities become a very real resource of the tourism industry. There has of course always been an entertainment/leisure component of the city centre economy, and world cities such as New York and London have had their entertainment districts, often overlapping their theatrelands as in Times Square/Broadway (Sassen and Roost, 1999) and the West End/Leicester Square. In other cities the decentralization of the popu-lation within urban areas, followed by some leisure activities coupled with more home-based leisure activities in the 1950s, 1960s and 1970s, resulted in a decline of these activities in the city centre (for the USA see Hannigan, 1998, Chapter 2). The revival of leisure activities has had a significant impact upon the regeneration of the city centre. At first, these activities frequently used existing and often cheap redundant buildings. But continued growth and expansion have witnessed the construction of many new structures either solely for these functions or within a mixed use building (Hannigan, 1998). Within some cities, urban entertainment centres have been constructed bringing together cinemas, nightclubs, bars, restaurants and health clubs, as at The Printworks in Manchester. In Dublin the intended cultural quarter at Temple Bar has as a result of rising rents become a very successful entertainment zone attracting many tourists (Montgomery, 1995b; McCarthy, 1998).

The growth of gambling is another form of entertainment which has impacted on some urban tourism destinations. In the past gambling aroused moral disapproval because of the harm that it could cause to family finances and because it was perceived as a misuse of money. It was also a cause of concern to civic authorities because of its links with criminal gangs. Consequently, gambling has often been forbidden or very tightly controlled, in the latter case frequently being restricted to a few geographical areas. As a result, gamblers have had to travel to specific locations in order to indulge in their favoured pastime, and destinations such as Monte Carlo (Monaco) and Las Vegas have grown and flourished on the industry. In recent years moral attitudes to gambling have changed with many people perceiving it as a harmless and amusing activity. At the same time promoters have started using the term 'gaming' and thereby hope to disassociate themselves from previous connotations. Governments have also shown themselves to be more liberal in their attitudes to licensing locations. With the growth of gambling, many cities and other places have sought to attract the trade, hoping to emulate places like Las Vegas, and gain tourists, jobs and taxes. One example of this process is to be found in Sydney, where the State of New South Wales went to some lengths to have a casino established (Searle and Bounds, 1999). In the USA there has been a spread of casinos from Las Vegas to Atlantic City (1976), to riverboats and native reservations and now more generally in cities. As gambling becomes more geographically widespread, the need for travel and thereby a tourism dimension is likely to become less.

Large cities because of their size, cosmopolitanism and anonymity have often attracted another type of activity with a significant tourism dimension which has not always been welcome. Sex tourism is a well-known feature of many cities featuring strip shows and prostitution. It has usually been concentrated in a particular part of the city, partly because clustering gives visibility and helps attract customers and partly because 'the authorities' wish to confine it to particular off-centre zones where it can be controlled and not give offence to the majority of the population. These 'adult entertainment zones', 'red light districts' or liminal zones are often found in the rundown areas of planning blight of the transition zone and also near railway stations (Ashworth *et al.*, 1988). They provide tourism promoters with a problem as to whether to ignore or accept them as a fact of life and exploit them for the benefit of tourism. Some cities such as Amsterdam, Hamburg and Bangkok have an international reputation for their sex tourism which probably needs little advertising. The situation has become more complicated with the acceptability of 'gay' or homosexual lifestyles and the emergence of gay zones from the famous Castro in San Francisco, the gay village in Manchester (Taylor *et al.*, 1996; Quilley, 1997) and the gay zones of Amsterdam (Hughes, 1998b). Other cities such as Munich (Cope and Barrie, 2001) are hoping to 'cash in' on the perceived high 'pink' spending. To attack such quarters would appear to be denying the human rights of gay individuals who may come to such places not just for sex but to escape from homophobic environments. Some local governments perceive these places as exotic zones giving an extra dimension to the excitement that the city can offer and therefore have no hesitation in advertising them to tourists. However, in the case of gay zones, the presence of voyeurs can only dilute the character of the area and possibly result in its demise. The significance of sex tourism will always be difficult to evaluate because of the debate about its moral appropriateness. It also shares with other activities such as culture the problem of differentiating those who are attracted to the city primarily because of it from those who merely take advantage of the opportunities that they find when they have come for another reason.

Case Study: Las Vegas

Las Vegas is one of the world's major urban tourism destinations receiving in the late 1990s over 42 million visitors a year, with its appeal largely based on entertainment and lacking the diverse economy and significant heritage that characterize most large cities. In 1970 it received only 6.7 million visitors and its population was a mere 273,000. By 1996 the metropolitan area had a population of 1.2 million, and it had 125,000 hotel bedrooms. It had also become one of the major convention cities in the USA, hosting 3.5 million delegates in 1997. Its development in the southern desert areas of Nevada, relatively remote from other large centres, is surprising in many ways, and possibly destined to be unique, although it inspires so much admiration that many cities look to it as a model or template of what they might achieve, particularly when many other tourism resources are lacking (see Gottdiener, 1997; Zukin, 1998; Gottdiener *et al.*, 1999; Parker, 1999).

In 1931 Las Vegas was a small town suffering from unemployment as the local mining economy collapsed. In a surprising move for a legislature dominated by members of the Mormon Church, the state of Nevada agreed to allow gambling to take place in Las Vegas. From 1931 to 1978 the town was the only area in the United States where gambling was legally permitted. For the next forty years the town was to grow steadily if not spectacularly with a reputation for gambling, sex and criminal activity. Gradually the criminal activity was reduced and to diversify its attraction, in 1959, a convention centre was constructed. To attract punters, many of the hotels put on shows and this was the beginning of the diversification to fun and entertainment. In the late 1980s another round of expansion began as mega-hotels were built. These are themed hotels as their names suggest – Aladdin, Bellagio (after an Italian resort), Caesar's Palace, Luxor, MGM Grand (Canyon), Mandalay Bay, Mirage, Monte Carlo, New York-New York, Paris, Treasure Island, and Venetian. All of these hotels have between 2,000 and 4,000 bedrooms and most have large shopping malls, as well as, of course, casinos. The fame of these spectacular hotels with their entertainments (Treasure Island features a mock sea battle by pirates) lures visitors to the resorts. Two-thirds claim that their prime reason for coming to Las Vegas is for a holiday. Only 5 per cent say they come to gamble but in fact 87 per cent do in fact gamble. Apart from the entertainment there are other things to do, such as golf and visiting the surrounding dramatic scenery. In the early 1990s the city attempted to sell itself as a family destination, but this has had only limited success. Nevertheless, the resort is diversifying; two casino hotels, the Bellagio (1998) and another in 2001 contain art museums, in the latter case operated by the Guggenheim Museum of New York. As casinos become legal in many states, and its monopoly disappears, the need to diversify becomes more urgent. In 2001 there was a real possibility of casinos being established in California, a state which supplies one-third of Las Vegas's visitors. Nevertheless, such was the optimism in the industry that the number of hotel bedrooms was forecast to grow from 124,200 in 2000 to 132,444 in 2003.

SPORT

Team sports have an important place in modern society. They provide not only ex-citement and entertainment but the opportunity to be part of a wider community by means of a shared interest. This wider community has been extended in recent years through the media and the processes of globalization (Whitson and Macintosh, 1993). Sports teams and self-identity are closely linked. There is a bond between a city team and its residents, while others aspiring to a high status may identify and follow a top league team. In the second half of the twentieth century sport was transformed from a local and often uncommercialized activity to a commodified product in which every aspect has become highly commercialized – from the selling of TV and broadcasting rights, sponsorship, corporate hospitality, advertising space, memorabilia and clothing, food and beverage concessions, players, stadium/arena names to the creation of visitor attractions and conference facilities and the establishment of a brand which can be sold around the world. Sport has become part of the entertainment industry and its 'big names' have become stars as in the rest of this industry. This commercialization of sport has occurred at the same time as, and perhaps in conflict with, the idea of sport as religion. As Blake wrote: 'Spirituality is far from dead and sport is an instance of its survival: sport is not just a secular faith but a religion, an object of many people's worship. Through this worship they can express their obsessions, fears and desires in exactly the same way as a churchgoer.' He goes on to say that similarly they can express their solidarity with (part of) mankind and, like other worshippers, they will need to make pilgrimages to the hallowed grounds and to museums to see images of their saints.

As with the arts, large cities, because of the size of their population, have developed major sports facilities and are the home bases of prestigious teams. In recent years there has been a tendency to see sport as more than simply a local amenity. Major sporting activities, whether regular fixtures or special events (see later section), are perceived to project a high status image of the city via media coverage which may attract economic development, persuade senior executives to live in the city, and attract visitors (Baade and Dye, 1988a, 1990). Sport may also increase civic pride, community spirit ('social bonding') and collective self-image. Since the Los Angeles Olympic Games in 1984 it has also been believed that the profits from hosting a mega-event could pay for high quality facilities which would be of permanent value to the community. In this section attention is focused on regular professional team sports and their facilities and a later section will examine special events. The key question is whether regular spectator sports can win a net inflow of visitors to the city, either on their own or in conjunction with other attractions (Baade, in Lawson, 1996).

In the USA, professional sports teams are privately owned and can move from one city to another and from the central city to the suburb (Johnson, 1986; Knack, 1986; Rosentraub and Nunn, 1978). Since about 1960 the number of teams moving from one city to another has increased. Many teams in older 'frostbelt' cities found themselves in a crowded market with either other teams in the same city or in a nearby one. By moving, often to a growing sunbelt city, they were able to dominate a city market and gain a better and subsidized publicly built stadium (Noll and Zimbalist, 1997). Large cities were prepared to build these stadiums for a number of reasons. Having a major team is perceived to indicate status, to be a 'big league city' and to be in a league where your team plays other teams from big cities (Whitson and Macintosh, 1993). Consequently, cities in pursuit of world-class status and having a role as an international destination, will seek to attract and retain top teams. Having a winning team, it is hoped, will bring visibility and the image of success and hopefully attract new businesses. There are presumed to be spillover benefits from the stadium as tourists spend money in the city. Building stadiums on the edge of downtown areas was also part of a regeneration strategy. To keep teams in the city and in the downtown area, and to attract them from elsewhere, municipalities have been prepared to offer inducements, including building and retaining ownership of a stadium which is then let to the team, usually on an uneconomic basis (Petersen, 1989). Of the 29 stadiums constructed in the USA between 1960 and 1990, 25 were publicly built (Baade and Dye, 1990) and of the 94 stadiums used by professional teams between 1953 and 1988, 67 were publicly owned (Baade and Dye, 1988a). This process has produced an over-supply of facilities in an industry where the number of teams in a league is limited, with the consequence that teams are in a buyer's market and there is the opportunity for 'owner extortion'. The rent for these stadiums rarely pays for all the costs, particularly debt servicing or loan repayments. Baade and Dye (1988a), Baade (1995, 1996a) and Baade and Sanderson (1997) could find no evidence to support these claims and concluded that in the final analysis the building of a stadium was based on non-measurable intangible benefits. To support this view they quoted the mayor of New Orleans: 'the Superdome is an exercise in optimism. A statement of faith. It is the very building of it which is important, not how much it is used or its economics.' In reality many cities were faced with the prospect of losing a major league team, a loss which would be severely felt by many of the electorate, with the result that the politicians were willing to consider a new sub-sidized stadium. It can be said therefore that payments create public consumption benefits. Many studies have attempted to demonstrate the economic gains from sport. Schaffer and Davidson studied the expenditure of the 321,000 attenders of the Atlanta Falcons (football) games in 1984 and suggested that the fans introduced nearly $12 million into the local economy (quoted in Bale, 1989). Even if the expenditure by local fans is ignored, the 30 per cent out-of-town attenders were responsible for 43 per cent of the economic impact. However, Noll and Zimbalist (1997) dispute these benefits. With major teams now spread more evenly across the country there is less need for spectators to travel long distances and also stay overnight, except when their team is playing away. Furthermore, in recent years an increasing proportion of tickets have been held by season holders limiting the opportunities for the casual tourist to attend. Even when there are visitors present, they may be visiting the city primarily for another reason.

The various team sports have different demand schedules and may require special facilities. A major baseball team will occupy a stadium for about 81 days of the year and require a special oval pitch. In contrast, an American football team occupies its stadium for only about 8–11 days in a year (although attendances are likely to be greater) and the game requires a rectangular pitch. Basketball teams play about 41 home matches and use an indoor arena. The low usage of these facilites must limit any impact they can have on tourism and economic regeneration. In recent years the open baseball and football stadiums have been replaced by enclosed domes: examples include the Astra Dome in Houston (1965), the Superdome in New Orleans (1975) and the SkyDome in Toronto (1989) with a retractable roof. Covered facilities, whether arenas or domes, have greater flexibility and can be used for many different purposes from sport and pop concerts to conventions and exhibitions (Petersen, 1989). Accordingly, in many cities, such as Atlanta and Indianapolis, the same authority has built the con-vention and sports facilities; they are adjacent to each other and are run jointly. To pay for the facilities a combination of sources may be used from tax-exempt bonds, sales taxes and lottery funds.

In North America the policy of subsidizing stadiums has been closely linked with other policies to revitalize the city centre and stop decentralization within the urban area. Newsome and Comer (2000) have shown that for the facilities of the major league teams in baseball, basketball, football and hockey there was a decentralizing tendency in the period 1965–85 which was reversed in the following period 1985–97. By 1997, 58 per cent of the facilities were in the downtown area. This may reflect not only the willingness of cities to subsidize these amenities, but the reviving attractiveness of downtown zones. In many cities the stadium had traditionally been near the city centre and municipalities fought to keep it there, particularly when a new, more modern facility, perhaps with better road access, was proposed for the suburbs. In other cities without a long-standing stadium, the first one was constructed in this zone (see Atlanta). In a few cities, such as Baltimore, an old stadium in a midddle suburb was replaced by a more modern one adjacent to the downtown area (Bale and Moen, 1995; Hamilton and Kahn, 1997). In Baltimore and Cleveland a small sports quarter has been created through the construction of two sports facilities. There are several advantages to this strategy of locating stadiums downtown, not least in its reinforcement of the tourism and recreational role of the city centre. In a few cases, such as the SkyDome in Toronto, the exciting architecture of the building has made it a visitor attraction in its own right with tours of the facility. Another advantage found in such cities as New Orleans is that the multistorey car parks built next to the sports facility can be used in the daytime by office workers and in the evening and at the weekend by spectators (Miestchovich and Ragas, 1986; Ragas *et al.*, 1987). Of course fans can also use the car parking facilities constructed for office workers. In Baltimore the move of the Orioles baseball team from the suburbs to a downtown stadium at Camden Yards resulted in a 75 per cent increase in attendance and some extra spending in the city centre although not in hotels as the city is too close to other large cities (Hamilton and Kahn, 1997). Because of the scale and low frequency of sports events, it is unlikely that on their own they will have a major impact on downtown regeneration, but as part of a comprehensive focused long-term strategy they can make a contribution (Rosentraub, 1997).

In Britain the dominant spectator sport is football which has a high density of teams and facilities. Consequently, a spectator is unlikely to have to travel far to find a match, unless it be as a fan to an away game, and so the tourist share of attendance is likely to be low (Collins, 1991). However, in recent years the gulf between the teams in the premier division and the other divisions has widened as television income, the ability to charge higher ticket prices and merchandising have enabled them to purchase the best players, giving real meaning to the term 'in a different league' (Mintel, 1998b; Johnstone *et al.*, 2000). The most successful teams obtain great publicity through television and have a national and international following with resulting increased tourist flows. One report has suggested that Newcastle United attracted 170,000 Norwegians for short weekend breaks (Stevens, quoted in Lawson, 1996). Although a city like Manchester was known throughout the world for its pioneering role in the industrial revolution long before Manchester United Football Club was established, today it is this team which is the flagship for the city and which will help it sell itself as a tourist city. Following the Taylor Inquiry into the Sheffield Hillsborough disaster, football clubs have been forced either to modernize existing stadiums or to move to new ones. There has been no consensus as to where these should be built and whether they should contribute to the regeneration of the inner city. Consequently, some have been built on the edge of the built-up area. However, nearly all stadiums have attempted to include other facilities which can be used to generate income, such as conferences, so that it is not 'dead space' for most of the week.

The more general role of sport in tourism and urban regeneration in Britain has only recently begun to be considered. Sheffield attracted much attention through its successful bid for the World Student Games held in the city in July 1991, but the losses incurred were not a good signal to other cities (Foley, 1991; Roche, 1992, 1994; Davies, 1996; Bramwell, 1997; Henry and Paramio-Salcines, 1999). However, the new facilities in regenerated areas have been used both for the benefit of local people and to attract other events. Both Birmingham and Manchester have bid unsuccessfully for the Olympic Games. Cardiff and Edinburgh have hosted the Commonwealth Games and Manchester is to do so in 2002, all gaining improved facilities in the process. There has been a wave of new indoor arenas in London (1989), Sheffield (1991), Birmingham (1991), Manchester (1995) and Newcastle (1995) which are used for sport as well as other forms of entertainment. Liverpool and Manchester have sought to use football to assist tourism through sports weekend breaks involving game and entertainment tickets as well as hotel accommodation. However, in Britain there are less than a dozen sports museums and most of these are relatively recent, whereas in the USA there are over 400 'halls of fame' which are overwhelmingly in honour of sportsmen and sportswomen (Redmond, 1991). In 1999 Manchester United's museum drew 274,000 visitors. In Europe many cities have invested heavily in sports facilities in order to host major events, including Barcelona and Duisberg. Many cities now sell themselves as cities of sport or sports cities, of which Sheffield is an example, in an attempt to exploit what they perceive to be a growing specialist market. Often building on existing resources, they attempt to diversify within the sports sector in order to enhance their standing (see case study of Indianapolis below). But sport on its own is rarely enough and they need to have an adequate range of other attractions.

Most of the research on sport and local economic development has been undertaken in the USA, where many studies (usually unpublished) have been commissioned both by municipalities and teams as part of their case for the public subsidy of stadiums and arenas (Baade and Dye, 1988a). These studies can focus either on the costs and benefits to the public sector (Johnson, 1986) or on the wider economic benefits to the area. When the public sector accounts show a deficit, emphasis is likely to shift to the wider economic benefits. Figures are often calculated to show how much spectators spend inside and outside the ground at regular fixtures. However, since most of the spectators are locals, a large share of the expenditure cannot be counted as additional income to the region, being merely displaced from other activities, unless it can be shown that in the absence of a local stadium the participants would have visited stadiums outside the region (import substitution). Given the large distances between US cities, it is likely that games attract some spectators for a short break vacation, although research suggests that for ordinary games only 5–10 per cent of spectators stay overnight. However, for big events like the SuperBowl this may rise to 90 per cent (Petersen, 1989). A study of the subsidized Louisiana Superdome in New Orleans found that when all the benefits were considered, the benefit to cost ratio was 12.4 to 1 (Ragas *et al.*, 1987). In contrast, in Britain, with its small distances, it is likely that nearly all spectators are either locals or day visitors. Unfortunately in Britain there is very little research on the economic impact of regular sports programmes. The American evidence would suggest that sports programmes can have their greatest economic impact when they are linked to other tourist attractions and when they are family leisure activities.

As regards the impact of sport on general economic development, this relationship is likely to be very difficult to disentangle since this is only one factor among many which will affect the growth performance of an urban area. Baade and Dye (1990) found no relationship between assistance to teams and the building of stadiums, and the growth of personal incomes in nine US metropolitan areas. In Britain, Liverpool Football Club was the the top of the league for many years in the 1970s and 1980s and yet Merseyside remained one of the poorest urban areas in the country. At the very local (site) level, sports facilities may have both positive and negative effects: positive because the prospect of large numbers of people may encourage investment in other activities (e.g. catering), and negative because crowds and congestion may discourage investment. Much may depend on the characteristics of the spectators. Baade and Dye (1988b) suggest that the maximum impact of a stadium is likely to be felt when it is close to other tourist attractions and hotels.

Case Study: Indianapolis

Many cities have included sport as part of their economic development strategy but few have put it at the forefront. One exception is Indianapolis in the Midwest of the USA, sometimes called 'Sports City USA'. In the 1960s and 1970s the city experienced economic stagnation as jobs were lost in the manufacturing sector, and as elsewhere population decentralization resulted in a decaying downtown and inner city area. The city was unable to attract new economic activities and was apparently not benefiting from its central location and low cost of living. One reason for this situation appeared to be its lack of a positive image or even an image at all (Schimmel, 1995). Then the public and private sectors joined together to create a regeneration strategy which included downtown rejuvenation, infrastructure improvements, tourism, conventions and world-class sport (Bamberger and Parham, 1984). In the late 1970s, under the leadership of the mayor, the concept of 'development through sport' was evolved; this contained within it the idea that specialization in sport would enable the city to carve out a separate identity (Wilkinson, 1990). At this time the city was known only for the Indianapolis 500 motor race, dating back to 1911. A convention centre was opened in 1972 (subsequently expanded three times), the Market Street Arena in 1974 and the Indianapolis (White River) Sports Center in 1979. However, a bid for the World Student Games failed and the ensuing post-mortem suggested that it was because the city had insufficient facilities. To remedy the deficiences, a not-for-profit Indiana Sports Corporation was established in 1980 to stimulate the development of sports facilities and the attraction of events. By 1982 a natorium and velodrome had been built, and in 1984 the $77.5 million, 60,000-seat RCA Dome was opened, linked to an enlarged convention centre. This was partly financed by $30 million of private grants and partly by bonds covered by a 1 per cent food and beverage tax (Petersen, 1989). Indianapolis has benefited in particular from the generosity of the Lilly Endowment Fund, established by the family that founded the pharmaceutical company of the same name. The dome is used for sports and other events such as concerts and conventions. The city used the facility to attract the Colts (American) football team from Baltimore (Johnson, 1986; Schimmel, 1995). Since 1984 other facilities have been added, including a regatta course, a soccer complex and a skating rink. Two major facilities were opened in the late 1990s: Victory Field for baseball in 1996 and Conseco Fieldhouse for basketball and other sports in 1999. In addition, hall of fame museums have been attached to the motor racing circuit and the RCA Dome, and a National Art Museum of Sport opened in 1991. Other visitor attractions, not directly related to sport, have also been developed.

As a consequence of having invested in these facilities, the city was able to win over 400 national and international sports meetings between 1977 and 1998, including the Pan-American Games in 1987. For the 1991 World Gymnastic Championships held in the RCA Dome, an impact study was undertaken by Herron Associates Inc. (1991). Herron found that of the 70,000 spectators, two-thirds came from outside the state and that there was a further non-local contingent of 1,600 competitors, officials and press personnel. These visitors spent $37.2 million in the area. Another type of impact has been that 22 sports organizations have located their headquarters in the city. The city has been able to attract many non-sports companies which have created many thousands of jobs and brought growth to the metropolitan area. Of course, it is difficult to evaluate the extent to which these firms have moved to the city because of the impact of sports, either in enhancing the lifestyle or changing the image. What is certain is that the development of sports and conventions has played a major role in the regeneration of the downtown area and in changing the image of the city (Rosentraub, 1997). Schimmel (1995), however, suggests that the policies of the public–private coalition have been very much in the interest of private sector firms who wish to raise the status and facilities of the city in order to attract senior staff and that while they have been able to sell the policies to the wider community on the basis of job creation, in fact expenditure on sports facilities has often displaced finance that might have been used, say, to improve housing for the poor. Rosentraub and Przybylski (1997) argue that while the city has been very successful in developing a sports industry, the direct effects on employment have been very small. However, the sports-led strategy has enabled the city, the state and the private sector to agree on a wide range of policies and the confidence that has come as a result of the successful sports policies over a number of years has spilled over into these other policy areas (Rosentraub *et al.*, 1994).

SPECIAL EVENT TOURISM

The term 'special event' is used to describe themed events which are one-off or occur infrequently outside the normal programme of activities (Getz, 1991a, 1997). For the customer or guest a special event is an opportunity for a leisure, social or cultural experience which is outside the normal range of choices or beyond everyday experiences. Special events are of finite length and are distinguished by an innate uniqueness. Even when special events are periodic, each one usually has a distinctive or individual programme. Frequently this uniqueness is sold as a once-in-a-lifetime opportunity. Most special events are distinguished by their celebratory or festive ambience. In most cases, special events have a significant public element with the organizers attempting to involve the local community. While attendance at the main events is usually by payment, there may be street parades and firework displays. Typical special events are ones that occur only on an annual basis in the same locality (e.g. the Edinburgh Festival), or move from one place to another (e.g. the Commonwealth Games). Another type of special event is the one-off celebration (e.g bicentenaries). Special events may have almost any theme and take any form (see Ritchie, 1984). A special event could be as simple as an annual street parade. Munich's Oktoberfest consists of parades and beer drinking. The arrival of the Tall Ships Race at an Atlantic port is an event which can attract millions of visitors. Some special events are connected with special personages, such as a coronation or a papal visit. Many special events are related to existing visitor attractions. An art gallery may have a special exhibition, perhaps using a theme and bringing in pictures on loan from elsewhere. When these feature a great and/or famous artist, this is often described as an 'art blockbuster' exhibition. A cathedral may be the setting for a choir festival.

The term hallmark event is used to describe an event held to enhance the awareness, appeal and profitability of a tourist destination in the short or long term (Getz, 1997). It is usually a recurring event which is or aspires to be a distinguishing feature of a destination. A mega-event is one distinguished by the high levels of tourism, media coverage, prestige and economic impact on the host community. It is an event of world importance and high profile which can have a major impact on the image of the host city (Hall, 1992; Syme *et al.*, 1989). This definition is mainly psychological, as it is difficult to specify a quantitative one that would be widely applicable (Witt, 1988). Special events can therefore be anything from the annual village carnival to the Olympic Games. Often, special events involve a considerable amount of spectacle which acts as a visitor draw. Most special events are only of short duration, lasting either a few days or a few weeks, but some such as World Expos last several months and even up to a year. In discussing the different types of special events, the major distinction is between the one-off mega-event and the annual fixed location special events. Mega-events have the potential to make a big impact, economically, in terms of physical regeneration, in changing the image of a place and in other ways (Roche, 1992). But to be effective they need to be planned as part of a wider strategy with long-term plans for the later use of facilities (Bramwell, 1997).

Many special events have a long history and some which almost went out of existence, such as the Mardi Gras and New Year carnivals, are being revived, but new ones are constantly being created, and Getz (1991a, 1992) provides evidence of their expansion. There are many reasons for their growth. Easier travel and globalization are factors in the development of international events. There are now many more international sports competitions and these special events have become a major travel generator. The increase in special events is not unconnected with the fact that they are increasingly being used as means of attracting tourists and raising the profiles and changing the images of places. The large special event, whether it is a festival, a sports competition or a political convention, gains tremendous television coverage which can give more effective publicity to a place than any other method (Guskind, 1988). In the past, most special events were conceived as purely local celebrations, but today the tourism motivation is often being added and sometimes events are deliberately being created to attract tourists. As with many of the other phenomena discussed in this book, special events have multiple purposes. Getz (1991a, 1997) and Hall (1992) list the many reasons for special events and their growth:

1. To offer a high quality cultural or sporting experience.
2. To involve the community in a civic celebration.
3. To encourage participation in the arts and sports.
4. To promote civic pride.
5. To attract visitors into the area and put the place on the tourist map.
6. To attract people outside the main season.
7. To attract media attention, raise the profile of the area, create a favourable image, combat negative images, and so attract investment from outside the area.
8. To add animation and life to existing attractions.
9. To encourage repeat visits.
10. To assist regeneration and improve the infrastructure of the area.
11. To lever government grants for sports, arts and culture.
12. To emulate the success of other communities.
13. To develop niche markets in a developing marketplace.

The current increase in the number of special events is a consequence of the competition which exists between places; no city can afford to miss out on this type of attraction. Getz (1992, 1997) notes that competition is forcing cities to discover new niche markets, new themes, to be more spectacular and to increase the scale and length of the event. However, there is a danger of saturation in the market, with the consequence that some older and less successful events may fail.

One of the advantages of special events is that they can be used by cities with few other attractions (i.e. quality visitor attractions) and which lack high visibility. Gold-blatt (quoted in Getz, 1997) studied special events in the USA and came to the conclusion that they were a significant part of the tourism-generating process of second-tier cities. Special events are also used by cities seeking to revive decayed downtown areas or to strengthen the role of the city centre. Many city councils have a special events unit to organize activities, often in partnership with other sectors, such as retailing. While these events are primarily aimed at bringing people from the suburbs back downtown, they are also an added attraction to tourists, creating the impression of vitality. Chicago's Mayor's Office of Special Events organizes up to 80 events a year on a city-wide basis with the downtown 'Taste of Chicago' attracting over 3 million visitors, of whom nearly one-fifth come from outside the metropolitan area (Getz, 1997).

The financing of special events is a topic relevant to their understanding. They can be organized to operate with a limited subsidy, to break even or to generate a profit. In the case of mega-events, that is events of world significance, national and regional governments can be expected to make a contribution as the event will not just showcase the city but the nation as well. A poor event would rebound on the standing of the nation and would damage its chances of hosting further mega-events. Local councils are often expected to subsidize special events, either because they are a community event or because they are expected to attract tourists and this will generate income to the community. With the general restrictions on local government finance in recent years other sources of finance have had to be found and this has generally come from the commercial sector with some form of sponsorship. Very few sponsors are altruistic and most are looking for some benefit. This may come if their name is associated with the title of the special event or with a particular part of it. They may also wish to have the opportunity to use the facilities for corporate hospitality. Within Britain sponsorship of the arts has grown to over £200 million a year (by 2000), but it may come with a price. Sponsors are only likely to want to be associated with large and successful events which gain much media publicity and with the type of events which have status and prestige. This makes it easy for an art blockbuster in a capital city such as London attracting patrons from financially well-linked groups and the middle classes to obtain sponsorship, but more difficult for a community-centred arts festival in a provincial town. As a consequence, London which is already well endowed with tourism resources is able to go on adding to them via special events while a smaller city in a peripheral region struggling to get on the tourist map is likely to find it more difficult. This is not to say that it is impossible but just harder, requiring more creativity.

Given the great variety of special events and the different types of places where they are held, it is difficult to generalize about their origin, operation and long-term effects. Special events can be studied from a number of perspectives: economic, social, political and planning (Roche, 1992, 1994, 2000). In terms of their economic impacts, studies have attempted to measure the number of people attending, their geographical origin, their social characteristics and their expenditure patterns. From these statistics an estimate can be made of the net income generated for the community and the number of jobs created (Myerscough, 1991). In addition, an attempt may be made to measure the level of knowledge of the event in other parts of the country and how this has changed the perceptions of the area. An assessment can also be made of the long-term effects, including the amount of inward investment and the growth of tourism. Other studies attempt to assess the impact on the local community, whether it was well received, whether the community felt they had ownership of the event and how many were involved in any way. Because of the wide diversity of special events, it is not possible to cover them all and attention will be concentrated on arts festivals, art blockbusters, sports events and world fairs (see Getz, 1991a, for a comprehensive treatment).

Arts Festivals

Getz (1991b) defines a festival as a themed public celebration which extends leisure and cultural opportunities beyond everyday experiences and choices. Originally the objectives of arts festivals were posited in purely local terms; to give local artists the opportunity to perform, to educate the local community as to the benefits of the arts and to bring in quality performers, but today they are more often seen as raising the profile of an area and providing the opportunity to attract tourists. The need to attract sponsorship has also steered them towards the 'high arts' so that, not surprisingly, they are seen by the local community as elitist. Arts festivals may cover several arts or focus on a single art such as classical music, jazz, literature, drama, film, etc., and within each genre there may be specialization. A few festivals of each type may have world significance, as with the Cannes Film Festival. In the UK there were 557 arts festivals in 1991, most of them having been in existence since the mid-1970s (Rolfe, 1992). However, five festivals accounted for more than half of all receipts. By far the majority of festivals were held in the May to October period, with those in cities occurring in mid-season when other activities fall away, and those in resorts in either the early or late summer to extend the season. Local government support was important in most cases, but commercial sponsorship has been increasing. Arts festivals attract mainly the middle class, and only the largest and most specialized attract a majority of attenders from outside the locality.

Many cities have attempted to introduce arts festivals in recent years. To attract attention and be able to draw people from a distance, they have increasingly been focused on a particular art form, such as film or jazz, but in a world awash with festivals late arrivals on the scene have found all the main themes taken. A recent innovation has been the introduction of year-long arts festivals which may move from one city to another. In Western Europe a City of Culture programme was begun in 1985 in which one city is given the title for a year and attempts to project itself across the continent in the hope that Europeans will travel to share in the event (see Glasgow below). Generally, the cities have been described as second-tier cities, but the programme has been so successful that there is considerable competition between places for the title which is now designated 'Cultural Capital of Europe'. From 2005 each country will have a year for which one of their cities can be nominated. In Britain a similar arts year for cities was developed in the 1990s, with each city associated with a theme. Cities bid for the title and the small amount of financial assistance that went with it. Birmingham's 1992 Year of Music was the first, followed by examples such as Manchester's Year of Drama in 1994 and Glasgow's Year of Architecture (1999). Once again, these festivals have multiple objectives of extending the arts experience of residents and raising the profile of the area, attracting visitors and acting as a catalyst for the improvement of facilities (Manchester City Council, 1991).

The success of an arts festival in terms of drawing an audience from outside its local area will depend in part on having a clear theme and achieving high quality. This is certainly true of British festivals such Aldeburgh and Edinburgh (Myerscough, 1988a) and the well-known European ones of Bayreuth and Salzburg (Frey and Pommenenehne, 1989). It is also likely that the more attractive the setting, the easier it is to draw an audience, and perhaps this is why older industrial cities may find it difficult to create a hugely popular event.

Some of the major arts festivals have been the subject of economic impact studies. The Edinburgh International Festival was established in 1947 and by the late 1980s, together with four other festivals and the Military Tattoo, was attracting 600,000 visitors for a three-week programme, generating income of between £30 million and £40 million. A study of 1990–91 found that the arts festival attracted a predominantly middle-class audience, whereas the Military Tattoo attracted a wider cross-section of the population (Gratton and Taylor, 1996; Scotinform Ltd and Leisure Research Services, 1991). However, whereas between 30 and 50 per cent of festival-goers visited another festival, there was little multiple visiting between the festivals and the Tattoo. Direct expenditure was estimated at £43.8 million, producing a net income to the area of £9.2 million, and creating 2,043 jobs or 1,319 full-time equivalents. An earlier pioneering study by Vaughan of the 1976 festival found that it attracted 33,200 overnight staying visitors and 100,000 day trips (Vaughan, 1977, 1980). In that year the Lothian Regional Council gave a subsidy of £206,000. Vaughan found that visitors spent £3.7 million and generated a net impact of £960,000, yielding a benefit–cost ratio of nearly 5 to 1. In the context of Edinburgh's full year of tourism, the festival was responsible for 19 per cent of the income generated, and the creation of the equivalent of 250 full-time posts. As Vaughan points out, these are only the easily quantifiable benefits. The publicity surrounding the festival raises the profile of the city and may encourage people to visit the city at other times of the year, and possibly firms may be influenced to locate in the city. However, arts festivals may also have negative impacts in the form of congestion during the event and the under-utilization of facilities during the rest of the year.

Since the late 1980s in Edinburgh a number of additional festivals and special events have been added to cover other parts of the year including folk, children's and science festivals in the spring and a Hogmany (New Year) celebration. By 1996 the audiences had reached 1.7 million and an impact study suggested an additional spend in the economy of £122 million and net impact of £30 million. Overall, it was claimed that 45 per cent of ticket sales were to locals, 20 per cent to residents of other parts of Scotland and 35 per cent to visitors from outside Scotland. By 1999 the subsidy to the International Festival had reached £1.9 million and their were extra costs to the local community in the form of litter collection, crowd control, extra hospital admissions and general congestion, but the benefits in terms of additional jobs and amenities to locals were considered to be advantageous.

The Art Blockbuster Exhibition

Although there have been sporadic temporary exhibitions which brought together a large collection of 'old masters' and the arts of ancient civilizations, their planned and regular use as a marketing device to attract large audiences is relatively recent (Haskell, 2000). The modern temporary art exhibition is characterized by its ability to bring together pictures from around the world and to concentrate on a theme whether it be one artist or the works of a particular school of artists. In the 1970s in New York the Metropolitan Museum of Art hosted the touring exhibition, Treasures of Tutankhamun, which played to a large audience. Later in 1980 the New York Museum of Modern Art staged a retrospective art exhibition of Picasso, with major works brought together from many art galleries around the world. In an area where seeing the original (authentic) work rather than a reproduction is paramount, this gave a once-in-a-lifetime opportunity to see a complete or nearly complete set of works by a particular artist. As a consequence, it became a 'must-see mega-show', an 'unmissable show' and one which people were prepared to travel long distances to see. Shows like this have been described as the 'Matterhorn of art tourism' and the 'cultural equivalent of the World Cup'. The success of the Picasso exhibition resulted in the concept being taken up by major art galleries around the world (Zeppel and Hall, 1992). Such exhibitions are costly to mount and potentially risky. In the late 1990s it was estimated that it cost £3 million to assemble, and to defray the costs the exhibition may be displayed twice, once in Europe and once in North America, and commercial sponsors are involved. These exhibitions, if successful, can be very profitable for the art gallery with income from ticket and shop sales. But there is always the risk that the artist or the theme will fail to attract sufficient visitors or sponsors. London's Royal Academy has had a 50 per cent success rate with these exhibitions. Its greatest success up to 2000 has been the 1999 Monet in the Twentieth Century exhibition which attracted 739,324 visitors. As discussed above, sponsorship is more likely to be obtainable where famous past artists are involved, such as Monet or Goya, and when the exhibition is located in a major city, such as London, Paris or New York, where elites will be easily attracted. For the major galleries in these cities the art blockbuster has become a regular feature, essential for their finances and profile (see *The Art Newspaper*, No. 111, February 2001 for attendance figures in 2000). In these cities the art blockbuster has become an additional attraction and a marketing tool which can be used to sell city break packages. Capital cities have developed venues which specialize in this type of exhibition such as the Royal Academy in London and the Grand Palais in Paris (EIU, 1993), while other major art galleries have had extensions so that they can mount these exhibitions. Critics claim that the success of these exhibitions, in terms of visitor numbers and income, has made them self-perpetuating, and that through their entry charges there has been a form of creeping privatization (Kay, 1996).

The Olympic Games

The four-yearly, 16-day summer Olympic Games is the world's greatest mega-event. The Olympic movement, which was reinvented in 1896, proclaims an ideology of sport for all and international friendship, although in practice the games concern elite athletes and depend on nationalistic competition. Each time the event is held, it gets bigger, with more countries represented, more sports, more spectacular opening and closing ceremonies and more impressive facilities. At the 27th summer Olympics in Sydney in 2000, 199 countries were involved and 28 sports. This compares with only 59 countries at the London games in 1948 and only 13 countries and 9 sports at the original Athens games in 1896 (Carreras, 1995). The competitive national element plus the various spectacles associated with the event ensure an interest well beyond the relatively few that follow sports. For the 2000 Sydney games up to 3.7 billion viewers world-wide were expected to watch the event. With television networks outbidding each other to have the rights to broadcast the event in their own country, and similarly, companies competing to obtain the commercial sponsorship rights, the event has been transformed from a loss-making one before 1984 to a profit-making one since (Gratton and Taylor, 1988a, b). It is this income which sets the Olympic Games apart from other large sports events such as the World Student Games and the continental games where TV interest and commercial sponsorship are much less (Collins, 1991). As a result, the Los Angeles games in 1984 made a profit of $250 million and the Seoul games in 1988 made $350 million.

This transformation of the economics of the games persuaded many cities of the benefits of hosting them. These cities hope that the profits to be made can be used to pay for the facilities that are required and which will be left behind as a legacy after the event. Given also the national visibility and prestige that goes with the Olympiad, host cities also hope that there will be an infusion of outside money and in particular that governments will pour money into the facilities and general infrastructure of the area. In some cases this may involve constructing a new stadium where there is an opportunity for stunning architecture to improve the image of the city. Since the Italians first began to build memorable stadiums in the 1930s, many cities have sought to have landmark sport facilities buildings (Stevens, 1994; Churchman, 1995). These stadiums may be also the flagship anchors for the regeneration of a decaying area. The act of winning the games is a catalyst for bringing forward and fast tracking general infrastructure investments that have been pending for years (Essex and Chalkley, 1998). In the case of the Barcelona games in 1992, a ring road was built, a new airport constructed and a derelict waterfront area cleared and redeveloped for an Olympic village. But it is also a catalyst for many less dramatic improvements. The prospect of a large number of visitors from around the world will encourage the city authorities to improve the appearance of the city centre and the entry routes. Public spaces such as squares, gardens and transport interchanges will be improved and there will be an extra attempt to clamp down on anti-social activities. For the host city, winning the games offers the prospect of world-wide publicity, global recognition and the enhancement of its image and reputation which should enable it to attract further investment, future events and more tourists. Short and Kim (1999) claim that: 'The games allow cities to change their global ranking and identity; they allow the possibility of the image to be transformed from anonymous provincial hicktown to happening global place.' For the 2000 games they say: 'the Olympics will reinforce Sydney's prime position in the Australian urban hierarchy and confirm its global recognition' (see also Searle and Bounds, 1999). With respect to tourism, hosting the Olympic Games has great promotional potential, an opportunity to showcase the city and to position the city on the international circuits of tourism. With respect to Sydney, Waitt (1999) argues that from the moment the bid was launched there was an attempt to 'redefine social realities' and create new 'place myths' about the city. If the city has many attractions and tourism potential, the new image established should enable it to win many visitors. In particular, it can be noted that the opening and closing ceremonies can be used to project images and messages about the city (Roche, 2000).

Accordingly, since the Los Angeles games of 1984 there has been fierce competition between cities to win the games and the prizes that go with it. Even to fail to win the games, having been the national champion, can be perceived as a good thing with several benefits (for the Manchester case, see Law, 1994). During the bidding process government money may have been provided to build some facilities and infrastructure, as bidding cities must show a significant degree of preparedness and credibility. Private finance may have been levered, both for the bid itself and for facilities, which would not have been forthcoming without the city having made its claim. Perhaps of greatest importance is the element of unity which the bid engenders. Politicians of different parties, leaders of the private sector and voluntary groups are able to come together around a bid and perhaps agree not only on the proposal itself, but also on the general direction in which the city should be moving. Almost certainly included in this will be a role for the tourist industry in the city, how it should be developed, and how the city should be marketed. However, bidding for the games is a risky process. Decisions made at the national and international level are not simply made on technical issues, but are deeply political and are alleged to be corrupt (Hill, 1996). Having a spotlight put on a city not only can magnify its strengths but also its weaknesses and problems (Morphet, 1996).

Only large cities can compete for mega-events like the Olympic Games. Only they have the basic infrastructures such as an international airport, a large hotel stock, media links, the amenities which many visitors to the games will expect, and the possibility of using the Olympic sports facilities in the long term, whether for local use or attracting other major events. It would be uneconomic for a small place to create all these requirements, only for many of them to have no use after the 16-day event. In reality, the competition to host the Olympics is a competition among large cities to either claim world status or to boost their position in the hierarchy of world cities.

The economic impact studies that have been made of special sports events like the Olympic Games involve two elements, namely, the costs and revenues to the organizers themselves and the impact of the event on the area. Post-event impact studies have been made of the Los Angeles games (Economic Research Associates, 1984) and of the Seoul games (Kim *et al.*, 1989; Kang and Perdue, 1994). The results of these studies have been used by cities making pre-event evaluations (for Manchester, see Hague *et al.*, 1990). The costs of the games involve direct expenditure on sports facilities, indirect expenditure on infrastructure from transport to hotels, the operating costs of the games themselves, and the consequent expenditure of all visitors, including competitors, team officials and the media. At Sydney in 2000 there were 11,000 athletes and 5,000 officials and coaches. These figures compare with only 4,700 competitors at the London games in 1948. However, it was also estimated that the number of media visitors to Sydney would exceed 17,000. The US NBC (TV) network alone brought 1,300 staff, more than the 925 in the US team. Overall, Barcelona expected about 600,000 visitors, and if this had been achieved it would have been one of the most successful Olympics as regards attracting tourists (Pyo *et al.*, 1988). The larger the injection of funds into the area from whatever source, the greater the impact of the event on the area. In the case of Los Angeles there was little expenditure on direct and indirect infrastructure, so that the impact was much less than in Seoul where this figure was much greater. At Barcelona in 1992, $3.8 billion was invested, but only 10 per cent of this was on sports facilities (Stevens, 1992).

Against these positive benefits there are claims of drawbacks (Hall, 1992, pp. 34–39; Hughes, 1993; Whitson and Macintosh, 1996; Higham, 1999). Because of the risks involved, such as cost over-runs on capital projects and lower than expected audiences, profits may not be realized, and possibly there will be losses as happened with the 1976 Olympics in Montreal. There is a tendency for pre-event studies to exaggerate the benefits. In such cases the local population will have to pay higher taxes to pay off the debts and in effect there may be some diversion of funds from welfare activities to the Olympics. The necessary improvements may involve the disturbance of communities of poor people and of tramps, beggars and travellers who have to be relocated. This is a fairly common occurrence at special events (Atkinson and Laurier, 1998). Others claim that the decisions to bid for and hold the Olympics are often made by a small cabal of local politicians and business people without widespread consultation and that this overrides the democratic process. Arguments for participation in the planning process are brushed aside with the excuse that with the deadline of the event there is no time for endless discussion (Hall, 1998). Public scrutiny of the event plans, infrastructure improvements and arrangements are often avoided by putting them under quangoes or public–private partnerships (for Sydney, see Hall, 1996, and also Thorne and Munro-Clark, 1989; Searle and Bounds, 1999; Waitt, 1999, p. 1063). Opponents of mega-events who claim to speak for ordinary people and who ask for 'bread not circuses' are derided as lacking vision and being against progress. Some claim that visitor numbers to host cities will be less when the whole year is taken into account because many visitors will be put off by the prospect of overcrowding and possibly high prices. Others are concerned about the effects on the local population who for a short period may have to suffer congestion and higher prices. Taxi fares were increased by 10 per cent during the Sydney Olympics. In order to give a 'good impression' to the visitors to the event, tramps, beggars and perceived threatening youths may be cleared from the streets, in what is claimed to be a denial of human rights. Although there may be improved facilities, these may be of the type only suitable for highly trained athletes and/or run by commercial organizations which charge high prices, so that the benefits to ordinary local people are reduced. In some cases, as at Atlanta in 1996, the city image may be harmed rather than improved through bad publicity about traffic chaos, shortage of hotel rooms and their location, crime and police brutality.

Of course, there are also long-term tangible and intangible benefits such as improved infrastructure, a legacy of facilities which will enable the city to host further sports events which bring in the tourists, improved image, the attraction of economic development and civic pride. In planning a mega-event such as the Olympic Games it is necessary to consider carefully how the legacy of facilities is going to be used, and how they relate to a long-term strategy for the development of tourism in the city, otherwise they and the extra hotel rooms built may be left empty or under-used. Very little research has been undertaken in these areas and because they are long term, it can only be done many years after the event and then there may be problems in attributing causes to the changes that have taken place. For the 1988 Calgary winter Olympics, Ritchie and Smith (1991) found that the city's visibility had increased in Europe and the USA as a result of hosting the event. However, awareness of the city had decreased after two years. The 1992 summer Olympics gave great publicity to Barcelona, showcasing a city with many relatively unknown attractions and considerable tourism potential. As a consequence tourist numbers have steadily risen during the rest of the 1990s from 1.73 million in 1990 to 3.12 million in 1999 (Smith and Jenner, 1999). At the same time the share of vacation visitors increased from 22.7 to 49.2 per cent and the number of conference visitors grew from 105,424 to 272,094 (www.barcelonatur-isme.com). In the case of visitors from Britain, aided by a budget airline, it has become one of the most popular short break destinations. Sydney too is benefiting from the expansion in hotel and conference capacity with a 129 per cent increase in conventions for 2001. Cities like Sheffield which built facilities to host the World Student Games claim that they have been able to host 300 sporting events since, between 1991 and 1999 generating over £30 million income (Dobson, 1996; Bramwell, 1997; Gratton and Dobson, 1999). However, the $A800 million Stadium Australia, which seats 110,000 and attracted 3 million visits for the two-week Olympics, has failed so far (March 2001) to find a regular sports team to be based here and has only five major events planned for 2001, and faces mounting losses.

World Fairs and Expos

The Great Exhibition held in London in 1851 was probably the first show to be called a world fair. Since then there have been 31 universal exhibitions and many cities have sought to have a world fair (Carreras, 1995). In 1928 the International Bureau of Expositions was founded in Paris to co-ordinate these events and ensure that there is only one each year (Hall, 1992, pp. 29–30). There are various and interlinked objectives for holding a world fair which have been listed by Ley and Olds (1988). The stated objectives include encouraging trade, increasing the visibility of a city and country, developing tourism, attracting economic development and increasing employment, stimulating the re-use of land and infrastructure improvements, the celebration of a past event, and the entertainment of the masses, as well as the often unstated one of obtaining extra funds from the higher levels of government. Ley and Olds suggest that the prime motive for holding a world fair is to boost the city, but as well as selling the city, there is also the selling of ideas. Most expos are linked in some way to the notion of the progress of civilization or modernity (Bennett, 1991). Not surprisingly, Expo 92 in Seville, Spain, had the theme of discovery. Other themes include education and international understanding (Greenhalgh, 1988). The host city usually prepares a special site for the event where new buildings and structures of hoped-for architectural distinction and image changing ability are erected. Early examples were London's Crystal Palace and Paris's Eiffel Tower and a more recent one is Seattle's Space Needle. These structures will remain a permament legacy to the area, as will any general infrastructure put in place. The fair itself usually contains exhibitions of both arts and manufactures, with pavilions provided also by foreign nations. World fairs usually last between five and seven months, but sometimes they last for a whole year. At Expo 92 in Seville, the pavilions had an area of 650,000 square metres, of which one-third was to be permanent; 110 nations were represented, and there were 50,000 cultural events. Total investment was put at £5.4 billion, of which only 20 per cent was on the fair itself, the remainder being on general infrastructure. Among the benefits to the city were new roads, an airport and a high speed railway. These, together with the fairground, should have a long-lasting effect on the development of the city and region. The organizers hoped for 20 million visitors, most of whom would be tourists. To cope with this influx, the number of hotel bedrooms was increased from 12,000 to 24,000.

Historically world fairs have attracted large numbers, thus making them important for tourism (Carreras, 1995). The most visited has been the world expo at Osaka, Japan, in 1970, which attracted 64 million people. However, recently numbers have declined, and Hanover in 2000 only attracted 18 million. It has been suggested that with so many alternative attractions and the basic concepts of world expos so readily perceived in the media, that it is unlikely that fairs will ever be so popular again.

Historical Celebrations

It has become commonplace for countries and cities to celebrate the anniversary of some landmark achievement in their history. In recent years, the USA (1976), France (1989) and Australia (1988) have all had bicentennial celebrations. Cities may celebrate the anniversary of their foundation or their raising to civic status as well as other events of national and international significance with which they have been involved. Thus Bristol, UK, celebrated in 1997 Cabot sailing the Atlantic to discover Newfoundland. Once again the motives are various from pure celebration to the idea of place promotion and visibility, including the attraction of tourists. The celebration can take various forms, including festivals, fireworks and outdoor spectacles, new buildings and infrastructures, possibly including new museums and art venues and world fairs. The event or events may last a few days to a whole year. In the case of national celebrations the events are likely to take place either in the capital city, a city with a particular connection or in venues scattered around the country. The outcome of historical celebrations has not always been positive. In Australia and the Americas indigenous peoples have objected to the idea that they were 'discovered', and have used the event to air their grieveances, while Spain discovered that 1492 was not only the year that Christopher Columbus set sail for America, but also the year in which Jews and Muslims were expelled. Elsewhere, the local populace have shown so little interest in the celebration that it has been seen to be false and merely a contrived event as a pretext for commercial promotion or political propaganda (Getz, 1992). The year 2000 was a special year for much of the world commemorating the beginning of a new millennium. There were many new projects such as museums and art galleries as well as national events. In Britain the New Millennium Experience housed in a dome in Greenwich failed to live up to expectations receiving only 6 million visitors, less than half the forecast numbers. Failure was put down to bad publicity, the lack of an inspiring theme or purpose and competition from so many other old and new visitor attractions. Once again the purpose in selecting the site, apart from its position on the Greenwich meridian, was to stimulate urban regeneration of a waterfront site.

Case Study: Glasgow

The city of Glasgow illustrates how a city can use arts and special events to assist regeneration. Although Glasgow is an ancient city, its rise in importance came in the nineteenth century with the growth of industries like shipbuilding and engineering. By the early twentieth century the population of the conurbation had reached 1.6 million and it had become a major commercial city with many fine buildings, large companies and strong institutions. Although Glasgow is much larger than Edinburgh, this latter city retained the title of capital of Scotland, with many associated administrative, legal and financial institutions and since 1999 has been the seat for a devolved Scottish Parliament.

Since World War I Glasgow has faced economic decline as many of its staple industries have bled away. In 1997 there were only 32,000 manufacturing jobs compared to 265,000 in 1951. Losses were particularly heavy in the recessions of the mid-1970s and early 1980s. Notwithstanding assistance from regional policy, new activities have not compensated for the decline; the population has been declining since 1961 and unemployment has remained stubbornly high. Apart from its relative remoteness, the city has suffered from a poor image involving low quality housing, militant labour and an industrial character which its leaders perceived to be a handicap in attracting the inward movement of jobs.

Since the early 1980s the city has been fighting back in a number of ways. The city council was one of the first in Britain to become entrepreneurial and take a pro-active approach to economic development (Boyle and Hughes, 1994). It has also benefited from government assistance which from 1975 to 1991 was mainly channelled through the Scottish Development Agency and since then through the Glasgow Development Agency. Its policies have developed incrementally and opportunistically and with the purpose of tranforming the image of the city. The first signs of a new movement to revitalize Glasgow appeared in 1983 when the Lord Provost (the Scottish equivalent of mayor) launched an indirect marketing campaign with the slogan 'Glasgow's Miles Better' (Paddison, 1993). In the same year a long-planned project to build a museum for the Burrell art collection was completed and an annual arts festival, Mayfest, was launched. By 1985 a public–private partnership organization, Glasgow Action, one of whose aims was to encourage tourism, had been founded to promote the city centre. Also in this year an exhibition and conference centre was opened, and festivals of choral, folk and jazz music and dance were started to enliven the summmer months. In 1987 a festivals unit was established by the city council. Plans made at this time resulted in Glasgow hosting a Garden Festival in 1988 and in a transport museum being relocated to a site opposite Glasgow's impressive art gallery, thus helping to create a cluster of tourist attractions (Figure 7.1).

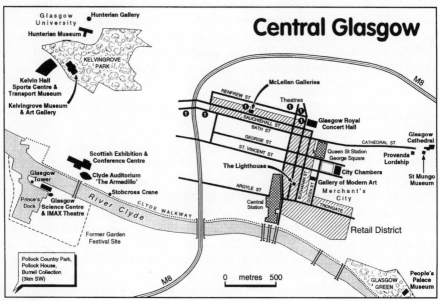

Figure 7.1 Central Glasgow

The momentum was kept going in 1990 when Glasgow became the European City of Culture, resulting in even wider publicity (Wishart, 1991). The year-long event used the existing extensive resource base and built on it with enhanced programming involving world famous artists and high profile performances. Museums and galleries had special displays and there were additional exhibitions. Buildings were cleaned and floodlit at night, a new £28.5 million concert hall was opened, the McLellan art gallery was refurbished for special touring and loan shows, and several parts of the city, such as the cathedral precinct, experienced physical improvements. In many ways this year was the culmination of several years of change which had included inner city revitalization programmes such as GEAR (Donnison and Middleton, 1987), and the opening of two new city centre covered shopping malls. Overall, 1990 was widely considered to have been a success with the city having been portrayed as 'dynamic and sophisticated' and having been put on the tourist map (Boyle and Hughes, 1991, Hughes and Boyle, 1992).

During the 1990 European Year of Culture the number of attendances at events and attractions reached 6.59 million, 74 per cent attending museums and galleries and 26 per cent attending theatres and concerts (Myerscough, 1988b, 1991). This was an increase of 40 per cent over 1989. Compared with the findings of an earlier survey (1986), the number of visitors from outside Glasgow had increased by 85 per cent and there was an estimated increase of 72 per cent over 1989. Visits to the main attractions increased from 1.4 million in 1981 to 3.2 million in 1990. The Year of Culture is estimated to have generated a net income to the city of £10–14 million and created around 5,500 jobs for the year. During 1990 the city received much publicity across Britain, and this appears to have changed the image held by people. A survey of residents of classes ABC1 in London and South-East England enquired about the perceptions held of British cities (see Table 7.5). Within a few weeks of the beginning of the event the perceptions held of Glasgow were significantly better than for other cities. This change of image was regarded as a success for the event.

Table 7.5 Perception of British cities, February 1990

| | Percentage agreeing | | | |
	Glasgow	Birmingham	Bristol	Edinburgh
Increasingly important for the arts	45	13	7	42
Rapidly changing for the better	48	18	11	11
Is rough and depressing	40	45	9	3
Has interesting museums	31	6	14	57
Has wide variety of theatres and music	26	17	14	60
Has good pubs/restaurants and night life	23	17	20	27
Would like to visit	36	12	32	67
Would be happy to live and work there	11	6	30	31

Source: Saatchi and Saatchi, quoted in Myerscough (1991), Table 132

During the 1990s Glasgow continued with its efforts to promote itself via special events and new visitor attractions. A festival of Visual Arts was held in 1996 and in 1999 Glasgow was Britain's City of Architecture. In both cases the city exploited the genius of its former native Charles Rennie Mackintosh, an architect and craftsman. Two buildings which he designed were opened to the public, one a school as an educational museum and the other, the Lighthouse, as a place for exhibitions and seminars. Other new visitor attractions have included the St Mungo Museum of Religious Life (1993), the Gallery of Modern Art (1996) and the Glasgow Science Centre (2001) located on the site of the Garden Festival. In 1995 Glasgow became one of three British Cities of Sport and the national Scottish football stadium in the city was refurbished with a museum added. An extension to the Scottish Exhibition and Conference Centre in 1997 enabled Glasgow to continue to be competitive in the industry. However, the late 1990s was a difficult time financially for the city as funding for its museums was hit when the Strathclyde Regional Council was abolished with the entire cost of running them falling on the city council and there was a fear that there might have to be closures.

In spite of all these developments it has been difficult to keep up the momentum in increasing the number of visitors. After the success of 1990, the number of British overnight visitors to Glasgow fell by nearly half in the early 1990s, perhaps partly affected by the recession, and they did not recover till 1998. Overseas visitor numbers have grown slightly, but they are only a third of the domestic numbers, albeit bigger spenders. Attendance at the older visitor attractions has not increased, and in the case of the Burrell Collection (see Chapter 5), there has been a continuing decline. Outside of tourism, the city claims that its promotional efforts have resulted in greater inward investment. Between 1986 and 1991, 18 service organizations were attracted to the city creating 7,340 jobs and between 1992 and 1997 there were 62 inward moves or expansions creating 13,000 jobs. The city council also claim that after special events the number of associations wanting to hold conferences in Glasgow increases.

At the beginning of the 1980s the idea that Glasgow (like other old industrial cities) could develop a significant tourism industry would have appeared extremely doubtful. But the city has had a fair measure of success by using special events and expanding its tourism resources. The fact that the city appears to be running to a standstill in terms of visitor numbers is a reflection in part of the challenge to develop tourism in this milieu and in part of the competition from other cities. The various programmes have not been without their critics (Boyle and Hughes, 1991). The make-over has sanitized the city and in the process obscured many of its real problems. Many are affronted by the identity which has been created which denies the working-class heritage. In the effort to reposition the city, the high arts have been used rather than any indigenous culture. Furthermore, a one-off festival which relies on imported performers does little to develop the cultural resources of the city (Booth and Boyle, 1993). Inevitably the launching of special events has been costly and many argued that the money would have been better spent on improving the welfare of the citizens.

CONCLUSION

While the topics of arts, entertainment, sport and special events have been treated separately, there is a high degree of interrelatedness and links with the other topics dealt with in this book. They are being developed by cities for a mixture of reasons, including raising the profile of a place, changing its image and attracting tourists. The mega-event is becoming a key part of this strategy, as it acts as a catalyst for change by persuading people to work together around a common objective and as a fast track for obtaining extra finance and getting building projects off the drawing board. This is not without its problems, since some would argue that it gives priority to development issues over those of welfare. The physical aspect of this strategy is that it has frequently been linked to inner city regeneration and in particular with that of the city centre. This is reinforcing the role of the downtown area as an entertainment centre.

Given the mixed motives and the intangibility of some of them, as with changing the image, it is often difficult to evaluate these policies. Sometimes success or failure can be measured in accountancy terms. Mega-events may make a profit or leave behind debts which the community will have to pick up for years to come. But good or bad publicity is more difficult to evaluate, particularly in terms of its effects on economic development. One consequence of the increase in special events is that no city can afford to rest on past achievements. Success one year is soon forgotten as others come along with their special events. Each special event is thus only part of a long-term campaign which must be repeated in some way if the progresss made is not to be lost. In this competition between cities, a continuing inflow of tourists and economic developement are the ultimate prizes to be won. For most major cities tourists will usually represent only a small percentage of patrons of regular arts, entertainment and sports activities. For the occasional high profile special event the share of visitors may rise. However, while tourists may only form a small proportion of the audience, they are part of a nexus of arguments which are being used to promote these activities as flagship activities for cities designed to raise the profile of cities and regenerate the downtown areas.

Surveys of audiences have found that arts events, including arts festivals, attract mainly middle-class participants, whereas spectacles such as sport, parades and carnivals attract a broader cross-section of the population. In terms of the economic impact of tourism there may well be a trade-off here. A smaller number of high income middle-class tourists may spend as much as a larger number of average income visitors. Whether a city goes for the middle-class market or the broader market will depend on its tourism strategy, and this may in turn depend on how it sees itself positioned in the marketplace.

Chapter 8

Secondary elements

In this chapter those elements of a city's tourism resources which, while not primary in the sense of being the main attractors of visitors, can be critical in whether it is successful or not as a tourist destination, are considered. These elements include hotels, shopping facilities, restaurants, pubs and transport.

Relatively few visitors would travel a long distance because a city has good hotels, interesting shops, a varied range of restaurants and an excellent transport infrastructure. However, they might be deterred from visiting a city if there is a shortage of hotel rooms, they are expensive, and if it is difficult to get to the city and, once there, difficult to move around. On the other hand, knowing that these elements are easily available, of good quality and not too expensive may provide an additional reason for visiting the city or tip the balance between one city and another when a decision is being made. Thus the provision of these elements is essential if a city is to become a successful tourist destination.

Table 8.1 Spending by UK tourists, 1998

| | Percentage of expenditure | | | |
	Overseas	Domestic	Combined*	Day
Accommodation	33.3	34.0	33.8	NA
Eating and drinking	20.6	25.0	22.8	30.0
Travel in UK	9.2	18.0	14.0	11.8
Shopping	26.0	15.0	20.0	29.0
Entertainment	2.3	5.0	3.8	9.0
Other	–	1.0	0.5	20.2

Note: * Overseas and domestic overnight staying visitors.
Source: *Tourism Intelligence Quarterly*, 22, 2000, No. 1, pp. 29–30

Another reason for considering them is that these are the principal forms of expenditure and therefore have most impact. Table 8.1 provides a breakdown of tourist expenditure in the UK in 1998 from which it can be seen that accommodation, eating and drinking, shopping and transport account for 91 per cent of all spending.

The importance of these activities is not only that they are the principal forms of expenditure and therefore have an economic impact, but also that the nature of these activities will determine the type of employment created. It is often suggested that these activities tend to create a significant proportion of low-skilled and low-paid jobs, although this can be exaggerated.

The aim of this chapter is to understand how these activities develop, their dynamics, their dependence on tourists, how they are located within cities and in general their contribution to the tourist industry.

HOTELS

Any large city which aspires to be an important tourist centre will require a substantial stock of hotel rooms. Not all tourists stay in hotels. Some will be day visitors, others will be staying with friends and relatives, and some may choose to stay in bed and breakfast establishments or unserviced accommodation. Compared with seaside resorts, camping and self-catering are not very important as tourist accommodation in cities. It is likely that the more important a city is as a tourist destination, the higher the proportion of visitors who will stay in some type of serviced accommodation: hotel, motel, inn, etc. It is the visitor who stays in a hotel who has the greatest economic impact. As Table 8.1 shows, up to 60 per cent of expenditure may be accounted for by the cost of accommodation and meals bought in hotel restaurants. It is therefore pertinent to examine the factors behind the growth of hotels in cities, the structure of the hotel sector, where hotels are located and the employment impacts.

The Demand for Hotels

As mentioned above, for most hotel users, staying in a hotel is a means to an end, not the end in itself. Thus the demand for hotels is a derived demand (Medlik, 1980; Goodall, 1989). The demand for hotel services can be broken down by market type into business, tourist, conferences and other (see Table 8.2).

Table 8.2 Composition of hotel markets, 1989

	Percentage of total			
	USA	*Canada*	*UK*	*Europe*
Government officials	0.0	10.1	1.7	2.0
Business travellers	39.6	30.8	39.9	40.0
Conference	21.6	16.8	13.0	12.0
Tourist (individual)	31.6	18.6	18.4	19.9
Group tour	0.0	13.7	9.9	16.1
Other	7.2	10.0	17.2	10.0

Note: Surveys cover properties with more than 25 rooms.
Source: Horwath International (1990)

The exact composition of demand will vary greatly from one hotel to another and particularly according to location. City hotels depend much more on business travel and less on the leisure market, whereas for resorts it would be the reverse. The business market consists of executives travelling to visit other company establishments to transact business, salesmen visiting clients, meetings between business people from different companies, as well as many other activities such as visiting artists to local theatres and official government business. The size of the business market will depend on the nature of activities undertaken in the city and the role of the city in the urban system, and it is unlikely to be simply correlated with population size. Industrial cities with a high proportion of manual jobs are likely to have less hotel stock for this market than a city which is important for finance, head offices and business services. The conference and leisure markets will also vary in size from one city to another. Although most cities are attempting to develop these markets, as described in Chapter 6, there have been differering degrees of success. As regards conferences, a large supply of hotel rooms is an essential ingredient in attracting business, but as was shown in Chapter 6, there can be a chicken and egg situation here. Without the trade the hotels will not be built, but without the hotels the trade will not be attracted. Under 'other markets' are included people travelling for personal reasons, such as to attend a wedding. A growing market is the traveller in transit where the demand is likely to be either on the edge of cities or between cities. The world's first motel was opened in the USA in 1926, but it was not until the post-war period that demand grew rapidly. Hotels also derive income from non-staying clients through providing meals in restaurants, space for receptions (e.g. weddings) and health clubs.

Hotels can be classified by size, facilities, tariff, ownership and location. The quality and price of services provided are often indicated by a starring system. Other terms used include luxury, first class, upscale and budget (Lundberg, 1989). Much business travel is at the upper end of the market, while the leisure traveller is often seeking cheaper accommodation, but there is no clear-cut distinction. As the leisure market has expanded in cities so has the quantity of low price including budget hotels. The nature of the market in any city will usually be reflected in the types of hotel, but an aspiring tourist city should attempt to offer accommodation of varying price and quality.

Table 8.3 English hotel occupancy by area type, 1990.

Type of area	Occupancy (%)	Average length of stay (days)
London	69	2.9
Large towns	60	2.0
Small towns	59	1.9
Countryside	55	2.1
Seaside	52	3.0

Source: British Tourist Authority (1991)

The demand for hotel accommodation would appear to have been growing steadily since the 1950s, arising from an expansion of the various component markets discussed above and in particular because of general economic growth (Laventhol and Horwath, 1984). The globalization of business has increased the amount of business travel, while conference and exhibition business and leisure travel has also been growing in the city, the latter aided by growing affluence and the factors identified in Chapter 2. This expansion of demand from the leisure traveller has required an increase in the supply of cheaper or budget-priced accommodation. This increased demand is shown in the growing supply and occupancy figures. The latter are collected by tourist organizations and consultants such as Panell Kerr Foster and Horwath International. Occupancy figures in cities vary from 50 to 80 per cent and reflect market conditions. Because tourism is less seasonal in cities, occupancy rates are higher than in other types of areas such as seaside resorts (Table 8.3). Recessions affect all the markets for hotel services, and obviously the state of the local economy will be another factor affecting occupancy rates.

Table 8.4 Hotel occupancy in Manchester city centre, 1991–95

	Percentage occupancy	
	Weekday	*Weekend*
January	59.0	38.8
February	66.0	38.1
March	70.6	49.0
April	67.4	44.7
May	69.0	43.9
June	65.8	43.5
July	67.2	51.8
August	52.8	45.0
September	70.7	54.3
October	81.3	52.5
November	79.6	50.5
December	57.5	40.0
Average 1991	67.2	46.0
1992	62.9	49.8
1993	69.3	54.5
1994	72.8	51.6
1995	77.9	56.7

Source: Greater Manchester Visitor and Convention Bureau (1992), and Marketing Manchester (1996)

The demand for hotel accommodation varies over the week and over the year. Business travel tends to be concentrated into weekdays, with low demand at the weekends. In contrast, leisure travel, particularly the short break, is concentrated at the weekend. Ideally, a city would fill its hotels during the week with business travellers and over the weekend with the leisure visitor. However, because these markets are rarely nicely balanced in this way, it is often necessary to offer cut-price rates at the weekend to attract customers. Table 8.4 shows the weekday and weekend occupancy rates in Manchester for 1991. This was a recession year and the figures also show that the weekend market was as yet weakly developed.

Unlike the market in seaside resorts, hotels in cities experience only minor seasonal variations in demand, as can be seen in the statistics for Frankfurt and London (Figure 8.1). The business and conference markets decrease around Christmas–New Year and in the summer holidays, while the short break market peaks in the spring–early summer and autumn periods. Major tourist cities like London and Paris which attract the holiday visitor have a summer peak. Some compensation at Christmas may be found through offering parties and special meals to the local market. A large conference or exhibition can sometimes make a huge demand on the available accommodation resources, keeping out other visitors, but in between such events occupancy can fall significantly.

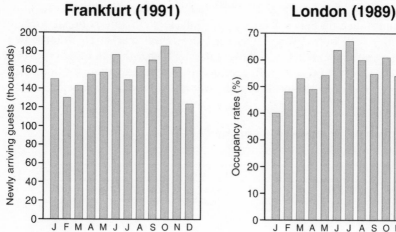

Figure 8.1 Seasonal variations in usage of Frankfurt and London hotels
Source: Frankfurt Tourism office (personal communication) and British Tourist Authority's *Digest of Tourism* statistics

The Supply of Hotels

Hotels can be built by either a hotel company or an independent developer and then leased to a hotel chain. In either case the investor will have to decide whether there is sufficient demand and of what type. With the redevelopment of city centres it is becoming quite common for hotels to be planned as part of a multi-use structure, and therefore built by a developer rather than a hotel company. Developers are becoming more important as the constructors of hotels as many hotel companies do not want their capital locked up in buildings. Indeed, many properties owned by hotels are being sold to institutions and then leased back. However, many free-standing hotels are still being built and owned by hotel companies.

Table 8.5 Hotel income and costs

Income (%)		Costs (%)	
Rooms	60.5	Employees	28.1
Food	23.5	Cost of goods	12.1
Beverages	8.9	Operating costs	30.7
Other	7.1	Tax	5.5
		Interests/profits depreciation	23.6

Source: Pannell Kerr Foster (1983) quoted in Lundberg (1994)

The basic economics of hotels are shown in Table 8.5, where it is seen that the prime income will come from the letting of rooms and also from the selling of food and beverages to guests. Another reason why the letting of rooms is of prime importance is that the profits on rooms are higher than those on meals and other services (Kotas, 1975). On the cost side, a significant proportion of the outlay goes on interest and depreciation. The greater the capital cost of the hotel, the higher these overheads will be, and hence the need for high occupancy rates. For this reason the break-even oc-

Table 8.6 Hotel price and occupancy in US cities, 1987

City	Average daily rate ($)	Occupancy (%)
New York	107.62	74.4
Boston	93.49	67.9
San Francisco	91.90	72.0
Washington	91.80	72.0
Chicago	86.19	67.0
New Orleans	73.70	64.2
Los Angeles	70.99	73.2
Philadelphia	69.66	70.5
Atlanta	65.64	62.6
Detroit	64.05	68.7
Dallas/Fort Worth	61.34	55.7
Seattle	60.09	62.6
Minneapolis	56.43	62.1
St Louis	55.72	64.2
Denver	50.62	54.5

Source: Pannell Kerr Foster (1987)

cupancy rate is usually lower for budget-price hotels than for luxury ones. Land and capital costs may be high in prosperous city centres and this may deter the construction of hotels. In the late 1980s the cost of a hotel bedroom in London was £175,000 (Business Ratios, 1989). Employee costs may also be higher in city centres. Given this situation it is not surprising that the cost of hotel accommodation varies considerably around the world, from one city to another, and between the city centre and the urban fringe areas. Figures for city hotel prices in the USA are shown in Table 8.6.

The physical requirements for a hotel building have been increasingly affected by the rising expectations of customers and the higher safety standards laid down by public authorities. Most patrons now expect an en-suite bathroom even in low-price accommodation. During the 1980s new luxury hotels developed providing the all-suite accommodation which consists of a living room, bedroom and kitchenette. Because of the increasing importance of conferences, suitable rooms for meetings must be provided and also small exhibition areas. The convention hotel is a specialized type of hotel, with up to 2,000 bedrooms, which has been developed since the 1960s in major cities and resorts. This super or mega-hotel may be ideal for conventions, but is often regarded as impersonal by the leisure tourist.

At the luxury end of the market, patrons have come to expect a very high standard of design, both inside and outside the building. The hotel becomes a combination of a landmark building and a rich man's house, and provides an experience for the visitor. According to Deyan Sudjic:

> The place of the hotel in the contemporary urban landscape is being redefined by a crop of hotels (large and small) in which design makes a big showing ... It is a redefinition that is some ways a rediscovery of what big city hotels used to be like, when along with department stores and railway stations they were the major landmarks of the newly industrialised cities. The point about hotels then was that they set out to be different from each other, to create a world that was private enough to keep people in their place, but public enough to offer somewhere worth showing off in ... All that was submerged in the Holiday-Inn-ification of world hotels. They designed-out the surprises, reassuring guests so they could know the same everywhere. This trend has run out of steam. (*Guardian*, 16 July 1996)

Since 1967 when John Portman opened an atrium hotel in Atlanta with its lobby soaring to the top of the hotel, architects have attempted to make hotels spectacular and dramatic in some way, often through having towers and wall-climbing lifts (Frieden and Sagalyn, 1989; Lundberg, 1994). These are sometime known, irreverently, as JC hotels because many people when they enter the building and look up and exclaim 'Jesus Christ!' As with other buildings in the city, the exterior is now becoming just as important. If the shape is distinctive, the hotel will have a strong image which will help it and perhaps the city attract visitors. Inside the building, there will be more facilities to cosset the traveller including swimming pools and gymnasiums. Many hotels are now themed and Deyan Sudjic has described them as 'urban theme parks for adults' (*The Observer*, 26 February 2000). Overall, the contemporary luxury hotel of today attracts customers by offering the promise of a unique experience and one that will visually entertain them (Gaardboe, 2000).

Many of the old city centre hotels were built at the end of the last century, or the beginning of the twentieth century. There appears to have been little hotel building in the period between 1929 and 1959 (Laventhol and Horwath, 1984). Many of these older hotels were built without en-suite facilities and did not meet modern safety regulations. The cost of adapting these hotels to current conditions is high, and in many cases the return on investment would not justify modernization. Not surprisingly, therefore, many of these hotels have been demolished, often to make way for office blocks. Some cities, such as Boston, found that in the 1950s and 1960s their hotel stock was declining. In a few cases these old hotels occupied architecturally fine buildings, and cities have been prepared to give grants towards the cost of modernization in order to retain historic and attractive urban landscapes. These old hotels rarely had conference facilities and this has been another reason for their demolition. Outside the city centre, particularly in Britain, many hotels were situated in converted large houses. These, again, have needed modernization. Failure to upgrade the hotel has resulted in many of them going downmarket, but this probably only postpones the day when they will be closed and demolished. While some hotels will survive these temporal changes, it is likely that the hotel building lifecycle is an important element in the changing mix of hotels in a city. Of course, the pressure to close and demolish hotels may arise from other external factors including the emergence of other more profitable uses of the land.

Another factor affecting supply is the hotel development cycle, akin to the office development cycle and other economic cycles. As demand grows for hotel accommodation, occupancy rates and profits increase. This encourages developers and hotel chains to invest in new properties, or extend existing ones, thus increasing the stock of hotel rooms. However, because the economy is often cyclical, it is frequently the case that this extra capacity comes on stream just as the economy takes a downturn and the demand for hotel accommodation falls. With more capacity and lower throughput, occupancy rates and profits fall. During a recession, some of the older and less profitable hotels may close. Low occupancy and low profits discourage any further building of hotels. It may then take several years of recovery before occupancy rates and profits reach former levels and even longer before increased demand stimulates further building. During the 1980s, hotel building in the USA and Britain went through a cycle from recession to boom and back to recession. Another feature of the cycle is that during the up-turn new types of hotel and new locations may emerge.

The supply of hotel accommodation has also been greatly affected by the changing enterprise structure of the industry. In the past the industry was characterized by the

Table 8.7 The ten largest corporate hotel chains in the world

Rank (1999)	Organization (HQ country)	Rooms	Hotels
1	Cendant Corp (USA)	542,630	6315
	(Days Inn, Howard Johnson, Travelodge, Ramada)		
2	Bass Hotels and Resorts UK)	471,680	2886
	(Holiday Inn, Inter-Continental)		
3	Marriott International (USA)	355,900	1880
	(Marriott, Renaissance)		
4	Accor (France)	354,652	3234
	(Formula 1, Ibis, Novotel)		
5	Choice Hotels (USA)	338,254	4248
	(Comfort Inn)		
6	Best Western International (USA)	313,247	4037
7	Hilton Hotels Corp (USA)	290,000	1700
8	Starwood Hotels (USA)	217,651	716
	(Ritz-Carlton, Sheraton, Westin)		
9	Carlson Hospitality (USA)	114,161	616
10	Hyatt Hotels (USA)	85,743	195

Source: *Travel Industry World Handbook* (2000)

fact that most hotels were independently owned and often family-run. If all hotels are counted in all locations, then the small firm is still seen to be important, although less so than in previous years. However, when the number of rooms and turnover is taken into consideration, the importance of the large firm can be seen. In the USA 0.9 per cent of the properties account for 10.8 per cent of rooms. In Britain in 1988 the corporate/large firm sector owned 15 per cent of the hotels but had 35 per cent of the bedrooms. This is true in all major Western countries and has been accompanied by the tendency for the major firms to go multinational and then transnational (Table 8.7). At the luxury end of the market important world chains include Hilton, Holiday Inn, Hyatt, Inter-Continental, Maritim, Marriott, Sheraton, Sofitel and Westin. At the budget end of the market are firms such as Campanile, Comfort Inn, Days Inn, Ibis and Travelodge. Some of the major chains attempt to cover all sectors of the market using a different brand name for each sector. In a few cases the hotel chains are franchises with each hotel separately owned and operated but conforming to the general formula of the chain. Many hotel chains are part of larger corporations which have diversified interests. Historically, hotels have been linked via holding companies with transport (railway companies and now airlines), breweries, leisure and property.

Large hotel chains have been able to develop because of the advantages that accrue to scale. They are able to use marketing techniques effectively in order to reach potential customers, to exploit brands and can deploy central reservation systems to advantage. They can agree special terms with major companies whose staff use hotels regularly and thus tie up the market. They know of major firms that need conference facilities and can offer these at a wide range of locations. They offer the same formula around the world so that customers know what to expect and make repeat visits to their properties. Because of their size, they can extract good terms from suppliers. All these factors give them an advantage over the independent firm. Having established themselves in one major national market, they then seek to have a presence in all other large markets, whether these are described as national or as resorts or cities. As such, they may be courted by cities that are revitalizing inner city areas and may even be given grants as an incentive to invest.

In the main the supply of hotel accommodation has been left to market forces with little intervention from the public sector other than those connected with planning regulations. However, a few governments have provided tax incentives to encourage the construction of hotels and thus stimulate tourism, an example being Dublin in Ireland. Where hotels are planned for regeneration areas there are often grants available and in particular hotels have frequently received grants or loans for location in proposed convention quarters.

Overall, it would appear that the supply of hotel rooms around the world has been steadily increasing since the 1950s. Problems of definition and coverage make comparisons over time and space difficult and imprecise. Not all countries require the registration of hotels and in some cases only those over a certain size are counted. Further, some countries count bedrooms and others bedspaces. However, in 1979 it was estimated that there were 7.5 million hotel rooms in the world, a figure which had increased to 11.1 million by 1989 and to 15.4 million by 1998 (Waters, *Travel Industry World Handbook*, 2000). In the late 1990s the number of hotel rooms world-wide was increasing by 3 per cent a year. The loss of some older hotels has been more than compensated for by the opening of new ones, not always of course in the same location. In the USA the number of hotel bedrooms increased between 1959 and the mid-1970s, when growth was interrupted by the oil crisis (Laventhol and Horwath, 1984). The stock then grew from 2.1 million bedrooms in 1979 to 3.0 million in 1989. After the 1973 recession the growth rate for 1975–78 averaged 1 per cent a year, but in the period 1982–86 it averaged 2.7 per cent a year, with higher rates for the economy/budget and all-suite hotels. The 1990 recession reduced the growth rate again (Waters, 1991). The emergence of budget-priced hotel chains has been both a response to a growing demand and a reason for the growth of that market, offering value for money to a new group of travellers. It may, however, have hit smaller and older establishments resulting in their closure.

Hotels and the City

The location of hotels in cities is an important topic for any understanding of urban tourism. Visitors will want hotels close to the places they wish to visit and so cut down local transport as much as possible, while developers will be looking for sites which are proven generators of patronage (Karver, 1982). The traditional location for urban hotels was the city centre, with many nineteenth-century hotels being constructed near railway stations (Ritter, 1985; Ashworth, 1989a). The city centre nearly always included the most expensive and luxurious hotels in the city (Figure 8.2). Other hotels in the city centre tended to be located on the fringe of the retail and business zones away from the highest land values (Egan and Nield, 2000). In British cities the cheaper hotels were often found along the main roads, not far from the city centre, in converted and extended large Victorian houses. Taken together these two groups of hotels provided a choice by price and location.

The past forty years have witnessed a change in the geography of urban hotels. Many new hotels have been built on the fringe of the built-up area, and have reinforced the idea that hotels occupy 'gateway' locations (Table 8.8). Some, such as motels and budget-priced hotels, are found along highways which connect with high speed inter-

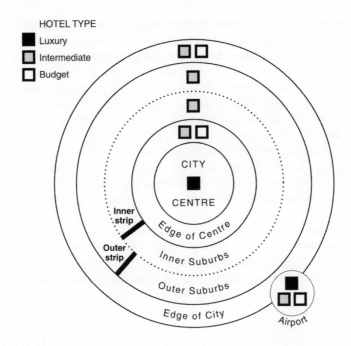

Figure 8.2 Urban hotels by type and location
Source: Adapted from Egan and Nield

Table 8.8 US hotel location, 1999

Location	Percentage of total	
	Property	*Rooms*
Urban/city centre	9.5	15.8
Suburban	35.8	32.9
Airports	6.7	9.1
Highway	41.7	29.6
Resorts	6.2	12.5

Source: *Travel Industry World Handbook* (2000)

city roads, and where generally land costs would be cheaper. Another cluster is found around the airport for the city, catering for the needs of departing and arriving travellers and also for business conferences attended by executives flying in from distant places. These new locations are relatively remote from the downtown where the main attractions and convention facilities are likely to be found. While some visitors may be willing to trade off convenience against cheaper lodging costs, many will not (Arbel and Pizam, 1977).

In recent years there has been also an increase in the number of hotels in the inner urban core. The development of hotels near conference and exhibition facilities was discussed in Chapter 6. In many American cities there are planned convention quarters containing these facilites (see Boston example). This expansion of hotels has been stimulated by the growth of other business and tourism, and as in earlier periods, particular location patterns can be discerned (Egan and Nield, 2000). Luxury hotels are usually able to pay for the most accessible and prestigious sites, although they must compete with other land uses, while the budget hotels are often pushed to sites on the edge of the city centre where land values have been low in recent years. In major world cities such as London and Paris there are often very large clusters of hotels (Pearce, 1987, pp. 180–189). In the case of London many hotels are found on the west side close to the roads that link the centre to Heathrow airport. However, hotels may be found in the midst of the attractions and even be part of them. In Singapore many hotels are located along the Orchard Road, the main shopping street and perhaps the principal attraction of the city. In Las Vegas the casinos are found in the main hotels and as described earlier, these establishments have been diversifying through other entertainments and retailing.

The construction of hotels in these urban core areas has been often encouraged by the planning, regeneration and fiscal policies of the city authorities. In order to encourage the redevelopment of fringe areas which may be expensive, grants are often given, or in some American cities tax exemptions. Hotels often feature in dockland redevelopment schemes and also in multi-use buildings.

Table 8.9 Top US hotel markets, 1998

Rank	City	No. of hotels	No. of Rooms
1	Las Vegas	287	125,983
2	Orlando	392	105,067
3	Los Angeles/Long Beach	672	82,582
4	Atlanta	603	81,352
5	Chicago	444	77,830
6	Washington, DC	405	73,543
7	New York	262	70,806
8	Dallas	396	59,714
9	Houston	349	49,873
10	Phoenix	331	49,473
11	San Diego	404	48,228
12	Anaheim/Santa Ana	368	46,145
13	San Francisco/San Mateo	321	44,933
14	Miami/Hialeah	272	43,486
15	Boston	248	39,155

Source: Smith Travel Research, quoted in *Travel Industry World Yearbook* (2000)

The size of the downtown and metropolitan area hotel stock is measured by the number of bedrooms and together with the range and price of accommodation is an important indicator of the success of a city as a tourist destination. It is a critical factor in determining whether the city can function as a conference and exhibition location (see Chapter 6), and its size will also reflect the importance of business and leisure tourism. For the USA the 15 largest hotel stocks by metropolitan area are shown in Table 8.9, where it is seen that the resorts of Las Vegas and Orlando are the most important. Downtown hotel capacity is much less, but many cities have between 5,000 and 10,000 bedrooms. The position is similar for many German cities, particularly when there is a *Messe* in the core area. In Britain outside London the hotel stock is much less, but has shown significant growth in recent years. Manchester city centre had only 1,300 hotel bedrooms in the early 1980s, but has since experienced a high rate of growth particularly in the late 1990s, and the total by 2000 was 3,400 (Law, 2000).

Hotels and Employment

Hotels have a distinctive employment structure. A small management staff is complemented by catering and cleaning staff. Many of the latter are unskilled, female and low paid (Bagguley, 1990; Wood, 1992). While some may be part-time, many jobs in hotels are full-time. The employment structure for the UK hotel industry is shown in Table 8.10, where it is seen that 45 per cent of all workers are part-time and that for women this figure rises to 54 per cent. Hotel work in cities is available throughout the year, since as mentioned above, the industry is not subject to seasonal variations. Although some decry these types of jobs, they are suitable and what is desired by many inner city residents. Upmarket hotels employ about one person per bedroom while the ratio is much less for budget-price establishments.

Table 8.10 UK hotel employment, 1989 and 1995

	Employment (000s)		Share (%)	
	1989		1995	
All jobs	238.1	100.0	340.9	100.0
Women				
Full-time	68.4	28.7	92.4	27.1
Part-time	81.1	34.1	108.7	31.9
All Women	149.5	62.8	201.1	59.0
Men				
Full-time	62.6	26.3	99.7	29.2
Part-time	26.0	10.9	40.1	11.8
All men	88.6	37.2	139.8	41.0

Source: Department of Employment (1991)

SHOPPING

In the general mind, tourism and retailing are not associated, but any analysis of the behaviour of tourists will show that a significant amount of time and money is spent on shopping. As Kent *et al.* (1983) have pointed out, surveys of tourists which ask the purpose of the trip rarely have mentioned shopping, but when asked what they did, visitors list shopping as one of the most important activities. This is not purposeful shopping for essential (convenience) goods, which, with the exception of those who go self-catering, is not required. For many people, shopping is a pleasurable experience and something they like to do when they have time, as they do on holidays, and are not under pressure to do domestic chores. Shopping has become an important leisure time activity whether on holiday or at home (Jansen-Verbeke, 1990). There is also the desire and a hope to see if there are different goods on sale at the destination compared to home. It is fun to discover interesting goods which can be bought on impulse (Jansen-

Verbeke, 1998). A survey of festival marketplaces in the USA found that 60 per cent of the patrons came with no specific purchase in mind (quoted in Jones Lang Wootton, 1989). A pleasant environment may make shopping more enjoyable and there is also the wish to take something unusual back to one's family and friends. So whether it is a day out, a short break, a long holiday or even a business trip, there is nearly always an element of shopping. Consequently it is not surprising that retail premises are nearly always found within, adjacent to or near the principal tourist attractions (Pearce, 1987, p. 193). In some cities where there are heavily trodden tourist routes the whole corridor may be lined with shops. A good example of this is Prague's Royal Mile which links the Old Market Square to the Castle via Charles Bridge. The outlets which are found in these areas vary from the simple gift/souvenir shop to outlets selling a wide variety of speciality goods. When there are many shops of this type, they become part of the attraction of the place. In Britain the historic cities of Bath, Chester and York, as a consequence of the large number of visitors that they receive, have become important retailing centres, far greater than their population would suggest. Retailing is therefore both an outcome of tourism but can also act as an attraction to tourists.

Very large and high quality retail centres, with a great variety of luxury goods, may be able to win tourists as the main attraction. Many people visit London and Paris because of their shops. In London tourists comprise 17 per cent of shoppers in Oxford Street and they are also important in Knightsbridge (where Harrod's is located as well as other shops). Some cities are noted for the excellence of a particular type of shopping and so may attract visitors, Milan's fame for fashion clothing being an example. Similarly it is reported that the very large West Edmonton Mall in Alberta, Canada, which has a large leisure component, attracts many tourists (Butler, 1991). The developers of a similar project, the Mall of America in Minneapolis opened in 1992, anticipated that customers would travel from a radius of 150 miles. However, these are likely to be rare examples, and in general retailing complements other attractions and is not the main draw in Western countries. However, the situation appears different in South-East Asia, where shopping is the main attraction in the cities of Hong Kong and Singapore. This may reflect poorer shopping facilities in the rest of the region and possibly fewer other attractions.

Major cities have been always important retail centres because of their large populations. As regional capitals they have drawn day visitors from their hinterland. In most European cities the city centre remains the most important retail node, but in many American cities downtown retailing has gone into serious decline (Law, 1988). This is a consequence of the decentralization of the population and the emergence of high quality retail centres in the suburbs. The old downtown shopping centre has been left to serve a poor and shrinking inner city population, and, even if it survives, is likely to be dominated by mass market goods which have little appeal to tourists and the downtown business workers who might form another market. In Britain and elsewhere, the 'High Street' has often been taken over by national chains, but there is still usually an up-market quarter where tourists might find goods of interest.

Tourists are particularly interested by what is now termed 'speciality' retailing. Speciality goods are, perhaps by definition, not found everywhere (Pysarchik, 1989). They are not mass produced, and in some cases are genuine craft goods. They could be described as luxuries in the sense that they are not goods which are essential for living. Among the goods sold are arts and crafts, including pottery, unusual and expensive designer clothes, books (both new and high quality second hand), perfumes and un-usual household articles. This type of retailing has always existed but it is only recently that it has been categorized as a distinctive market sector. With this recognition, more developers are attempting to bring the various elements together to create speciality shopping areas.

One model which takes this idea and extends it is the concept of the 'festival marketplace', which combines speciality shopping, eating and drinking and entertain-ment. This formula was pioneered in the USA by James Rouse, a developer of shopping malls (Rouse, 1984). He was brought in to redevelop the Faneuil Hall–Quincy Market area of Boston in the early 1970s after the old vegetable market had closed down. The city sought to find a new use for the fine old buildings, which Rouse restored, and in which he installed the new function (Whitehall, 1977). Opened in 1976, it became an immediate success, attracting office workers, suburbanites and tourists in large num-bers. Part of its appeal was that it remained open all evening and at the weekend.

The success of the project resulted in a spate of imitations across the USA and later in Canada, Britain and Australia. Rouse was asked to develop schemes in New York (South Street Seaport), Baltimore (Harborplace), Milwaukee (Grand Avenue), St Louis (Union Station), and Atlanta (Underground Atlanta). Most of these projects received large public subsidies as an incentive to undertake urban regeneration, with re-developed waterfronts being amongst the most popular type of sites. Similar schemes were undertaken in San Francisco (Ghiradelli Square) and Toronto (Queens Quay). By the late 1990s there were 25 festival marketplaces in the USA. In Britain the model of Quincy Market was used for London's Covent Garden, and later festival marketplaces were constructed at the Albert Dock, Liverpool and Ocean Village, Southampton. Other examples of festival marketplaces are Sydney's Darling Harbour (Hall, 1998) and Cape Town's Victoria and Alfred Waterfront (Dodson and Kilian, 1998). Not all festival marketplaces have been successful (Guskind and Pierce, 1988). On its own a festival marketplace is unlikely to be a sufficient draw for tourists, but if it is within a wider revitalization strategy which includes other visitor attractions, then it can en-hance the amenity and help create a critical mass (Frieden and Sagalyn, 1989; Sawicki, 1989). Close attention must be given to the quality of the shops, the tenant mix, their environment and security, as the example of the first and failed Underground Atlanta shows (Kent, 1984). Successful festival marketplaces are usually found in a thriving city centre where there are a large number of office workers in the daytime and within a populous metropolitan area (Jones Lang Wootton, 1989).

Critical social theorists have analysed the reasons for the success of festival marketplaces. Boyer (1992) has studied New York's South Street Seaport and Goss (1996) Aloha Tower in Honolulu. Goss argues that festival marketplaces are a dream-house for contemporary capitalism creating illusions of an idealized past which was sanitized, where people of all classes mixed without tensions in open spaces and where shoppers purchased goods from individual merchants. These illusions have been created through the carefully designed architecture which evokes the past and provides open spaces, and through the selection of tenants who include a significant number of small retailers.

One conclusion that can be drawn is that retailing is being added to many attractions both to enhance the experience and provide extra income for the establishment. Most visitor attractions have shops, as do airports, and the large casino hotels of Las Vegas have added shopping malls to their list of facilities.

RESTAURANTS

One of the obvious requirements of the visitor to the city is food and drink. This may be to meet an essential need and/or to be a pleasurable experience in itself, part of the enjoyment of going somewhere different. The potential or existing tourist city must therefore ensure that the right kind of catering facilities are provided. It has already been noted that the festival marketplace combines retailing, entertainment and eating and drinking, but this is likely to be only a small part of a much wider scene of restaurants. A successful tourist city should have a wide array of restaurants in or near the city centre. In order to understand why this occurs in some cities and not in others, it is useful to discuss the general development of restaurants in urban areas, whether serving local residents, visitors or both.

In recent years there has been a great increase in the demand for restaurants, here defined very broadly as any establishment which serves food and drink which can be consumed on the premises. There are many reasons for this, but most importantly it arises from greater affluence and changing lifestyles (Smith, 1983). More people are travelling further away from home, whether for work, to shop or for leisure purposes, and while away will need food and drink. More women are working and are less willing to prepare meals on their return home, and as an alternative they and their families are eating out. There are more one-person households, including young adults, some of whom are single again following a divorce, and this group is more likely to eat out. Finally, more people are eating out as a leisure activity. The trend is particularly strong among the more educated.

Statistics confirm the growing importance of eating out. In the USA in the late 1980s the average adult ate out 192 times a year. Another way of stating this is to say that on average people had 3.7 meals away from home each week, with a figure of 4.2 for men and 3.7 for women (Waters, 1989). By 1990, 43 per cent of a household's food expenditure was spent on meals outside the home, compared to only 25 per cent in 1955. In Britain the number of adults eating out for leisure has grown from 18 million in 1979 to 25 million in 1989. The recession of the early 1990s caused a temporary setback to the growth of the industry, but eating out increased rapidly in the late 1990s (Mintel, 1998, 1999b, 2000a). Eating out is widespread across all ages but is particularly significant in the pre-family and empty nester groups. Some 80 per cent of the former eat our regularly while in the latter group the participants are looking for a good experience.

Pillsbury (1987, 1990) has classified eating out into two types, described as body food and soul food. Body food is consumed to keep the body going. It may be simple, taken quickly and relatively cheap. It is the kind of meal taken during a work break, in the middle of a shopping trip or prior to engaging in a leisure activity. While soul food does satisfy basic needs, it is sought after as an enjoyable experience. The food will be more sophisticated, the cost greater, the surroundings more important and the time taken much longer. It is also a social event, rarely undertaken alone, and often as part of an important personal relationship, or as a special family or group occasion. It may also be the type of meal offered as part of a business transaction. Eating in good restaurants is perceived to be one of the best experiences of life. Dining in upmarket surroundings may also improve the self-esteem of an individual (Lundberg, 1989).

Restaurants can be also obviously classified by their type of cuisine. Compared to the past, there is an enormous variety of foods available ranging from the ethnic, such as Chinese, Indian and Italian, to the traditional, seafood, gourmet cuisine, to the menu of the fast food chains such as burgers or chicken. The fact that these new ranges of cuisines are available is perhaps why dining out has become such a popular leisure activity. Restaurants are also classified by price, from the expensive to the moderate to the budget.

The demand for restaurant facilities obviously varies throughout the day, throughout the week and from one season to another depending on location. Restaurants can be busy around lunchtime and again in the evening. In the daytime customers are more likely to be shoppers, local workers and perhaps business people. In the early evening the patrons are more likely to be people on their way to other activities such as the cinema, concert or theatre, while from the mid-evening they are more likely to be having an enjoyable night out by having a meal. The latter, whether local or a visitor, may or may not be aware of the choice on offer. Some will therefore be in the position of searching for a good restaurant with the type of meal they want and at a price they can afford. There may still be business people and perhaps conference attenders and tourists. This weekday pattern may change at the weekend when the business element disappears. Seasonal factors may reflect several influences, such as business fluctuations, tourist flows, and special events such as Christmas and New Year, when many people are out.

These comments suggest that the market for restaurants can be classified in various ways into different components, and that particular establishments will tend to specialize, serving a distinctive market niche. Thus some restaurants will primarily cater for the business market, others the gourmet market, others the quick snack for office workers and shoppers, and so on. The richness of the gastronomy of a city may not simply depend on whether it has some highly rated upscale restaurants, but may lie in the range of experience and type of eatery which it can offer to the visitor.

As the demand for eating out has increased, so has the supply of restaurants. In the USA in the late 1970s there was one restaurant for every 7,000 persons; by the late 1980s this had increased to one for every 2,700 (Waters, 1989). The number of outlets increased from 560,000 in 1983 to 657,000 in 1990. Of these about 120,000 were classified as fast food businesses.

Like other sectors of the economy, the restaurant business is increasingly dominated by large corporations. By the late 1980s in the USA, corporations controlled 56 per cent of the outlets, and this was very important at the cheaper end of the market and in the fast food sector. These corporations gain economies of scale in the purchasing of food and equipment and in marketing. Some of the corporation-owned restaurants form only part of a much larger enterprise, perhaps specializing in drink or the leisure industries. Restaurants are also found within hotels department stores and other places. At the high quality end of the market there are many independent businesses, and here there is large entry and exit rate. In the USA, 50 per cent fail within the first year and 65 per cent within two years (Lundberg, 1989). Many of these businesses have been founded by chefs who often have poor management abilities and find it difficult to hold and recruit staff.

Turning to the spatial distribution of restaurants in cities, an adage states (as for other retail activities) that the three most important factors for success are location,

location and location (Farrell, 1980). However, Smith (1983) and Pillsbury (1987) found this to be too simple to be of great use when they sought to understand restaurant location in Kitchener-Waterloo and Atlanta, respectively. Two important ideas in understanding restaurant location are accessibility and visibility. The former may mean that a large number of pedestrians are passing by, or that it is located on a busy highway. In 1980 P.T. Smale, a director of the UK fast food chain, Wimpey International, described how the location of an outlet was chosen. 'At present we consider such things as customer counts, other multiple retailers, car parking, entertainment, etc. Once the sales potential is established we will search for a site that is the right rent at about 5–7 per cent of projected sales.' The concept of visibility describes the fact that restaurants often cluster, not simply because they all choose the same accessible location. Customers who are going out for a meal and who do not know the reputation of individual restaurants are attracted to clusters of establishments where they feel confident that they will be able to find an outlet to their liking. This may apply to fast food outlets along main roads. Customers can make for a cluster without the need to decide which outlet they are going to patronize (Smith, 1985).

Pillsbury (1987) found his division of restaurants into those providing body food and those providing soul food to be helpful in his search for an explanation of the pattern of restaurants in Atlanta. Body food establishments, and particularly fast food ones, sought accessibility. They were located in the city centre, in malls and office parks, near where people worked, shopped and attended leisure activities and along the main arterial roads, described as 'Hamburger alleys'. Soul food establishments were found in the city centre, usually on the fringe of the retail and business quarters, accessible to business people and conventioneers, and elsewhere in what were described as 'ambient clusters'. These were often found in upmarket housing areas or gentrified neighbourhoods, but Pillsbury maintained that while there was a local market base, they attracted patrons from all over the city. These areas had developed elite restaurants, and had a certain ambience which patrons found attractive. Once established, these districts obtained visibility, which enabled them to continue to attract both new customers and entrepreneurs. These ambient clusters will develop only in parts of the city where the market conditions are right, and will not be found in poorer and deprived parts of the city.

Using this analysis, it can be seen why in many cities the downtown area contains the largest and most varied cluster of restaurants. For body food, an essentially derived form of demand, there are shoppers, office workers and the patrons of leisure facilities such as theatres to maintain a stock of establishments. For soul food there are business people, conference attenders and often a historical legacy has helped to maintain a stock of quality restaurants. This traditionally has been the place to go for a good meal. Many cities, particularly in Europe, have historic quarters which have become the location for upmarket outlets, having the right ambience. In Cologne, in Germany, the riverfront district south of the cathedral is an example of this phenomenon. Elsewhere, immigrant quarters have developed providing ethnic food. Manchester's Chinatown is an example of this process.

From this analysis it might be thought that most cities and most city centres are well resourced to supply the gastronomic needs of visitors, but this is not always so. The decline of the American downtown has weakened its base of restaurants. Upmarket retailing has often decentralized to the suburbs. Entertainment functions have often been reduced. There may be only a weak convention business. For many white people the area may be associated with a black population and therefore a place to be avoided, particularly in the evening. Accordingly, the number of restaurants, particularly high class ones, open in the evening, may have greatly diminished. It would be a distinct disadvantage to have to tell visitors staying downtown that if they want a good meal in the evening they will have to travel to the suburbs. In this situation many American cities which are attempting to develop tourism have given consideration to this topic. The festival marketplace, which has eateries and stays open all evening, has been one answer to this problem. Baltimore's Harborplace (1980) and Atlanta's Underground (1989) are examples of this type of response. Another has been to encourage the creation of a restaurant (and perhaps retailing) quarter in a historic part of the downtown area. In St Louis, the last remaining part of the waterfront in the downtown area, Lacledes Landing, has been so designated and supported by improvement grants. In many cities the redeveloped waterfront has become the location for restaurants.

In Britain the increase in restaurants has coincided with the campaigns by many cities to strengthen the evening economy and create the 24-hour city. Licensing laws (for alcohol) have been relaxed and bars, clubs and restaurants can stay open much later. Instead of being deserted after 6 o'clock during the week, city centres have become much busier. One consequence of this is that there are more people around and feelings of insecurity are removed, which in turn encourages more people to visit the city centre. For tourism the benefit is that a lively city centre will have greater appeal to visitors. This is a feeling that many British visitors get when they visit the cities of mainland Europe which have suffered much less than Anglo-American ones from the consequences of decentralization.

Given this increase in eating out and the growth in the number of restaurants, it is not surprising that employment has grown rapidly. Many of these jobs are low paid, part-time and on a casual basis. Often jobs in this sector are second jobs and are informal, with the result that they may not be recorded in the official statistics. There has been an increase in the share of women and young people in the labour force as employers seek to cut costs (Wood, 1992). In the USA in particular, many young people take jobs in catering as a means of working their way through college, so that the spatial coincidence of educational institutions and tourism is beneficial. Similar practices are growing in Britain where grants were replaced by loans in 1998.

TRANSPORT

Transport is important for urban tourism in at least two ways. First, there is the journey to and from the city, and, second, there is the issue of movement within the city. Both of these could influence whether a potential tourist decides to visit a city. In each situation the factors of speed/time, comfort and cost play a role. Of the two, access to the city is likely to be more critical. Providing a visitor can get to a city satisfactorily and definitely wants to go to that city, they are unlikely to be put off by poor transport within the city. As the question of access to the city was discussed in Chapter 4, it will not be repeated again. Instead this section will concentrate on movement within the city.

Movement within the city involves at least two aspects: the journey from the arrival point to the accommodation and then movement around the city. Most cities are attempting to provide fast frequent links between the airport and the city centre. Rail transport is preferred because it has its own separate track and it can be fast and not interfere with other traffic. Many cities still rely on coach services and of course many passengers prefer to hire a taxi, particularly if they are going to a point not well served by public transport. For those arriving by train or coach the arrival points are usually fairly central, and a short taxi ride can take the traveller to their final destination.

The ideal tourist city has a compact central area in which are found all the sights, the main visitor attractions and entertainments so that it is possible to walk from one place to another without the need for public transport or a taxi, preferably in a mainly pedestrianized zone. There are a number of cities which are like this, Florence and Vienna being examples. However, many tourist cities such as London and Paris have a large central area, while others have their attractions scattered within and beyond the city centre so that walking, except for the most athletic, is impossible. In these cities the visitor must choose between using either a taxi or some form of public transport: bus, tram, surface rail or underground system. These public transport systems have been developed in the main to serve the local population to enable them to travel to work, to shop and for recreation, and may not be ideal for the tourist in terms of providing routes to the main attractions or in frequency of running. Urban transport systems are still evolving and in recent years there has been an increase in investment in underground rail systems and surface tram systems with the intention of shifting traffic from congested roads. Many cities still adhere to the ideal of an integrated transport system with the possibility of easy transfers between modes. Unfortunately in some cities this principle has been negated through the privatization of the different modes. This has prevented the purchase of tickets which can be used on the different systems. However, the visitor to a city wants a simple system with through ticketing or the purchase of day tickets which can be used on all modes. These have proved popular in many cities and provide a convenient form of transport for the tourist. In London international visitors account for 25 per cent of passengers on the Underground and in taxis in the central area (Trew, 1999).

The use of public transport by visitors will depend to a large extent on the information about the local system available to them. Many tourists buy guide books for the city they are about to visit before they set out on the journey and from these they can gather information about local transport. Others obtain guide books and further local information on arrival and can thus discover information on local transport. However, for the less popular urban destinations few guide books are published and the ones that are will not be available in distant airports, so that the arriving tourist will be ill informed. Other tourists may be at a disdavantage because there is no literature in their language. All these factors will affect the movement of the visitor in a strange city and also thus their enjoyment or satisfaction.

In some cities the use of transport can be part of the attraction and enjoyment of the place as well as a means of getting from A to B. In Venice where there are no motor vehicles, water buses (and taxis) provide the main means of crossing the city and at the same time a way of seeing and admiring the ancient palaces along the Grand Canal. In many cities on rivers and estuaries river buses and ferries provide a way of seeing the city. No trip to Sydney would be complete without a trip around the harbour from which the Opera House, the bridge and the skyline can be viewed. In Amsterdam. the numbers carried on boat trips makes it the premier visitor attraction. Elsewhere, there are novel forms of transport which provide a way of seeing and experiencing a city. These might include the tram cars of San Francisco, the old double-decker trams of Hong Kong and the cable ride across Barcelona harbour. In many British cities there are tour buses which can be used to provide an initial orientation tour as well as a form of transport linking the main sights and attractions. Indeed, it might be suggested that an imaginative city seeking to make itself more attractive would invent a transport system which provided both an experience and a means of carrying the tourist around the city, as happens in theme parks.

CONCLUSION

The topics examined in this chapter are all very important for the success of tourism in cities. In general, they can be regarded as secondary elements in that they do not provide the main reasons why tourists visit cities, although, as has been shown, in a few instances they can be very important motivators of travel. Every aspiring tourist city needs good hotels, good retail outlets, quality restaurants and efficient transport facilities. They are a necessary requirement to attract visitors, but not a sufficient one on their own. In so far as these resources are not of the highest standards, tourists may choose to go to other places. A convention planner, other things being equal, may choose the city which has the best access by scheduled air routes.

The importance of these activities is seen in the income gained from tourists and the jobs which they create. They also often contribute to regeneration through the investment in fringe areas of the city centre and in some cases through the images given to the city by new buildings. It is also important that tourists have a good experience in hotels, shops and restaurants, and as they travel around the city in order that there might be repeat visits or recommendations to others to visit the city.

Chapter 9

The impact of urban tourism

The aim of this chapter is to assess the impact that tourism is having on cities. Earlier chapters have considered specific aspects of tourism and examined these impacts. In this chapter an attempt will be made to draw the discussion together. The impact of tourism will be considered both from the view of the individual city – how can the impact of tourism on city X be evaluated? – and from the impact of tourism on cities in general – how are cities being changed as result of the growth of tourism? This latter question cannot be divorced from wider issues of how the world is changing and what is the connection between these trends and tourism.

The basic issues of any economic and more general impact study into the effects of tourism in a city are: the number of visitors; how much income they inject into the local economy; the number of jobs created; the kind of jobs created; the impact tourism has on the maintenance of amenities; the impact of tourism on physical regeneration; the impact of tourism on the image of the city (and thus its general attractiveness to inward investment); and any other effects such as the displacement of funds from other sectors to tourism. These concerns can be classified into what might be described as narrow economic impact and wider impact, the latter being more tenuous and therefore more difficult to measure. The former are generally quantitative, while the latter are usually qualitative and of a critical cultural nature. Some of the implications of these assessments of impact will be discussed further in the concluding chapter.

ECONOMIC IMPACT OF TOURISM

The adoption of tourism as an economic development strategy by so many cities in the 1980s has not been without debate and questioning. Critics will need to be satisfied that the amount of public money being spent can be justified, and that the aims of the tourism strategy are being achieved. Such questions can be answered only through impact studies. Given the prominence of urban tourism, it is surprising that so few have been undertaken, or at least so few that can be regarded as reliable. One reason for this situation may be that tourism is difficult to measure. When, say, a car factory or car factories are built in a city, it is relatively easy to see where the jobs have been created, although even here there is the problem of multiplier effects. However, the impact of tourism is spread across many sectors, from the visitor attractions, to hotels, restaurants, shops, transport and other activities, so that it is more difficult to calculate the impact. To be reliable, assessments of impact require many detailed surveys, which are both time-consuming and costly. There is consequently a search for short cuts, the use of simple ratios, and the borrowing of results from other cities or wider surveys. In the USA in particular, many convention and visitor bureaux supply quantitative information about the state of the industry in their city, but in the absence of any reference to detailed surveys it must be assumed that the consultants employed have used concise methods, and that these results are open to question (Hughes, 1982). Unfortunately, in many cases, the results of these studies by consultants are not available for detailed scrutiny. Because of the confusion and misunderstanding surrounding the economic impact of tourism, this chapter will seek to explain the methods used, as well as presenting results from cities where impact studies have been undertaken.

The list of questions posed in the introduction can be divided into those which can be answered by one survey and those which require more than one because they are examining the impact of the industry over time. This latter aspect gets to the heart of the urban tourism strategy, which is to assist the economic and physical development of the city. Only by reviewing the progress of tourism over a number of years can an assessment be made as to whether these objectives are being achieved. Asking whether the urban tourism strategy has been successful involves a series of related questions: is the number of visitors increasing? What is the rate of growth of the different components? How does their rate of growth compare with national and international rates? Is the income increasing? How far can the success achieved be attributed to the policies implemented? Once these questions have been answered, cities will be in a position to evaluate their policies and produce revised ones.

So far it has been suggested that impact studies are concerned with the whole of the tourism industry, but as has been seen in earlier chapters, they may be concerned with individual projects or with sectors of the industry. The viability of individual projects is usually studied by their sponsors before the go-ahead for the scheme is given, whether these are in the public or private sectors. After-studies may occur where there has been public funding, to ascertain that the investment has been to good effect. Once again the project may be looked at in narrow economic terms or in terms of its wider effects. In Britain the Department of the Environment commissioned a study to evaluate the success of tourism projects which had received public assistance (Central London Polytechnic *et al.*, 1990). Sector studies may involve the convention industry, the arts or cultural industries, or sport, and these have been referred to in earlier chapters.

In essence, the methodology of economic impact studies is relatively easy to understand, although its implementation is fraught with problems. First, these studies establish the number of visitors. Second, these studies calculate the amount spent in the local economy by these visitors and its further impacts through multiplier effects. The money spent in the local economy is used by firms to make purchases and to pay staff, with possible further impacts. Thus the monetary impact of tourists can be classified as direct, indirect and induced. Third, these studies attempt to calculate the number of jobs which have been created as a result of this spending, producing a figure which is likely to have the most significance for local politicians. In the rest of this chapter these topics will be examined in more detail, and will be illustrated with the results of impact studies. However, it will be apparent from what has already been said and what follows that because of the different definitions and methods used, it is extremely difficult to compare the results of impact studies in different cities.

Visitors

The first task of any impact study is to decide who is to be counted as a visitor or tourist, a definitional problem that has been discussed in earlier chapters. The official definition of a tourist is a person who spends more than 24 hours away from home, but this excludes the day tripper, a type of visitor who is important to most cities. Since cities often draw in commuters from a wide area it is necessary to distinguish the regular commuter who may travel over 20 miles each day, from the visitor who is coming to the city for a day out. Even in this latter category there is the question as to whether the visitor whose sole purpose is shopping should be included. Many studies have excluded shoppers on the basis that shopping is a function for which the large city has always had a regional role. However, given that there are often several shopping centres in a metropolitan area and that shopping is increasingly perceived as a leisure activity, this distinction is not always easy to justify. In some studies the day tripper has been defined on the basis of an arbitrary distance, say 20 or 100 miles, beyond which it is assumed that anyone coming to the city is making a special trip. It is unlikely that there will ever be a universally agreed definition, but if the information about visitors can be classified in an agreed way, then useful comparisons can be made.

Visitors staying overnight can be classified in various ways, the most obvious being between those who use serviced accommodation such as hotels and those who stay with friends and relatives. The great advantage of this division is that it can be related to expenditure patterns, there being a great difference between these categories. Visitors can also be classified according to the purpose of their visit, primarily between the business traveller and the leisure tourist, but possibly with a further division to include the conference and exhibition delegate. Another classification may be based on origin and this may be significant when there is an international component among the visitors. Foreign visitors often spend more than domestic ones, but within the international division there may be important differences. For Britain, American visitors are generally big spenders while those from continental Europe are not. This may reflect the fact that within the latter group there are many young people who have come to learn the English language.

The calculation of visitor numbers is extremely difficult. There are no frontier posts around cities to record arrivals and departures. Visitors staying in hotels can be counted if there is co-operation from the establishments. In some European countries it is, or has been in the past, a legal requirement to register hotel guests, particularly foreigners, and this could be a reliable source for this type of visitor. Otherwise, the co-operation of the hotel industry is required and this may not be given on the grounds of commercial confidentiality. In some areas sample surveys are done of hotel occupancy, and if the total stock of hotels is known, then through multiplication an estimate of the number of hotel room nights can be obtained. Further details from these surveys may provide details of the types of visitors and the length of stay. For other types of visitors, those staying with friends and relatives, and day trippers, there are no records and some form of survey is required.

Most surveys of tourists take place at key visitor sites. The number of sites used will vary from city to city, depending on the nature of the attractions, and according to the resources available for the survey. Surveys could take place at locations where there is a popular vista or outside museums, theatres or sports arenas. The costs of these surveys is high and therefore they are likely to be limited to a few days in the year which are considered to be representative. Specific days will be chosen to represent the different seasons of the year and days in the week, and the hours in the day will also be carefully chosen. The questionnaire will obtain information about the visitor, including age, sex, number in party, home area, purpose of visit, length of stay, sites visited or to be visited, other activities (such as shopping and use of resaurants), expenditure patterns and impressions of the city. The answers to these questions will need to be classified very carefully and may not be without problems. In particular, there are often difficulties in categorizing the purpose of the visit. There can be often several purposes for the visit, either major/minor or equal ones. Answers such as 'just for a change' are difficult to classify using the normal headings.

The reliability of these types of visitor survey is often questioned. Visitors interviewed in the middle of a trip cannot give an account of the whole trip. They may not be able to recall accurately the expenditures they have made. Indeed, in many cases they may not be aware of the expenditures made on their behalf by a tour operator. Alternative methods involve interviewing visitors only at the end of a visit, posting questionnaires to tourists after their visit, or giving visitors a diary as they enter the city to record the required information (Frechtling, 1987). However, all these techniques suffer from similar problems and in addition it may be more difficult to obtain a representative sample.

This information can then be related to other statistical information to provide an estimate of the total number of visitors. Thus if the general survey reveals that 20 per cent of all tourists visit a particular museum or attraction and the total number of tourists, i.e non-local, admissions is known from surveys in the attraction, then a multiplier of five could be used to obtain the total number of visitors to the city. If one-sixth of the tourists are staying in hotels and the number of hotel stayers is known, then a multiplier could be used again (Merseyside Information Services, 1991). Once the total number of visitors has been calculated, the survey data can be used again to provide estimates of numbers of tourists by different categories. The reliability of this method will depend on the surveys picking up a representative sample. Street surveys might not pick up the business traveller or the convention delegate or some other specialist type of visitor. Thus the technique of confining surveys to the main attraction may produce results only for the leisure visitor sector. To overcome this problem, other surveys may be necessary, either in hotels or convention centres. There is scope clearly for error in all these surveys from a failure to be representative. The flow of tourists may be very uneven, perhaps because of special events, or the weather, variations which cannot be picked up from surveys. Outside researchers may not be aware of these variations and thus draw false conclusions about visitor flows.

In some countries national sample surveys of both domestic and foreign tourists can be disaggregated to provide information on the number of visitors to metropolitan areas. In the USA the US Travel Data Center developed a Travel Economic Impact Model (TEIM) in the early 1970s which estimates the economic benefits from travel to counties and cities (Frechtling, 1987). Given the size of the national sample, the data thus provided are subject to a degree of error.

Using the results from a number of cities, the scale and nature of visitors to cities can be discussed. To begin with, information from Merseyside (which includes Liverpool) and Munich is used as these are among the few cities where there is comprehensive data (Table 9.1).

Table 9.1 Visitors to Merseyside and Munich

	Merseyside		*Munich*	
	No. (million)	*(%)*	*No. (million)*	*(%)*
Overnight, hotel, etc.	1.4	4.7	3.1	5.7
VFR	2.1	7.1	1.6	2.9
Day	25.4	88.2	49.8	91.4
Total	28.9	100	54.5	100

Source: Merseyside Information Services (1991), and Munich City Tourist Office

In terms of absolute numbers, day visitors are overwhelming in both cases, representing between 88 and 91 per cent of all visitors. The category of visitors to friends and relatives varied between 3 and 7 per cent, while those staying in hotels represented about 5 per cent. Further information shows that Munich had 2.2 million overnight business visitors and 16.1 million day business visitors, equal to one-third of all visitors. In contrast, Merseyside only had 137,000 overnight and 764,000 day business visitors, equalling just 3 per cent of all visitors. A strong economy like Munich's attracts many business visitors and will provide a good base for the hotel industry. In Merseyside's case a weak economy does not provide a good base for the hotel trade. In the above examples the visitor numbers have simply been added up, but obviously hotel users will have a greater economic impact as they stay longer and spend more. Further information about Munich's non-business day visitors reveals that 73 per cent travelled from their homes, 20 per cent came from a holiday location and the remaining 7 per cent were in transit, stopping *en route*. Munich attracted 11.3 million visitors for its festivals, including 6.7 million for its Oktoberfest.

As could be expected, many more cities have data about the number of visitors staying overnight in hotels. Figures for the major world tourist cities were given in Table 1.1. When only hotel visitors are considered, the importance of business travel and conventions greatly increases. In Munich (1988) 56 per cent of the hotel stayers were business travellers and 16 per cent were attending trade fairs and congresses. For Glasgow in 1985, 40 per cent of overnight stays were business people and conference delegates. Most overnight-staying visitors in cities are on a short visit only, the average length being about two nights.

In some cities research has been limited to a core area and the results cannot be used for the entire metropolitan area. For Baltimore, annual surveys have taken place between 1980 and 1988 in and around the Inner Harbor (for the most recent see Jeanne Beekhuis and Co, 1988). These suggest that after a rapid increase in the early 1980s, visitor numbers have stabilized at around 2.7 million a year from outside the metropolitan area, composed of 45 per cent day visitors and 55 per cent overnight stayers.

About 25 per cent of the visitors come as individuals, 69 per cent in a party (average size 2.47) and only 6 per cent with group travel.

Income

Using the expenditure information obtained from the visitor surveys, an estimate of the income which tourists bring to the city can be made. This is usually done by classifying tourists into categories such as day visitors, those staying with friends and relatives, leisure tourists staying in hotels, business travellers and convention delegates. Each of these categories will have a different pattern of expenditure, as the figures for Hong Kong show (Table 9.2). The exact categories chosen will depend on the characteristics of tourism in the metropolitan area. If the numbers in each group have been estimated and their expenditure known, then through multiplication an estimate of total tourist expenditure can be obtained. Using the details of expenditure, this can be broken down into figures for hotels, restaurants, visitor attractions, shops and local transport. This, of course, is a misleading guide to economic impact, since much of the money will either be used to purchase goods from outside the area or be repatriated as profits to companies headquartered elsewhere (Frechtling, 1987). Once again, national models such as TEIM in the USA may be used to estimate expenditure. One problem of these models is how to allocate transport expenditure, in either the home or destination area. Simpler simulation techniques may also be used if, say, the total income of hotels in an area is known and a ratio can be applied to estimate total expenditure.

Table 9.2 Average per capita expenditure per day by tourists in Hong Kong, 1988

Type	Expenditure ($US)
Holiday-makers	240
VFR	70
Convention delegates	470
Incentive travel	700

Source: HKTA Visitor Survey, quoted in Bull (1991), p. 13

The second stage is to make an estimate of indirect expenditure. This requires further survey work to ascertain how the income is used in the firms identified above as receiving the tourist expenditure. Some of this will be used to pay staff. Some will be used to make purchases, some of which will come from the local economy and some from outside. Those made from the local economy will create a further impact via employment and possible purchases from the local economy which could require further survey work. Some of the income will be used to pay taxes and again these need to be divided between local and national ones. Using these results it is posssible to obtain an estimate of the impact of the second and subsequent rounds of expenditure in the local economy. As with other surveys, there may be problems in obtaining co-operation and getting precise information, the absence of which could prejudice the results. If there are input–output tables for the metropolitan economy, it may be possible to cut down some of the survey work.

The third stage of estimating the economic impact is to calculate the induced impact. This will come from the expenditure of those dependent on tourism for their income.

The second round will have provided an estimate of this household income. Either through further survey work or through input–output analysis tables can the break-down of this expenditure be obtained and the income divided between local and non-local spend. The local spend will be the induced impact.

Adding these three effects together will provide the total impact, and if this is put above the direct spend a simple ratio multiplier coefficient can be obtained. However, this would be a very unreliable, since it ignores the income that has left the area. The normal or Keynsian multiplier takes only the income spent in the area and puts it above direct expenditure to obtain a coefficient. For the general public these figures of total income are fairly meaningless and if there are no comparable figures for the met-ropolitan economy their significance is difficult to evaluate.

In 1988 Munich's tourism generated DM 4.6 billion, of which nearly half was spent on retailing, one-third on hotels and catering, and the rest on entertainment, local transport and other items. About 10 per cent of this income was generated by con-gresses. For Amsterdam in 1987, tourism generated 1.5 billion guilders, of which 57 per cent was spent by international visitors (Pearce, 1992).

Ahmadi (1989) has classified visitors to Baltimore City in two ways, according to type of accommodation and purpose of activity (Table 9.3). Hotel visitors formed 16.5 per cent of the total, but were responsible for 31.5 per cent of the tourist days, 56.7 per cent of the direct expenditure (and 57.9 per cent of the jobs). In contrast, 79.3 per cent of the visitors were day trippers, defined here as travelling over 30 miles, but they accounted for only 37.5 per cent of the expenditure. In terms of the purpose of the trip, there were three main groups: conventioneers, sightseers and visitors to events. Conventioneers were relatively small in number, but had a larger impact, while the greater number of event visitors had a smaller impact.

Table 9.3 Visitors to Baltimore City, 1988

(a) By accommodation			
Topic	Hotels	VFR	Day trippers
Numbers	654,000	165,000	3,143,000
Numbers (%)	16.5	4.2	79.3
Days	1,634,000	413,000	314,000
Days (%)	69.2	17.2	13.3
Daily spend ($)	143.61	58.87	49.43
Direct spend ($m)	234.71	23.99	155.32
Direct spend (%)	56.7	5.8	37.5
Jobs	7304	683	4628

(b) By activity				
	Conventions	Sightseeing	Shopping	Events
Days (%)	8.29	69.72	0.33	21.66
Direct spend ($m)	86.30	258.17	0.79	66.76
Direct spend (%)	20.8	62.4	0.19	16.61
Jobs	2684	7875	24	2032
Jobs (%)	21.3	62.4	0.2	16.1

Source: Ahmadi (1989)

Tourism economic impact studies naturally concentrate on the expenditure of tourists, and ignore the expenditure of residents on those activities which are used by the visitors. However, one benefit of developing resources to attract tourists could be that local residents have less need to travel to other cities. If there are only one or two aquariums or legalized gambling centres in a country, then those who want to make use of these facilities will have to travel to them. But if they become widespread, that is they are found in most cities or regions, then the need to leave home will be greatly reduced, unless there is a qualitative difference in these facilities. In this sense the enhancement of the tourism product can result in what the economists call 'import substitution'.

Jobs

The number and type of jobs that tourism generates are often regarded as the most important type of impact. For many cities the main reason for encouraging tourism has been the need to find new forms of employment to replace the jobs lost in older and declining industiries. However, the calculation of employment impact is perhaps the most difficult to establish of the three areas being investigated. As mentioned above, these jobs are scattered across many sectors and cannot easily be identified. The most relevant data for calculating the employment impacts are the income data identified as being used to pay staff costs, but this cannot always easily be translated into jobs. Usually some ratio drawn from national input–output tables is used to estimate the employment which a given amount of income will generate. More sophistication can be obtained if the income is broken down by sector and then the specific ratios applied. This still makes it difficult to identify the types of jobs that have been created by occupation, whether full-time or part-time, or seasonal, although industrial studies may be used to infer the likely breakdown for a particular city.

Since one motive for encouraging tourism in urban areas has been the aim of re-ducing unemployment, the question is often asked to what extent has this been achieved. Of course, the level of unemployment in an area is a result of many factors from demographic ones to the differing fortunes of its industries. Even if tourism is successful at creating a large number of jobs, unemployment will not fall if other activities are shedding labour and the number of young people coming into the labour market is greater than those who are leaving it. Other questions asked are whether the new jobs created in tourism are drawing labour from the ranks of the unemployed, and if there is a trickle-down effect to the most disadvantaged in society. Given that some, but by no means all, of the jobs in tourism are low-skilled ones, it might be thought that there should be the possiblity of the unemployed finding work in the sector. There is little evidence on this point, but it is not necessary for there to be a direct use of the unemployed for there to be an impact. As other studies have shown, when a new form of employment is introduced into an area it often draws labour from existing activities and only a small proportion from the unemployed (Salt, 1967). However, those firms that have lost labour then have to recruit again and they in turn may recruit from the unemployed. In this way the unemployed are taken into the labour force, although it may be difficult to get the long-term unemployed motivated to work.

The geography of tourism employment and the unemployed may be another factor which influences the extent to which there is an impact of this type. Since tourism is often concentrated in the city centre and many of the unemployed are found in the surrounding inner city zones, the possiblities of an impact would appear high. Studies of the home address of tourism workers have shown that many do in fact live in the inner city (MacDonald, 1996),

Table 9.4 Tourism employment in cities: selected examples

City (date)	Total	Direct	Indirect and Induced
London (1984)	380,000	230,000	150,000
London (2000)		275,000	
Paris (1997)		181,085	
New York City (1990)		124,000	
New York City (1997)	244,400	134,200	110,200
Chicago (1999)	131,800		
Toronto (1998)	119,000		
Munich (1988)	57,000		
Dublin (late 1990s)	30,000		
Birmingham (1998)	27,350	19,550	7,800
Glasgow (1998)	21,000		
Baltimore (1988)	16,400		
Liverpool (1998)	11,595 (or 8464 FTE)		

Sources: Various

A few statistics will illustrate the impact of tourism on employment in cities (see Table 9.4). The greatest number of jobs generated by tourism in cities not surprisingly are found in the major capital cities of London and Paris. For London in 1984 it was estimated that between 210,000 and 230,000 jobs had been created directly by tourism with a further 150,000 created indirectly. The combined figure was equal to about 10 per cent of all jobs in London and about a quarter of all tourism jobs in the United Kingdom (London Tourist Board, 1987). By 2000 the number of direct jobs had risen to 275,000. Estimates of employment are available for most major US cities which use the US Travel Data Center's TEIM to calculate impact. In Atlanta in 1987 it was estimated that tourism generated 65,000 jobs, of which 35,000 were accounted for by hotels and that, of these, 35 per cent were due to convention delegates. For Baltimore in 1988 about 20,000 jobs in the metropolitan area were attributed to tourism, of which 16,400 were found in the central city. Of the latter jobs, 62 per cent were generated by sightseers, 21 per cent by conventioneers and 16 per cent by visitors to special events. In Britain there are estimates for only a few cities. Studies of tourism on Merseyside suggested that the number of jobs created by the industry had increased from 13,500 jobs in 1985, 14,000 in 1990, to 18,080 in 1998 (DRV Research, 1986; Merseyside Information Services, 1991; TMP, 2000). For Bradford, where tourism became a key thrust of its economic development strategy in the early 1980s, Jeffrey (1990) suggested that the number of jobs increased only from 3,772 in 1981 to 4,133 in 1987. In Germany the 1988 study of Munich suggested that tourism generated 57,000 full-time equivalent jobs or 7 per cent of all employment. Unfortunately, there are few statistics which break down employment into full-time and part-time or by industry type and occupational level.

Other Methods

Owing to the cost of undertaking surveys, attempts have been made to develop simpler yet reliable methods of calculating impacts. One such method is the use of the counterfactual. This was used by Barnett (1984) when calculating the employment impact of tourism in the small historic city of York, England. The counterfactual method asks the basic question, what would the situation be if there were no tourism industry? To answer this question, a town of a similar size but without a tourist industry is taken and its employment structure compared, highlighting those industries where tourism could be expected to have an impact. Thus, the additional jobs in hotels could be presumed to arise from tourism. When these categories have been summed, an estimate of tourism impact is obtained. In the case of a small city like York it was relatively easy to compare it with an industrial town of the same size, but the method would be more difficult to apply to larger cities where it might be impossible to find a comparable city where there was no tourism industry.

Vaughan (1986) and Jeffrey (1989, 1990) have used two non-survey techniques to estimate employment in tourism. The first method relies on calculating the number of visitor nights. These may be obtained from sample surveys of hotel (and guest-house) occupancy, with the ratios being applied to the total accommodation stock. Altern- atively, national surveys of domestic and foreign tourists can be used to obtain visitor nights, although the disaggregated data to district levels may not be very reliable. Survey data, obtained from elsewhere, can then be used to estimate spend per 24 hours and thus a figure of total expenditure broken down into the main categories can be obtained. Again, using survey data from elsewhere, these figures can be converted into employment estimates (Table 9.5). These statistics cover only overnight tourists staying in serviced accommodation, and exclude visits to friends and relatives and day visitors.

Table 9.5 Workforce per £100,000 of turnover in selected businesses in Merseyside

Business type	Direct workforce	Secondary workforce	Total
Hotels and guest houses	8.3	1.7	10.0
Rented self-catering	19.2	0.9	20.1
Restaurants and pubs	6.7	1.1	7.8
Shops	3.6	0.4	4.0
Attractions	8.7	1.6	10.3

Source: DRV Research (1986)

A second technique uses the regularly collected employment figures which are broken down into classes or categories. Crude estimates can be obtained by simply adding together what are referred to as 'tourism and related industries'. In Britain these are published in *Labour Market Trends* and can be calculated at the local level. However, this technique includes all workers in such classes as restaurants as being part of the tourism industry when in fact only a proportion of sales would go to people from outside the local area. Morrell (1985) has attempted to improve the technique by cal- culation of the proportion of employment which can be attributed to tourist demand (Table 9.6). These ratios can then be applied to the statistics of employment for a particular urban area to estimate the total number of jobs which can be attributed to tourism. Such a figure will cover all types of tourism including day trips. However, since it is likely that the proportion of tourism-related employment in each class will vary from area to area, any estimate for a particular area must be subject to a degree of error. These figures also need to include estimates of the number of self-employed, seasonal employment and induced effects of employment of workers' expenditure (Vaughan, 1986).

Table 9.6 Estimated proportion of total employment directly related to tourism

Class	Proportion directly employed in tourism
Retail distribution 1	0.0803
Retail distribution 2	0.0803
Hotels and catering	0.4901
Railways	0.0627
Other inland trains	0.0254
Sea transport	0.1064
Air transport	0.8254
Transport supplementary services	0.1795
Miscellaneous transport	0.2200
Recreational services	0.2160
Personal services	0.0811

Source: Morrell (1985)

URBAN TOURISM AND REGENERATION

In earlier chapters of this book it was shown that the case for developing tourism in many older industrial cities was based on the idea that it would assist regeneration. Tourism could help change the image of a city and raise its profile, and this in turn would assist it to attract various types of investment from manufacturing industry to office-based activities. Tourism would also help physical regeneration as new resources such as visitor attractions and convention centres were built on derelict or under-used land and ancillary activities brought back in to use old buildings. The employment aspects of regeneration have already been discussed. In this section an attempt will be made to assess how far these objectives have been achieved.

There is no doubt that the activities associated with tourism have the ability to transform the image and raise the profile of a city. Special events have put the spotlight on cities such as Barcelona and Sydney. New visitor attractions such as the Guggenheim Museum in Bilbao can raise the visibility of a city. But media interest can only focus on a limited number of new phenomena so there is competition to attract their attention. Even when it is attracted, it may not last long, so that the impact of one high profile news item may decline within a few years. At the same time any city faces negative news stories which it cannot easily control. Unfortunately although much has been written about image (see earlier chapters), there has been little research on the long-term image characteristics and changes over time to make any assessment of the impact of tourism.

Assuming that the image of a city is changed, what impact does this have on attracting investment to the city? Following the transformation of the image of a city it should be possible to examine the flow of inward investment and assess whether there was any causal relationship. Certainly cities such as Glasgow claim that image campaigns such as 'Glasgow's Miles Better' and the 1990 European City of Culture have resulted in a flow of office activities and jobs to the city (see Chapter 7). Proving this is more difficult. When business people are surveyed about the reasons why a location decision was made, they nearly always give a list of rational economic reasons, as they think they are expected to do. So they might suggest that the sole reasons were connected with labour supply, labour costs and property rent levels. They rarely mention non-economic reasons such as lifestyle opportunities for the executives, or if they do, not as the main reasons. These economic reasons are almost certainly important, for no rational firm would move if they were not satisfactory. However, the influence of image often operates at an earlier stage when executives are drawing up a short list of places to be considered. It is at this stage that having knowledge of or an image of a place is important and where any prejudices might operate. The influence of lifestyle opportunities is also likely to be greater if the firm has a high proportion of professional and managerial staff. Consequently proving that image is important in economic decision-making is usually only possible through an examination of the evidence of inward flows. If there is an upward shift in the amount of inward investment following an image change and there are no other changes occurring at the same time which could be influential, then it could be inferred that there was a causal link.

There can be little doubt that the expansion of activities associated with tourism has had an effect on the physical environment, as has been intended. From waterfronts to decaying industrial areas on the fringe of city centres, tourism projects have been used to anchor these regeneration schemes. New buildings have been constructed and old buildings brought back into use, and the physical environment surrounding them enhanced. For flagship projects, there has frequently been a spillover effect on the surrounding area as other activities have been attracted in the form of hotels, restaurants and shops. The public funds used to lever private investment have been shown to be well spent (Central London Polytechnic, Leisureworks and DRV, 1990). The effects do not always come immediately and projects to regenerate an area may take up to two decades to come to fruition. This may be because of either the slowness in getting public funds in place and/or the effects of the economic cycle which may delay private investment.

The Costs of Urban Tourism

The public sector is expected to take a lead role in the development of the activities associated with tourism in cities, in the provision of basic resources such as visitor attractions and stadiums, in the construction of general infrastructure and in the subsidization of special events as well as grants to the private sector to lever investment. The justification for these expenditures is in terms of the benefits that will flow from tourism to the community from jobs to better facilities, but the costs could outweigh any gains. As earlier chapters have shown, the costs arise from losses at events and attractions, from the displacement of investment from welfare activities and from opportunity costs.

Like any other economic activity, there is a speculative element in investment in tourism activities. Projects are justified on the basis of expected income from visitors, either as entrance charges or general expenditure in the community, and this is set against costs such as the construction of facilities. Unfortunately these costs may be higher than expected, due to the cost overruns on construction, and the benefits will be less because forecast visitor numbers have not been achieved. When this happens, the public sector generally has to bear the cost, which is then passed on to local people. Across the activities discussed in this book, there is a tendency to be optimistic about the balance of costs and benefits; to justify stadium building in the USA on the basis of inflated tourism income; to gamble on the amount of TV rights and sponsorship that can be obtained for special events; and to find consultants who will provide visitor forecast numbers high enough to obtain the income required for a proposed visitor attraction. In the latter case, failure to get the figures right can result in closure, as happened with the National Centre for Popular Music in Sheffield. Of course, forecasting is difficult, and while there have been many over-estimates, there have also been some under-estimates, as with the Guggenheim Museum in Bilbao and the Tate Modern in London. One of the reasons why there has been a tendency to over-estimate the benefits is that cities are very ambitious to have what Loftman and Nevin (1995, 1996) have described as 'prestige projects'. These may produce what Baade and Dye (1990) have described as 'intangible' benefits; higher status in city league tables, civic pride and satisfaction to city voters.

Public expenditure on tourism projects may result in the displacement of funds from the normal welfare activities of city councils. This may not be easy to prove without detailed investigative work and comparative analysis, requiring the skills of an accountant to unearth the details. In the case of the International Convention Centre in Birmingham, this sleuth work was undertaken by Loftman and Nevin (1994) arousing considerable antipathy from the city leaders. They were able to demonstrate that the city council diverted some of the funds required (there were external grants as well) from the educational budget which as a result was lower per child than in other local authority areas. Not only was less spent on the actual teaching but the buildings were allowed to fall into disrepair. For Cleveland, USA, Keating (1997) was also able to demonstrate that one consequence of tax abatements on the downtown tracts where tourism projects were found was a reduction in the amount spent on education. Elsewhere the losses of the World Student Games held in Sheffield had to be paid for by the city through higher debts and higher annual debt charges which exerted a downward pressure on what could be spent on welfare services.

Even if there is no displacement of funds from welfare services, there is always the question of 'opportunity costs'; could the money have been better spent on other services which better met the needs of local people? This is not a question that can be answered with any objectivity. Cities in th USA have avoided some of these issues by funding tourism projects from 'room or lodgings taxes' and sometimes 'sales taxes', so shifting the costs on to the visitor.

One frequent criticism of tourism projects is that it is all 'public sector costs and private sector gains'. American cities pay for the stadium and the sports teams' owners make the profit. Cities pay for loss-making visitor attractions and hotels proprietors make the profits from the visitor. The public sector subsidizes a special event and restaurant and pub enterprises reap the dividends. This of course is to simplify the case and ignore the other benefits to the community from better facilities to jobs. In the end, city leaders have to decide whether the balance of costs and benefits is right.

TOURISM, GLOBALIZATION AND STANDARDIZATION

By the end of the twentieth century globalization was considered by many commentators to be one of the main processes affecting the economic and social development of communities, regions and countries. By globalization is meant the increasing inter-dependence of the different parts of the world. Of course, ever since the age of discovery there have been increasing links between the various parts of the world, but it is suggested that the scale, intensity and impact are now very significant for most aspects of life. Global trade is increasing as barriers to the flow of goods are either abolished or eliminated. Similarly, large sums of money flow and are traded around the world, greatly aided by improved telecommunications. The major corporations seek to be global, as consumers are more willing to accept standardized products and there are economies of scale to be gained. Globalization affects culture and ideas via the media and there is the possibility of English becoming the *lingua franca* of the world. In this process, the power of the nation–state to exert an influence on events appears weakened. Of course, the impact of globalization is uneven across the world; it is greatest in the three main developed areas, North America, western Europe and East Asia (the Triad) and least in the less developed parts of the world such as Africa. Globalization is focused on the main cities, the 'world cities' such as London and New York which are powerful financial, corporate, creative/media and communication points in the system.

The movement of people is both a consequence of globalization and a contributor to the process. Business people travel around the world in pursuit of trade for their transnational employers. Conferences and exhibitions are increasingly international and global. Leisure travel over longer distances is growing rapidly and is no longer the privilege of only the very affluent. All of this tourism has been aided by declining regulations with respect to passports, visas and currency exchange. While easier global travel has opened up all types of places to tourism from warm water resorts, great cultural monuments, to safaris, major cities have benefited because they are the transport hubs in the system through which travellers pass to reach these other places and where they often stop off *en route*. They are also visited by the business tourist, who often provides the base market for the establishment of air routes and hotels. Global tourism is encouraged by national governments who are ambitious to gain a share of this growing trade and maintain a positive balance of trade. Global corporations are both following tourists and preceding them to open up new territory for travellers. The major hotel groups such as Holiday Inn are spread around the world, as are caterers such as McDonald's, retailers like the Body Shop, and also brands such as Coca Cola.

This globalization of the tourism industry has inevitably resulted in the standard-ization of the product. Hotels around the world become very similar as they must appeal to clientele accustomed to and expectant of a particular set of standards. As restaurants and retailers erect their façades and logos, street landscapes become more alike. At the same time there is a diffusion of ideas for the tourism product around the world. Successful models are replicated elsewhere. As the container revolution killed off old port areas, Baltimore's formula was copied around the world with anchor visitor attractions, festival marketplaces and convention centres. Cultural tourism is developed via new museums, concert halls and theatres sited in hopefully what will be landmark buildings. Sport has been incorporated into the strategy with new stadiums being constructed. Nearly all of this development has taken place in the past 30 years, and most of it more recently. For much of this time there were similar architectural styles with bland concrete and glass exteriors being adopted frequently. The result has been serial reproduction with cities becoming more and more alike, their individuality confined to a few historic buildings. This homogenization is not merely external, confined to building types and cityscapes. Local cultures are obliterated in the process as the world's major cuisines are offered in each city, theatres offer the latest Andrew Lloyd Webber musical and the art blockbuster is trundled around yet another Guggenheim outpost. To help the tourist, English language signs are erected everywhere and Latin script is used for firm names in countries with a different alphabet such as Japan. All these processes remove the sense of place which used to make visiting a foreign city enjoyable.

The processes of globalization are working strongly across the world and they impact on cities because they are the nodal points in the system. It is inevitable that tourism in cities will reflect the standardization which results from this process. However, because cities have resources which attract tourists, they contribute to the process of globalization.

TOURISTS AND LOCALS

What is the impact on the tourist of visiting another city? Idealists and optimists have long hoped that international tourism would be a force for good in the world, helping the visitor to understand other cultures and societies and thereby reducing any misunderstandings and potential for conflict that might exist between two nationalities. Pessimists have argued that seeing another culture might merely reinforce any prejudice that existed. Also they have argued rightly that there is often very little real contact between hosts and guests, and that any contact that happens is likely to be those serving them in restaurants and hotels. Is there an urban tourism aspect here?

Urban and rural settlements have often been contrasted with urban societies, because of their size, being regarded as anonymous and impersonal while the small rural community is perceived to be close-knit. For urban residents the vast majority of their fellow citizens are unknown and without affiliation to a group an individual can feel very alienated from the rest of society, with little commitment to maintain and improve it. This is likely to be more so for the short city break visitor who is delightfully free from any commitment to a place and also free to criticize without having any responsibility to do anything about it (Pocock, 1997). On the other hand, the big city offers more opportunities for a visitor to learn about the society they are visiting, from museums and heritage centres to cultural activities. Even if only a small glimpse of the country is seen, the visitor can return home with a desire to learn more. It is too much to expect that tourism will be a solution for the conflicts and misunderstandings that exist between peoples. The tourist who starts out with a positive attitude to the people and country that they are visiting is likely to return home with an enhanced understanding, while the visitors who thinks that all foreigners are inferior will have this view reinforced.

LOCALS AND THE TOURIST

Apart from the economic impacts discussed above, how does tourism in the city affect the locals? Much of the writing on this topic has focused on the fact that tourism tends to reinforce the hegonomy of an international and middle-class culture. It is the affluent person who can afford to travel, and therefore the city that wishes to attract their expenditure must cater to their tastes. So, cultural events are likely to be 'high art' rather than mass or popular culture. When Glasgow was proposed as the European City of Culture, some residents hoped that it would celebrate Glasgow's culture, and although there was a bow in the direction of popular culture, the city's main thrust was towards culture that would appeal across Europe (Boyle and Hughes, 1991).

Local people can benefit from the new tourism resources that are created, from visitor attractions to concert halls, and it has been shown that in a city such as London a significant share of the capacity is dependent on tourists, although this is less so in other cities. Nevertheless while tourists contribute from their pocket, they contribute in no other way. In that sense they are parasites, consuming what is there, but contributing nothing to its development. They want a lively city, but expect others to provide it (Roberta Gratz, quoted in the *Guardian*, 13 September 2000).

Where urban tourism is successful and concentrated, local people will suffer from congestion on roads and in pedestrian areas and also face the need to queue. They may feel that in the main tourist areas the prices of goods and servics are higher. In some cities such as San Francisco residents have been forced to move to allow for an expansion of hotels and tourist facilities. If the city has attracted criminal elements because of tourism, residents will suffer as well.

CONCLUSION

This chapter has examined some of the main approaches used to assess the impacts of tourism in cities, drawing together some of the points made in earlier chapters. In general, public authorities have only been interested in the economic impact, where the results of studies can be used to justify public intervention and expenditure in this field. Whereas in other sectors it is relatively easy to assess the economic impact of an industry and the changes taking place, it is much more difficult in tourism because the impact is spread over many activities and it is difficult to obtain hard facts on the actual number of visitors. Because reliable information is expensive to collect, there is a tendency to take short cuts using ratios obtained in other studies to make estimates. One consequence of the fact that a variety of methods are used is that the figures from different studies may not be comparable. Other problems which make comparisons difficult are that figures may relate either to the direct effects only or to direct plus indirect and induced effects. Additionally, some studies relate to a central city only, while others to the entire metropolitan area, no doubt reflecting the commissioners of the studies. While it is useful for those working in the field of tourism to have some information to illustrate the importance of the sector and any growth that is taking place, it is surprising how few economic impact studies have been undertaken either by tourism organizations or commissioned from consultants. This may be because of the costs involved which if taken from limited budgets would divert resources away from promotional efforts. However, a few tourism organizations, such as Merseyside's, have regularly undertaken impact studies and have used the consumer surveys as a vehicle also for obtaining feedback from visitors about their experience and other information that would be useful in marketing.

Surveys to assess the non-economic impacts of tourism in cities are very rare and have usually been undertaken by academics and their students. In a few cities residents have been surveyed to obtain their views about tourism, although this is more common in smaller cities, towns and villages than the large city with which this book is mainly concerned. Non-economic effects tend to be less tangible than the economic ones and take place over a longer period so that assessing their significance is less easy. If the effects are widely found and of multiple causation it is less easy to attribute them to tourism. However, it would be useful if cities undertook regular surveys to evaluate the wider impacts of tourism and not just the narrow economic ones.

The results that have been discussed in this and earlier chapters demonstrate that in some cities tourism is having a significant effect on the economy, particularly by providing jobs, in assisting the physical regeneration of decaying zones, in transforming the image of cities, in assisting in the attraction of mobile investment and in strengthening the influence of international culture in cities. The fact that this influence varies from one city to another, and is sometimes weak in the cities that are most hopeful of the impact of tourism is a topic that will be discussed in the next chapter.

Chapter 10

Conclusion

The aim of this book has been to map the nature and characteristics of tourism in large cities. It has been shown that tourism is growing rapidly in many cities around the world, that it is becoming a driving force in their economies although it generally remains only one component in their multi-functional economies rather than dominating, that its expansion is a conjunction of demand and supply trends, that it is a multi-motivated travel destination, that visitors generally stay only for a short period, that thousands of jobs are being created which are predominantly all the year round, that the industry has a multi-faceted character and that it has links to many other strands in the life of the city. Many of the projects with which tourism is connected are multi-purpose so that its contribution is often difficult to evaluate. Because of its disparate nature it can sometimes be overlooked but at other times it can be a prism which reflects the manner in which the large city is adapting itself in a rapidly changing world. Until relatively recently, tourism, that is the attempt to win visitors, was a often a small-scale activity and unrecognized, but now it is becoming much larger and the various components are beginning to recognize that they are part of the tourism industry. This chapter will examine the nature of the urban tourism complex, whether there is a complex and whether there is a coalition of interests focusing on tourism. It will then consider the factors which influence success in tourism followed by a discussion on whether there is an urban destination lifecycle.

THE URBAN TOURISM COMPLEX

The concept of an industrial complex or cluster has become very fashionable in recent years. It can be defined as a group of firms, geographically concentrated in space, which are linked through a focus on a particular activity and which gain strength and the potential for growth through their links. Not all the firms are in the core activity and many will have links with other activities. There may be an element of specialization which produces external economies of scale. Today a key ingredient is perceived to be the manner in which firms share information and thus reinforce their ability to compete in their economic environment. The cluster thus becomes a learning region. The prime example of a complex today is Silicon Valley in California where there is research and manufacture of advanced electronics with associated supporting activites including venture capital firms. How far can this concept be applied to urban tourism?

The focus for any urban tourism complex is a group of enterprises which need to attract consumers including a significant element of tourists. As has been discussed earlier, these would include visitor attractions, the conference and exhibition sector, the arts and entertainment, sport, hotels, catering, some aspects of retailing and possibly the transport sector. While some of these activities could and do operate independently, they gain greater strength and in some cases viability by being clustered in the city centre. By being close to each other they reinforce the attractiveness of the area and thus are able to bring in more consumers. Many examples of this effect have been noted earlier in the book; the convention industry is more successful when there are other attractions nearby, festival marketplaces cannot function on their own, a cluster of related visitor attractions will have greater pulling power and tourism benefits more from sports facilities when they are adjacent to the leisure industries of the downtown area. Related to this idea of synergy is the concept of a critical mass. When a certain size has been reached, there is the potential for further growth as both consumers and enterprises will be drawn to the area. The latter will consist of visitor attractions, hotels, restaurants, etc. Of course, the possibility of growth assumes a continuation of the expansion of demand and the absence of overwhelming competition.

When the industry has reached a certain size, when the enterprises in the various components recognize the importance of tourists, it is likely that they will begin to come together in networks, initially narrow (e.g. hoteliers) and later as a broader coalition of interests to campaign for the interests of the industry. These campaigns will mainly consist of putting pressure on the public sector to spend money on anything from promotion, special events, new or improved visitor attractions, upgraded physical environments, etc. In some of these campaigns the tourism industry will be joined by other industries such as the construction industry. The public sector is itself a part of this coalition either indirectly through its ownership of visitor attractions or directly when it accepts the need to develop the industry.

SUCCESS IN URBAN TOURISM

How do we explain the differing success which cities have had in attracting visitors? What have been the factors which have enabled some cities to be successful, and others which have caused some cities to be less successful? What should a city do to be successful? Of course, there is no homogeneous urban tourism, rather, cities attract visitors for a variety of reasons from culture to sport to fun so that any list of factors has to be weighted by the characteristics of the type of tourism that has been developed or is desired. Here are some key features necessary for success:

- The size and characteristics of the local population. Many tourism resources have been developed for and are maintained, at least in part for the local population, from museums to restaurants. The richer the population, the better these resources are likely to be. In addition, a large population will encourage a sizeable flow of visits to friends and relatives.

- The size and characteristics of the local business economy. High order business activities (e.g. head offices) will stimulate business travel and corporate meetings. Business travel has often been the initial stimulus for the development of air routes and hotels, which later can be used by the leisure traveller.
- Heritage. An appealing heritage is a very important reason why many people want to visit a particular city. This can include historic buildings and cityscapes as well as cultural associations and ambience from the past.
- Scenery. Although scenery is not usually considered important, waterfront cities and those with a backcloth of mountains have proved very attractive to visitors, which, as well as giving a great experience, also provide a dramatic image.
- Leadership and partnerships. Having a strategic vision is essential if a city is to move forward in the development of tourism resources and in the promotion of them to visitors. In many cities this has come from the public sector, a strong mayor in the case of Baltimore, but in other cities the vision has come from either a private sector coalition or a public–private partnership. This type of leadership is very important in those older industrial cities which have lacked strong appeal in the past. This vision must be pursued consistently over a long period.
- Regional and state factors. Capital cities, as showcases for the state, attract much greater funding, both public and private, than other cities, for museums, theatres and special events, which is to their great benefit as regards tourism resources. More recently cities in poorer regions have attracted funds for regeneration and in some cases these have been used to create tourism resources.
- The creation of uniqueness. The last chapter discussed the standardization of cities and the threat that this poses to tourism. Cities will only attract visitors if they can offer something different, special or unique. This might come from heritage and scenery as listed above, but can be created. The case of Bilbao illustrated the role which architecture can play in this respect. Cities are seeking to create these land-mark buildings whether they are a museum or convention centre. In the past Las Vegas was able to exploit its unique position as the only legal gambling centre in the USA.
- Image. Linked with uniqueness is the projection of a strong image, without which the potential visitor will not be aware of a place or want to visit. This image can be developed via new buildings (museums, stadiums, hotels, etc.) and special events, but capital cities have the great advantage that their image is constantly being propagated by the media.

The distribution of these factors is uneven. Some cities start with a tremendous advantage over others. One theme that has emerged in this book is the difference between capital cities and older industrial cities. But the situation is not static and a city's position in the hierarchy of tourism cities is not fixed for all time. New developments and opportunities are emerging all the time and the entrepreneurial city will be quick to grasp these. In addition, the urban tourist is looking for novelty. There is no loyalty to cities, and each decision the tourist makes where to go this year is an opportunity for a city.

COMPETITION BETWEEN CITIES

This fickleness of the tourist is one reason why cities are in competition with each other. They are not only competing for visitors but for conventions, sports events (and teams in the USA), cultural festivals, branches of museums and other visitor attractions, funding and also economic investments. But this competition has potential costs. In order to win either visitors or the resources listed above they must invest themselves. As was shown in the last chapter, there are many instances where funds have been diverted from other expenditures such as schools or welfare. Competition also results in the over-production of resources; there is too much capacity in convention centres, museums, theatres and special events. There are not enough visitors to go round and some investments, those regarded as the weakest, will fail. Their failure may be attributed to poor design, not being fashionable or bad management, but there is also the context of competition and over-supply. Providing resources in tourism is speculative and sometimes speculation ends in failure with the public sector usually paying the cost.

IS THERE AN URBAN DESTINATION LIFECYCLE?

The area destination lifecycle originally proposed by Butler (1980) has attracted a great deal of attention in tourism studies and has been applied particularly to seaside resorts and island destinations. Can this model be applied to cities and especially to large cities? There are a number of issues here (Grabler, 1997). Is the city a product or a bundle of products? What indicators should be used to measure whether the city is growing or declining? How long a period is necessary to determine whether the city is passing through different phases? What factors might cause a decline of demand? What role might inter-city competition play in the decline of demand?

The large city differs from many other types of destination in being not just one product but a bundle of products; it is a multi-purpose destination. In Chapter 5 the visitor attraction lifecycle was discussed. Within a city different attractions may go through a lifecycle, but it is unlikely that they will all be at the same stage simultaneously with the consequence that while one is declining, another will be growing. Given today's management training, most attraction managers are aware of the lifecycle and are planning either to rejuvenate their product or to introduce special events to maintain visitor numbers. A city that is successful is also likely to be gaining additional attractions thus compensating for any that are going into decline. Cities are also developing special events to stimulate visitor numbers.

One reason why visitor numbers at a destination may decline is that it becomes too successful. In the case of a city such as Venice, there is a finite carrying capacity (Van der Borg, 1998). Its narrow streets can only take so many visitors and when there is congestion, the visitor experience deteriorates to the extent that potential tourists may be deterred from coming. In most large cities tourism is spread over quite a large area with the result that congestion is only serious at a few points, the urban honeypots, in the system. Many popular visitor attractions have introduced timed entry to obviate bottlenecks in the system or are opening for longer hours during the peak season. As yet there are no signs that the most popular tourist cities are losisg trade because of congestion.

Competition from other urban tourism destinations could be another reason why a city's visitor numbers decline. With so many cities competing in the marketplace and with tourists being so fickle, no city can sit on its laurels and assume that it will continue to be a success. Decline for this reason cannot be ruled out and if it is followed by a lack of investment as happened with seaside resorts, could result in a spiral of decline. However, there is no evidence of this at the moment.

Most cities are experiencing a growth of visitors. The trend is not continuously upwards, and this is not unexpected. Visitors numbers may stagnate or fall for a year or two because of various factors. Recessions affect both domestic and international visitor flows. International movements are affected by currency changes and the fear of terrorism. Most of these factors are temporary and cause only a blip on the growth path. Glabler's (1997) interpretation that the figures of the early 1990s suggested that cities were reaching the stagnation phase was therefore premature. Of course, there can be no certainty that tourism in cities or even any type of tourism will continue to grow, even though this appears likely at present. The need to constrain the use of fossil fuels could force governments to impose fuel taxes which could so raise costs that travel is reduced. But the unpopularity of such a move is likely to delay any action for a long time.

THE NEED FOR MORE RESEARCH

The study of urban tourism is still a relatively new subject, and despite the burgeoning literature in the 1990s, there is still much scope for research. Many firms and promotional bodies are beginning to undertake research and surveys, but the type of question asked is still very simple and basic, getting little further than who are you; where do come from; what have you come for; how long are you staying; and who did you come with? There is a need for much more research about the nature of demand and on the interaction of tourism with the local economy and society.

On the demand side there is a need for research on how tourists come to decide to visit a city; do they have many cities in mind from which one is selected; how have they become interested in these cities or a particular city; what is the role of image and the visibility which cities have in the media; are they attracted by particular aspects of the city (e.g. visitor attractions) or just the city in general; and what is the appeal of cities? For the longer term, questions could be asked about how regularly people visit cities; has a foreign short city break become as usual as having a two-week summer holiday; are different cities visited each time; what characteristics would cause a return visit; and how are cities chosen in succession? There is also need for more in-depth research on the visitor experience; how was the time filled; what was expected to be the most interesting and what was found to be the most interesting experience in the city; as well as the questions that are being asked about basic satisfaction with the visit (e.g. quality of experience in hotels, visitor attractions, restaurants and transport).

Academics have become interested in the relationship between tourism and the local community, whether there is any clash between developments in tourism and local culture and local needs. In many cities academics often give the appearance of having an issue and to be looking for evidence to prove it. When evidence is presented, it comes from such small and apparently insignificant groups that it hardly supports the idea that there is a major issue here. What is needed is more extensive research on this type of local impact and how widespread is the feeling that tourism is having a negative impact on local life.

Within urban studies the concept of growth coalitions and public–private partnerships has been very important since the late 1980s, but relatively little research has focused on tourism. Much of the research has involved major regeneration projects in which there is a tourism component, but this aspect has received very little attention. Research is required on the growth coalitions for tourism and into the nature of the public–private partnerships that have evolved. Which groups are involved; what is their motivation; and what effect do they have? Hoteliers, visitor attraction operators and air industry firms have an obvious interest in the growth of tourism in a city, but what about other economic activities and how does the city government perceive its interest? Property owners, developers and construction firms often show an interest, but their links with tourism and its growth are more indirect. A comparative study of the composition of tourism marketing operations would be useful here. The question of whether there is a tourism industry or a cluster of activities was mentioned in Chapter 1, and research on this topic is also warranted. How important does tourism in a city have to be before it generates a community of interest with networking and common efforts to boost the industry?

References

Ahmadi, M. (1989) *The Economic Impact of Tourism in Maryland: A Multiregional Analysis*. Baltimore, MD: Department of Economics and Employment Development.

Allwinkle, S.J. and Speed, C. (1996) Tourism and cultural cities: a sustainable perspective. In M. Robinson and P. Callaghan (eds) *Tourism and Culture*. Sunderland: Business Education Publishers.

American Association of Museums (1992) *Data Report from the 1989 National Museums Survey*. Washington, DC: American Association of Museums.

Arbel, A. and Pizam, A. (1977) Some determinants of hotel location: the tourist's inclinations. *Journal of Travel Research*, **15**, 18–22.

Ashworth, G.J. (1989a) Urban tourism: an imbalance in attention. In C.P. Cooper (ed.) *Progress in Tourism, Recreation and Hospitality Management*. London, Belhaven.

Ashworth, G.J. (1989b) Accommodation and the historic city. *Built Environment*, **15**, 92–100.

Ashworth, G.J. and Tunbridge, J.E. (1990) *The Tourist-Historic City*. London, Belhaven.

Ashworth, G.J. and Voogd, H. (1990) *Selling the City: Marketing Approaches in Public Sector Urban Planning*. London: Belhaven.

Ashworth, G.J. and Voogd, H. (1991) Can places be sold for tourism? In G. Ashworth and B. Goodall (eds) *Marketing Tourism Places*. London: Routledge.

Ashworth, G.J. and Voogd, H. (1996) Marketing of Tourism Places: What are we doing? In M. Uysal (ed.) *Global Tourist Behavior*. New York: International Business Products.

Ashworth, G.J., White, P.E. and Winchester, H.P.M. (1988) The red-light district in the west European city: a neglected aspect of the urban landscape. *Geoforum*, **19**, 201–212.

Astroff, M.T. and Abbey, J.R. (1998) *Convention Sales and Services*. 5th edn. Cranbury, NJ, Waterbury Press.

Atkinson, D. and Laurier, E. (1998) A sanitised city? Social exclusion at Bristol's 1996 International Festival of the Sea. *Geoforum*, **29**, 199–206.

AUMA (2001) *AUMA Handbuch Messeplatz Deutschland, 2001*. Cologne: AUMA.

Avraham, E. (2000) Cities and their news media images. *Cities*, **17**, 363–370.

Baade, R.A. (1995) Stadiums, professional sports and city economies: an analysis of United States experience. In J. Bale and O. Moen (eds) *The Stadium and the City*. Keele: Keele University Press.

Baade, R.A. (1996) Professional sports as catalysts for metropolitan economic development. *Journal of Urban Affairs*, **18**, 1–17.

Baade, R.A. and Dye, R.E. (1988a) An analysis of the economic rationale for public subsidization of sports stadiums. *Annals of Regional Science*, **23**, 37–42.

Baade, R.A. and Dye, R.E. (1988b) Sports stadiums and area development: a critical review. *Economic Development Quarterly*, **2**, 265–275.

Baade, R.A. and Dye, R.E. (1990) The impact of stadiums and professional sports on metropolitan area development. *Growth and Change*, **21** (2), 1–14.

Baade, R.A. and Sanderson, A.R. (1997) The employment effect of teams and sports facilities. In R.G. Noll and A. Zimbalist (eds) *Sports, Jobs and Taxes: The Economic Impact of Sports Teams and Stadiums*, Washington, DC: Brookings Institution Press.

Bagguley, P. (1990) Gender and labour flexibility in hotel and catering. *Services Industry Journal*, **10**, 737–747.

Bale, J. (1989) *Sports Geography*. London, E & F.N. Spon.

Bale, J. and Moen, O. (1995) *The Stadium and the City*. Keele: Keele University Press.

Ball, R.M. and Metcalfe, M. (1992) Tourism at the margin: pitts, pots and potential in the Potteries locality. *Proceedings of the Tourism in Europe Conference: The 1992 Durham Conference*. Newcastle: Centre for Travel and Tourism.

Bamberger, R.J. and Parham, D.W. (1984) Leveraging amenity infrastructure: Indianapolis' economic development strategy. *Urban Land*, **43** (11), 12–18.

Barnett, R.R. (1984) Tourism's contribution to employment in York. Unpublished report to York City Council.

Berg van den, L., Borg van der, J. and Meer van der, J. (1995) *Urban Tourism: Performance and Strategies in Eight European Cities*. Rotterdam: European Institute for Comparative Urban Research.

Bianchini, F. (1991) Urban renaissance? The arts and urban regeneration process. In S. MacGregor and B. Pimlot (eds) *Tackling the Inner Cites: The 1980s Reviewed, Prospects for the 1990s*. Oxford: Clarendon Press.

Bianchini, F. (1994) Night cultures, night economies. *Town and Country Planning*, **63**, 308–310.

Bianchini, F. (1995) Night cultures, night economies. *Planning Practice and Research*, **10**, 121–126.

Bianchini, F., Fisher, M., Montgomery, J. and Walpole, K. (1988) *City Centre Culture: The Role of the Arts in the Revitalization of Towns and Cities*. Manchester: Centre for Local Economic Strategies.

Bassett, K. (1993) Urban cultural strategies and urban regeneration: a case study and critique. *Environment and Planning A*, **25**, 1773–1788.

Baudrillard, J. (1988) In M. Poster (ed) *Jean Baudrillard: Selected Writings*, Cambridge: Polity Press.

Beaverstock, J.V., Taylor, P.J. and Smith, R.G. (1999) A rosta of world cities. *Cities*, **16**, 445–458.

Beioley, S. (1999) Short and sweet: the UK short break market. *Insights*, May, 63–78.

Bennett, B. (1991) The shape of things to come: Expo 88. *Cultural Studies*, **5** (1), 30–51.

Berkowitz, B.L. (1984) Economic policy really works: Baltimore, Maryland. In R.D. Bingham and J.P. Blair (eds) *Urban Economic Development*. Beverly Hills: Sage.

Berry, B.J.L. (ed.) (1976) *Urbanization and Counterurbanization*. Beverly Hills: Sage.

Birmingham Development Department (1987) *Action Programme for Tourism in Birmingham*. Birmingham: Birmingham City Council.

Birmingham Economic Information Centre (1998) *The Tourism Sector in Birmingham*. Birmingham: Birmingham City Council.

Birmingham Economic Information Centre (1999) *Tourism Strategy for Birmingham*. Birmingham: Birmingham City Council.

Blau, J.R. and Hall, R.H. (1986) The supply of performing arts in metropolitan places. *Urban Affairs Quarterly*, **22**, 42–65.

Booth, P. and Boyle, R. (1993) See Glasgow, see culture. In F. Bianchini and M. Parkinson (eds) *Cultural Policy and Urban Regeneration*. Manchester: Manchester University Press.

Bourdieu, P. (1984) *Distinction*, London: Routledge and Kegan Paul.

Boyer, C. (1992) Cities for sale: merchandising history as South Street. In M. Sorkin (ed.) *Variations on a Theme Park: The New American City and the End of Public Space*. New York: Farrar, Strauss and Giroux.

Boyle, M. and Hughes, G. (1991) The politics of the representation of 'the real': discourses from the Left on Glasgow's role as European City of Culture, 1990. *Area*, **23**, 217–228.

Boyle, M. and Hughes, G. (1994) The politics of urban entrepreneurialism in Glasgow. *Geoforum*, **25**, 453–470.

Bramwell, B. (1993) Planning for tourism in an industrial city. *Town and Country Planning*, **62** (1/2), 17–19.

Bramwell, B. (1997) Strategic planning before and after a mega event. *Tourism Management*, **18**, 167–176.

Bramwell, B. and Rawding, L. (1994) Tourism marketing organizations in industrial cities: organizations, objectives and urban governance. *Tourism Management*, **15**, 425–434.

Bramwell, B. and Rawding, L. (1996) Tourism marketing images of industrial cities. *Annals of Tourism Research*, **23**, 210–220.

Brawn, B.M. (1992) The economic contribution of conventions: the case of Orlando. *Journal of Travel Research*, **30**, (3), 32–37.

British American Arts Association (1989) *Arts and the Changing City: An Agenda for Urban Regeneration*. London: British American Arts Association.

British Tourist Authority and English Tourist Board (1988a) *The Short Break Market*. London: British Tourist Authority.

British Tourist Authority and English Tourist Board (1988b) *The Visiting Friend and Relatives Market*. London: British Tourist Authority.

Bromley, R., Thomas, C. and Millie, A. (2000) Exploring safety concerns in the night-time economy: revitalizing the evening economy. *Town Planning Review*, **71**, 71–96.

Brown, A., O'Connor, J. and Cohen, S. (2000) Local music policies within a global music industry: cultural quarters in Manchester and Sheffield. *Geoforum*, **31**, 437–451.

BTA/ETB (British Tourist Authority and English Tourist Board) (annual) *Visits to Attractions*. London.

BTB/ETB (annual) *Sightseeing*. London.

Buckley, P.J. and Witt, S.F. (1985) Tourism in difficult areas: case studies of Bradford, Bristol, Glasgow and Hamm. *Tourism Management*, **6**, 205–213.

Buckley, P.J. and Witt, S.F. (1989) Tourism in difficult areas II: case studies of Calderdale, Leeds, Manchester and Scunthorpe. *Tourism Management*, **10**, 138–152.

Bull, A. (1991) *The Economics of Travel and Tourism*. Melbourne: Pitman.

Business Ratios (1989) *The Hotel Industry*. Hampton: Business Ratios.

Butler, R.W. (1980) The concept of the tourist area cycle of evolution: implications for the management of resources. *Canadian Geographer*, **24**, 5–12.

Butler, R.W. (1991) West Edmonton Mall as a tourist attraction. *Canadian Geographer*, **35**, 287–295.

Capstick, B. (1985) Museums and tourism. *International Journal of Museum Management and Curatorship*. **4**, 365–372.

Carreras, C. (1995) Mega-events: local strategies and global tourist attractions. In A. Montanari and A.M. Williams (eds) *European Tourism: Regions, Spaces and Restructuring*. Chichester: John Wiley and Sons.

Cazes, G. and Potier, F. (1996) *Le Tourisme Urbain*. Paris: Presses Universitaires de France.

Central London Polytechnic, Leisureworks and DRV Research (1990) *Tourism and the Inner City: An Evaluation of the Impact of Grant Assisted Tourism Projects*. London: HMSO.

Chadwick, P.A. (1987) Concepts, definitions and measures used in travel research. In J.R.B. Ritchie and C.R. Goeldner (eds) *Travel, Tourism and Hospitality Research*. New York: John Wiley.

Champion, A.G. (ed.) (1989) *Counterurbanization*. London: Arnold.

Churchman, C. (1995) Sports stadia and the landscape. *Built Environment*, **21**, 6–24.

Clark, C. (2000) Changes in leisure time: the impact on tourism. *Insights*, A, 103–109.

Clift, S. and Forrest, S. (1999) Gay men and tourism: destinations and holiday motivations. *Tourism Management*, **20**, 615–25.

Collinge, M. (1989) Tourism and urban regeneration. Paper given at the Vision for Cities conference, London.

Collins, M.F. (1991) The economics of sport and sport in the economy: some international comparisons. In C.P. Cooper (ed) *Progress in Tourism, Recreation and Hospitality Management*, vol. 3, London, Belhaven.

Comedia (1991) *Out of Hours: A Study of the Economic and Cultural Life in Twelve Town Centres*. London: Comedia.

Comedia Consultants (1989) *Developing a Cultural Industries Strategy for Coventry*. Coventry: Coventry City Council.

Coopers and Lybrand Deloitte Tourism Leisure Consultancy Services (1990) *UK Conference Market Survey*. London: Coopers and Lybrand Deloitte.

Costley, T. (2000) The British conference market. *Insights*, January 2000, B33–45.

Couch, C. and Farr, S.-J. (2000) Museums, galleries, tourism and regeneration: some experiences from Liverpool. *Built Environment*, **26**, 152–163.

Cope, R. and Barrie, N. (2001) *European City Reports*. London: Travel and Tourism Intelligence.

Countryside Agency (1999) *Leisure Day Visits: Report of the 1998 UK Day Visits Survey*. Northampton: Countryside Agency.

Crilley, D. (1993) Architecture as advertising: constructing the image of redevelopment. In G. Kearns and C. Philo (eds) *Selling Places: The City as Cultural Capital, Past and Present*. Oxford: Pergamon Press.

Cuadrado-Roura, J.R. and Rubalcaba-Bermejo, L. (1998) Specialisation and competition amongst European cities: a new approach through fair and exhibition activities. *Regional Studies*, **32**, 133–148.

Cwi, D. (1980) Models of the role arts in economic development. In W. Hendon, J. Shanahan and A. McDonald (eds) *Economic Policy for the Arts*. Cambridge, MA: Abt Books.

Davidson, R. (1994) *Business Travel*. Harlow: Longman.

Davies, L. (1996) Sports tourism and economic development. In M.E. Robinson *et al.* (eds) *Culture as a Tourist Product*. Sunderland: Business Education Publishers.

Deloitte and Touche Consulting Group: Hospitality Division (1997) *A Survey of Continental European Visitor Attractions*. St Albans: Deloitte and Touche Consulting Group.

Denman, R. (1988) *A Response to the Visits to Friends and Relatives Market*. London: English Tourist Board.

Dobson, N. (1996) Is sport a sustainable option for Sheffield? In M.E. Robinson *et al.* (eds) *Culture as a Tourist Product*. Sunderland: Business Education Publishers.

Dodson, B. and Kilian, D. (1998) From port to playground: the redevelopment of the Victoria and Alfred Waterfront, Capetown. In D. Tyler, Y. Guerier and M. Robertson (eds) *Managing Tourism in Cities: Policy, Process and Practice*. Chichester: John Wiley and Sons.

Donnison, D. and Middleton, A. (eds) (1987) *Regenerating the Inner City: Glasgow's Experience*. London: Routledge and Kegan Paul.

DRV Research (1986) *An Economic Impact Study of the Tourist and Associated Arts Developments in Merseyside*. Bournemouth: DRV Research.

Economic Research Associates (1984) *Community Economic Impact of the Olympic Games in Los Angeles*. Los Angeles: Economic Research Associates.

Egan, D.J. and Nield, K. (2000) Towards a theory of intraurban hotel location. *Urban Studies*, **37**, 611–621.

EIU (1993) The market for cultural tourism in Europe. *Travel and Tourism Analyst*, 6, 30–46.

English Tourist Board (1984) *The UK Conference Market: Providing for the Future*. London: English Tourist Board.

Essex, S. and Chalkley, B. (1998) Olympic Games: catalyst of urban change. *Leisure Studies*, **17**, 187–206.

ETB Research Services (annual) *Visits to Attractions*. London: English Tourist Board.

ETC Research and Intelligence (2000) *Sightseeing in the UK 1999*. London: English Tourism Council.

Exhibition Industries Federation (1989) *The UK Exhibition Industry*. London: Exhibition Industries Federation.

Exhibition Industries Federation (1991) *The UK Exhibition: The Facts*. London: Polytechnic of North London.

Exhibition Venues Association (2000) *UK Exhibition Facts*, vol. 12, Mayfield, East Sussex.

Fainstein, S.S., Gordon, I. and Harloe, M. (1992) *Divided Cities: New York and London in the Contemporary World*. Oxford: Blackwell.

Farrell, K. (1980) Insights into site selection. *Restaurant Business*, 1 July, 115–120.

Fenich, G.G. (1992) Convention center development: pros, cons and unanswered questions. *International Journal of Hospitality Management*, **11**, 183–196.

Fodness, D. (1990) Consumer perceptions of tourist attractions. *Journal of Travel Research*, **28**, 3–9.

Foglesong, R. (1999) Walt Disney World and Orlando: deregulation as a strategy for tourism. In D.R. Judd and S.S. Fainstein (eds) *The Tourist City*. New Haven, CT: Yale University Press.

Foley, P. (1991) The impact of the World Student Games on Sheffield. *Environment and Planning C*, **9**, 65–78.

Frechtling, D.C. (1987) Assessing the impacts of travel and tourism-introduction to travel impact estimation. In J.R.B. Ritchie and C.R. Goeldner (eds) *Travel, Tourism and Hospitality Research*. New York: John Wiley.

Frey, B.S. and Pommenehne, W.W. (1989) *Muses and Markets: Explorations in the Economics of the Arts*. Oxford: Blackwell.

Frieden, B. and Sagalyn, L.B. (1989) *Downtown Inc: How America Rebuilds its Cities*. Cambridge, MA: MIT Press.

Gaardboe, M. (2000) Urban tourism: global projects of architectural excellence. *Built Environment*, **26**, 130–141.

Gardiner, C. (1991) The West End Theatre Audience Survey 1990/1. *Cultural Trends*, **11**, 18.

Gartrell, R.B. (1994) *Destination Marketing for Convention and Visitor Bureaus*. Dubque: Kendall/Hunt Publishing.

Getz, D. (1991a) *Festivals, Special Events and Tourism*. New York: Van Nostrand.

Getz, D. (1991b) Festivals, special events and tourism. In D.E. Hawkins and J.R.B. Ritchie (eds) *World Travel and Tourism Review*, vol. 1. Wallingford: CAB International.

Getz, D. (1992) Trends in event tourism. In J.R.B. Ritchie and D. Hawkins (eds) *World Travel and Tourism Review*, vol. 2. Wallingford: CAB International.

Getz, D. (1997) *Event Management and Event Tourism*. New York: Cognizant Communication Corporation.

Gilbert, D.C. (1990) Conceptual issues in the meaning of tourism. In C.P. Cooper (ed.) *Progress in Tourism, Recreation and Hospitality Management*, vol. 2. London: Belhaven.

Glaser, J.R. (1986) USA museums in context. In Scottish Museums Council (ed.) *The American Museum Experience: In Search of Excellence*. London: HMSO.

Go, F. (1991) The international conventions and meetings market. In D.E. Hawkins and J.R.B. Ritchie (eds) *World Travel and Tourism Review*, vol. 1. Wallingford: CAB International.

Gold, J.R. and Ward, S.V. (eds) (1994) *Place Promotion: The Use of Publicity and Marketing to Sell Towns and Regions*. Chichester: John Wiley and Sons.

Gomez, M.V. (1998) Reflective images: the case of urban regeneration in Glasgow and Bilbao. *International Journal of Urban and Regional Research*, **22**, 106–121.

Gonzalez, J. (1993) Bilbao: culture, citzenship and quality of life. In F. Bianchini and M. Parkinson (eds) *Culture and Urban Regeneration*. Manchester: Manchester University Press.

Goodall, B. (1989) Tourist accommodation: a destination perspective. *Built Environment*, **15**, 78–81.

Goodwin, M. (1993) The city as commodity: the contested spaces of urban development. In G. Kearns and C. Philo (eds) *Selling Places: The City as Cultural Capital, Past and Present*. Oxford: Pergamon.

Goss, J. (1996) Disquiet on the waterfront: reflections on nostalgia and utopia in the urban archetypes of festival marketplaces. *Urban Geography*, **17**, 221–247.

Gottdiener, M. (1997) *The Theming of America; Dreams, Visions and Commercial Spaces*. Boulder, CO: Westview Press.

Gottdiener, M., Collins, C.C. and Dickens, D.R. (1999) *Las Vegas: The Social Reproduction of an All-American City*. Oxford: Blackwell Publishers.

Grabler, K. (1997) Cities and the destination life cycle. In J.A. Mazanec (ed.) *International City Tourism: Analysis and Strategy*. London: Pinter.

Grabler, K., Mazanec, J. and Wober, K. (1996) Strategic marketing for urban tourism: analysing competition among European tourist cities. In C.M. Law (ed.) *Tourism in Major Cities*. London: International Thomson Business Press.

Gratton, C. and Dobson, N. (1999) The economic benefits of hosting major sports events. *Insights*, July, A31–36.

Gratton, C. and Taylor, P. (1988a) The Olympic Games: an economic analysis. *Leisure Management*, **8** (3), 32–34.

Gratton, C.A. and Taylor, P. (1988b) The Seoul Olympics. *Leisure Management*, **8** (12), 54–59.

Gratton, C. and Taylor, P.D. (1996) Impact of festival events: a case study of Edinburgh. In G.J. Ashworth and A.G.J. Dietvorst (eds) *Tourism and Spatial Formations*. Wallingford: CAB International.

Graveline, D. (1984) Convention centres. *Urban Land*, **43** (7), 2–5.

Gray, H.P. (1970) *International Travel – International Trade*. Lexington, MA: Heath Lexington.

Greater Glasgow Tourist Board and Convention Bureau (1995) *Glasgow Tourism Strategy and Action Plan (1995–1999)*. Glasgow: Greater Glasgow Tourist Board.

Greenhalgh, P. (1988) *Ephemeral Vistas: The Expositions Universelles, Great Exhibitions and World Fairs, 1851–1939*. Manchester: Manchester University Press.

Greenhill, E.H. (1988) Counting visitors or visitors who count? In R. Lumley (ed.) *The Museum Time Machine*. London: Routledge.

Griffiths, R. (1993) The politics of cultural policy in urban regeneration strategies. *Policy and Politics*, **21**, 39–46.

Griffiths, R. (1995) Cultural strategies and new modes of urban intervention. *Cities*, **12**, 253–265.

Griffiths, R. (1998) Making sameness: place marketing and the new urban entrepreneurialism. In N. Oatley (ed.) *Cities, Economic Competition and Urban Policy*. London: Paul Chapman.

Griffiths, R., Bassett, K. and Smith, I. (1999) Cultural policy and the cultural economy in Bristol. *Local Economy*, **14**, 257–264.

Guggenheim (1999) *Report: Second Anniversary*. Bilbao, Guggenheim Bilbao.

Guggenheim (2000) *Report: Third Anniversary*. Bilbao, Guggenheim Bilbao.

Gunn, C. (1988) *Tourism Planning*. New York: Taylor and Francis.

Guskind, R. (1988) The biggest photo opportunity of them all. *Planning (APA)*, **54** (7), 4–11.

Guskind, R. and Pierce, N.R. (1988) Faltering festivals. *National Journal*, **20** (38), 2307–2311.

Hague, D., Jones, T., Pandit, N.R. and Richardson, P.K. (1990) The economic impact of the Manchester Olympics. Unpublished report to the Manchester Bid Committee.

Haider, D. (1992) Place Wars: new realities of the 1990s. *Economic Development Quarterly*, **6**, 127–134.

Hall, C.M. (1992) *Hallmark Tourist Events: Impacts, Management and Planning*. London: Belhaven Press.

Hall, C.M. (1996) Hallmark events and urban reimaging strategies: coercion, community and the Sydney 2000 Olympics. In L.C. Harrison and W. Husbands (eds) *Practicing Responsible Tourism: International Case Studies*. New York: John Wiley and Sons.

Hall, C.M. (1998) The politics of decision making and top-down planning: Darling Harbour, Sydney. In D. Tyler, Y. Guerrier and M. Robertson (eds) *Managing Tourism in Cities*. Chichester: John Wiley and Sons.

Hall, T. and Hubbard, P. (1996) The entrepreneurial city: new urban patterns: new urban geographies. *Progress in Human Geography*, **20**, 153–174.

Hall, T. and Hubbard, P. (eds) (1998) *The Entrepreneurial City: Geographies of Politics, Regimes and Representation*. Chichester: John Wiley and Sons.

Hamilton, B.W. and Kahn, P. (1997) Baltimore's Camden Yards Ballparks. In R.G. Noll and A. Zimbalist (eds) *Sports, Jobs and Taxes: The Economic Impact of Sports Teams and Stadiums*. Washington, DC: Brookings Institution Press.

Hannigan, J. (1998) *Fantasy City: Pleasure and Profit in the Postmodern Metropolis*. London: Routledge.

Harvey, D. (1989) From managerialism to entrepreneurialism: the transformation of urban governance in late capitalism. *Geografiska Annaler*, **71B**, 3–17.

Haskell, F. (2000) *The Ephemeral Museum: Old Master Paintings and the Rise of the Art Exhibition*. New Haven, CT: Yale University Press.

Heath, T. and Strickland, R. (1997) The twenty-four hour city concept. In T. Oc and S. Tiesdale (eds) *Safer Cities: Reviving the Public Realm*. London: P. Chapman.

Hendon, W. and Shaw, D. (1987) The arts and urban development. In G. Gappert (ed.) *The Future of Winter Cities*. Beverly Hills: Sage.

Henry, I.P. and Paramio-Salcines, J.L. (1998) Sport, culture and urban regimes: the case of Bilbao. In M.F. Collins and I.S. Cooper (eds) *Leisure Management, Issues and Applications*. Wallingford: CAB International.

Henry, I.P. and Paramio-Salcines, J.L. (1999) Sport and the analysis of symbolic regimes: a case study of the City of Sheffield. *Urban Affairs Review*, **34**, 641–666.

Herron Associates Inc (1991) *1991 World Gymnastics Championships Impact Report*. Indianapolis: Herron Associates Inc.

Hewison, R. (1991) Commerce and culture. In J. Corner and S. Harvey (eds) *Enterprise and Heritage: Crosscurrents of National Culture*. London: Routledge.

Higham, J. (1999) Sport as an avenue of tourism development: an analysis of the positive and negative impacts of sports tourism. *Current Issues in Tourism*, **2**, 82–90.

Hill, C.R. (1996) *Olympic Politics*. Manchester: Manchester University Press.

Hinch, T.D. (1996) Urban tourism: perpectives on sustainability. *Journal of Sustainable Tourism*, **4**, 95–109.

Holcombe, B. (1993) Revisioning place: de- and re-constructing the image of the industrial city.

In G. Kearns and C. Philo (eds) *Selling Places: The City as Cultural Capital, Past and Present*. Oxford: Pergamon Press.

Holcombe, B. and Luongo, M. (1996) Gay tourism in the United States. *Annals of Tourism Research*, **23**, 711–13.

Honigsbaum, M. (2001) McGuggenheim? *Guardian*, 27 January, 4.

Hooper-Greenhill, E. (1994) *Museums and Their Visitors*. London: Routledge.

Hoyle, B.S., Pinder, D.A. and Hussain, M.S. (1988) *Revitalising the Waterfront: International Dimensions of Dockland Redevelopment*. London: Belhaven.

Hughes, C.G. (1982) The employment and economic benefits of tourism reappraised. *Tourism Management*, **3**, 167–176.

Hughes, C.G. (1988) Conference tourism: a salesman's dream. *Tourism Management*, **9**, 235–238.

Hughes, G. and Boyle, M. (1992) Place boosterism: political contention, leisure and culture in Glasgow. In J. Sugden and C. Knox (eds) *Leisure in the 1990s: Rolling back the Welfare State*. Eastbourne: Leisure Studies Association.

Hughes, H.L. (1986) Tourism and the live performance of opera and classical music. *Journal of Arts Policy and Management*, **2** (3), 12–16.

Hughes, H.L. (1989a) Tourism and the arts. *Tourism Management*, **10**, 97–99.

Hughes, H.L. (1989b) Entertainment. In S.F. Witt and L. Moutinho (eds) *Tourism Marketing and Management Handbook*. New Jersey: Prentice Hall.

Hughes, H.L. (1993) Olympic tourism and urban regeneration. *Festival Management and Event Tourism*, **1**, 157–162.

Hughes, H.L. (1997a) Holidays and homosexual identity. *Tourism Management*, **18**, 3–7.

Hughes, H.L. (1997b) Urban tourism and the performing arts. In P.E. Murphy (ed.) *Quality Management in Urban Tourism*. Chichester: John Wiley and Sons.

Hughes, H.L. (1998a) Theatre in London and the inter-relationship with tourism. *Tourism Management*, **19**, 445–452.

Hughes, H.L. (1998b) Sexuality, tourism and space: the case of gay visitors to Amsterdam. In D. Tyler, Y. Guerrier and M. Robertson (eds) *Managing Tourism in Cities: Policy, Process and Practice*. Chichester: John Wiley and Sons.

Hughes, H.L. (2000a) The elusive cultural tourist. In M. Robinson *et al.* (eds) *Reflections on International Tourism: Expressions of Culture and Meaning in Tourism*. Sunderland: Business Education Publishers.

Hughes, H.L. (2000b) *Arts, Entertainment and Tourism*. Oxford: Butterworth-Heinemann.

Hula, R.C. (1990) The two Baltimores. In D. Judd and M. Parkinson (eds) *Leadership and Urban Regeneration: Cities in North America and Europe*. Beverly Hills: Sage.

Imrie, R. and Thomas, H. (eds) (1999) *British Urban Policy: An Evaluation of Urban Development Corporations*. London: Sage.

Jansen-Verbeke, M. (1986) Inner city tourism, resources, tourists and promoters. *Annals of Tourism Research*, **13**, 79–100.

Jansen-Verbeke, M. (1988) *Leisure, Recreation and Tourism in Inner Cities*. Amsterdam: Netherlands Geographical Studies.

Jansen-Verbeke, M. (1989) Inner cities and urban tourism in the Netherlands: new challenges for local authorities. In P. Bramham *et al.* (eds) *Leisure and Urban Processes*. London: Routledge.

Jansen-Verbeke, M. (1990) Leisure + Shopping = Tourism product mix. In G. Ashworth and B. Goodall (eds) *Marketing Tourism Places*. London: Routledge.

Jansen-Verbeke, M. (1998) The synergism between shopping and tourism. In W. Theobald (ed.) *Global Tourism*. Oxford: Butterworth-Heinemann.

Jansen-Verbeke, M. and van Rekom, J. (1996) Scanning museum visitors: urban tourism marketing. *Annals of Tourism Research*, **23**, 364–375.

Jeanne Beekhuis & Co. (1988) *Expenditure and Characteristics of Visitors to the Inner Harbor and Related Downtown Sites in Baltimore*. Washington, DC: Jeanne Beekhuis & Co.

Jeffrey, D. (1989) *The Impact of Tourism in Yorkshire and Humberside*. Bradford: Department of Environmental Science, University of Bradford.

Jeffrey, D. (1990) Monitoring the growth of tourism related employment at the local level: the application of a census based non-survey method in Yorkshire and Humberside, 1981–1987. *Planning Outlook*, **33**, 108–117.

Johnson, A.T. (1986) Economic policy implications of hosting sports franchises. *Urban Affairs Quarterly*, **22**, 411–433.

Johnson, J. (1991) Attractive experiences. *Leisure Management*, May, 42–45.

Johnstone, S., Southern, A. and Taylor, R. (2000) The midweek match: premiership football and the urban economy. *Local Economy*, **15**, 198–213.

Jones Lang Wootton (1989) *Retail, Leisure and Tourism*. London: English Tourist Board.

Judd, D.R. and Collins, M. (1979) The case of tourism: political coalitions and redevelopment in central cities. In G. Tobin (ed.) *The Changing Structure of Cities: What Happened to the Urban Crisis?* Beverly Hills: Sage.

Judd, D.R. and Fainstein, S.S. (eds) (1999) *The Tourist City*. New Haven, CT: Yale University Press.

JURUE (1983) *The Economic Impact of the International Convention Centre*. Birmingham: JURUE.

Kang, Y.-S. and Perdue, R. (1994) Long-term impact of a mega-event on international tourism to the host country: a conceptual model and the case of the 1988 Seoul Olympics. In M. Uysal (ed.) *Global Tourist Behaviour*. New York: International Business Press.

Karver, J.R. (1982) There's more to lodging than location. *Urban Land*, **41** (10), 14–17.

Kay, P. (1996) Creeping privatisation: the pros and cons of tourism for public art museums and blockbuster exhibitions. In M. Robinson, N. Evans and P. Callaghan (eds) *Tourism and Culture: Culture as a Tourist Product*. Sunderland: Business Education Publishers.

Keating, W.B. (1997) Cleveland: The comeback city. In M. Lauria (ed.) *Deconstructing Urban Regime Theory: Regulating Urban Politics in a Global Economy*. Thousand Oaks, CA: Sage.

Kent, W.E. (1984) Underground Atlanta: the untimely passing of a major tourist attraction. *Journal of Travel Research*, **22**, 2–7.

Kent, W.E. and Chestnutt, J.E. (1991) Undergound Atlanta: resurrected and revisited. *Journal of Travel Research*, **29** (4), 36–39.

Kent, W.E., Shock, J. and Snow, R.E. (1983) Shopping: tourism's unsung hero(ine). *Journal of Travel Research*, **21** (4), 36–39.

Kim, J.-G. *et al.* (1989) *The Impact of the Seoul Olympics on National Development*. Seoul, Korean Development Institute.

Knack, R.E. (1986) Stadiums: the right game plan? *Planning (APA)*, **52** (9), 6–11.

Koster, E.H. (1996) Science culture and cultural tourism. In M. Robinson, N. Evans and P. Callaghan (eds) *Tourism and Culture: Culture as a Tourist Product*, Sunderland: Business Education Publishers.

Kotas, R. (ed.) (1975) *Market Orientation in the Hotel and Catering Industry*. Guildford: University of Surrey Press.

Kotler, P., Haider, D.H. and Rein, I. (1993) *Marketing Places: Attracting Investment and Tourism to Cities, States and Nations*. New York: Free Press.

KPMG Peat Marwick (1993) *The Economic Impact of the International Convention Centre, the National Indoor Arena, Symphony Hall and the National Exhibition Centre on Birmingham and the West Midlands*. London: KPMG.

Krippendorf, J. (1987) *The Holiday Makers: Understanding the Impact of Leisure and Travel*. Oxford: Heinemann Professional Publishing.

Labasse, J. (1984) Les congrès: activité tertiaire de villes privilegiées, *Annales de Geographie*, **88**, 688–703.

Ladkin, A. and Spiller, J. (2000) The European exhibition market. *Travel and Tourism Analyst*, **2**, 49–63.

Laurier, E. (1993) Tackintosh: Glasgow's supplementary gloss. In G. Kearns and C. Philo (eds) *Selling Places: The City as Cultural Capital, Past and Present*. Oxford: Pergamon.

Laventhol and Horwath (1984) Checking into hotel development. *Urban Land*, **43** (2) 12–14.

Law, C.M. (1967) The growth of urban population in England and Wales, 1801–1911. *Institute of British Geographers Transactions*, **41**, 125–145.

Law, C.M. (1985) Urban tourism in the United States. *Urban Tourism Project Working Paper*, No. 4, Salford: Department of Geography, University of Salford.

Law, C.M. (1988) *The Uncertain Future of the Urban Core*. London: Routledge.

Law, C.M. (1991) Tourism as a focus for urban regeneration. In S. Hardy, T. Hart and T. Shaw (eds) *The Role of Tourism in the Urban and Regional Economy*. London: Regional Studies Association.

Law, C.M. (1992) Urban tourism and its contribution to urban regeneration. *Urban Studies*, **29**, 599–618.

Law, C.M. (1993) *Urban Tourism: Attracting Visitors to Large Cities*. London: Mansell.

Law, C. (1994) Manchester's bid for the Millennium Olympic Games. *Geography*, **79**, 222–231.

Law, C.M. (ed.) (1996) *Tourism in Major Cities*. London: International Thomson Business Press.

Law, C.M. (2000) Regenerating the city centre through leisure and tourism. *Built Environment*, **26**, 117–129.

Law, C.M. and Tuppen, J. (1986) *Tourism and Greater Manchester: The Final Report of the Urban Tourism Research Project*. Salford: Department of Geography, University of Salford.

Lawson, F.R. (1985a) *Exhibition Trends 1984*. Guildford: University of Surrey.

Lawson, F.R. (1985b) *Major UK Exhibitions 1983 and 1985*. Guildford: University of Surrey.

Lawson, F.R. and Wilkie, B. (1985) *Major UK Exhibitions 1983 and 1984*. Guildford: University of Surrey.

Lawson, T. (1996) After it's all over. *Geographical Magazine*, **68**, 20–23.

Leiper, N. (1990) Tourist attraction systems. *Annals of Tourism Research*, **17**, 367–384.

Levine, M.V. (1987) Downtown redevelopment as an urban growth strategy: a critical appraisal of the Baltimore renaissance. *Journal of Urban Affairs*, **9**, 103–123.

Ley, D. and Olds, K. (1988) Landscape as spectacle: world fairs and the culture of heroic consumption. *Environment and Planning D: Society and Space*, **6**, 191–212.

Lim, H. (1993) Cultural strategies for revitalizing the city: a review and evaluation. *Regional Studies*, **27**, 589–595.

Listokin, D. (1985) The convention trade: a competitive economic prize. *Real Estate Issues*, **10**, 43–46.

Llewelwyn-Davies, *et al.* (1996) *Four World Cities: A Comparative Study of London, Paris, New York and Tokyo*, London: Llewelwyn-Davies.

Loftman, P. and Nevin, B. (1994) Prestige project developments: economic renaissance or economic myth? A case study of Birmingham. *Local Economy*, **4**, 307–325.

Loftman, P. and Nevin, B. (1995) Prestige projects and urban regeneration in the 1980s and 1990s: a review of benefits and limitations. *Planning Practice and Research*, **10**, 299–315.

Loftman, P. and Nevin, B. (1996) Going for growth: prestige projects in three British cities. *Urban Studies*, **33**, 991–1019.

Lohmann, M. (1991) Evolution of short break holidays. *Tourist Review*, **46**, 14–22.

London Tourist Board (1987) *The Tourism Strategy for London*. London: London Tourist Board.

Lovatt, A. and O'Connor, J. (1995) Cities and the night-time economy. *Planning Practice and Research*, **10**, 127–133.

LTB (annual) (London Tourist Board and Convention Bureau) *Survey among Overseas Visitors to London*. London: LTB.

Lundberg, D.E. (1994) *The Hotel and Restaurant Business*. 6th edn. New York: Van Nostrand.

Lyall, K. (1982) A bicycle made for two: public–private partnerships in Baltimore. In S. Fosler and R. Berger (eds) *Public–private Partnerships in American Cities*. Lexington, MA: Lexington Books.

MacCannell, D. (1976) *The Tourist: A New Theory of the Leisure Class*. New York: Schoken Books.

MacDonald, R. (1996) A study of tourism in Liverpool, Unpublished PhD thesis, University of Durham.

MacLaurin, D.J. and Leong, K. (2000) Strategies for success: how Singapore attracts and retains the convention and trade show industry. *Event Management*, **6**, 93–103.

McCarthy, J. (1998) Dublin's Temple Bar – a case study of culture-led regeneration. *European Planning Studies*, **6**, 271–281.

McCarthy, J. and Lloyd, G. (1999) Discovering culture-led regeneration in Dundee. *Local Economy*, **14**, 264–268.

McInroy, N. and Boyle, M. (1996) The refashioning of civic identity: constructing and consuming the 'New' Glasgow. *Scotlands*, **3**, 70–87.

McNeill, D. (2000) McGuggenisation? National identity and globalisation in the Basque country.

Political Geography, **19**, 473–494.

McNulty, R. (1985) Revitalizing industrial cities through cultural tourism. *International Journal of Environmental Studies*, **25**, 225–228.

Madsen, H. (1992) Place-marketing in Liverpool: a review. *International Journal of Urban and Regional Research*, **6**, 633–640.

Manchester City Council (1991) *Manchester: City of Drama Bid for the Arts 2000 Initiative.* Manchester: Manchester City Council.

Manchester Polytechnic (1985) *Manchester City Centre Theatre Survey.* Manchester: Manchester Polytechnic.

Marketing Manchester Visitor and Convention Bureau (1996) *The 1996 Audit of Tourism Business in Greater Manchester.* Manchester: Marketing Manchester.

Martin, A. (1998) West End theatres impact. *Insights*, September, A31.

MAS Research Marketing and Consulting (1989) *North West Area Short Break Holidays.* London: MAS Research Marketing and Consulting.

Maslow, A.H. (1970) *Motivation and Personality.* New York: Harper and Row.

Mazanec, C. (ed.) (1997) *International City Tourism: Analysis and Strategy.* London: Pinter.

Medlik, S. (1980) *The Business of Hotels.* London: Heinemann.

Merriman, N. (1991) *Beyond the Glass Case: The Past, the Heritage and the Public in Britain.* Leicester: Leicester University Press.

Merseyside Information Services (1991) *Visitors to Merseyside 1990.* Liverpool: Merseyside Information Services.

Middleton, V.T.C. (1988) *Marketing in Travel and Tourism.* London: Heinemann.

Middleton, V.T.C. (1994) *Marketing in Travel and Tourism.* Oxford: Butterworth-Heinemann.

Miestchovich, I.J. and Ragas, W.R. (1986) Stadium parking attracts office developers in New Orleans. *Urban Land*, **45** (6), 14–17.

Mintel (1998a) Eating out. *Mintel Leisure Intelligence*, June 1998.

Mintel (1998b) Football business. *Mintel Leisure Intelligence*, September 1998.

Mintel (1999a) No frills/low cost airlines. *Mintel Leisure Intelligence*, February 1999.

Mintel (1999b) Eating out. *Mintel Leisure Intelligence*, August 1999.

Mintel (1999c) Short breaks abroad. *Mintel Leisure Intelligence*, September 1999.

Mintel (2000a) Eating out. *Mintel Leisure Intelligence*, February 2000.

Mintel (2000b) City breaks. *Mintel Leisure Intelligence*, March 2000.

Mintel (2000c) Short breaks in the UK. *Mintel Leisure Intelligence*, May 2000.

Montgomery, J. (1994) The evening economy of cities. *Town and Country Planning*, **63**, 302–307.

Montgomery, J. (1995a) Urban vitality and the culture of cities. *Planning Practice and Research*, **10**, 101–109.

Montgomery, J. (1995b) The story of Temple Bar: creating Dublin's cultural quarter. *Planning Practice and Research*, **10**, 135–172.

Morphet, J. (1996) The real thing. *Town and Country Planning*, 312–313.

Morrell, B. (1985) *Employment in Tourism.* London: British Tourist Authority.

Mullins, P. (1991) Tourism urbanization. *International Journal of Urban and Regional Research*, **15**, 326–342.

Murphy, P.E. (ed.) (1997) *Quality Management in Urban Tourism.* Chichester: John Wiley and Sons.

Myerscough, J. (1988a) *The Economic Importance of the Arts in Britain.* London: Policy Studies Institute.

Myerscough, J. (1988b) *The Economic Importance of the Arts in Glasgow.* London: Policy Studies Institute.

Myerscough, J. (1991) *Monitoring Glasgow 1990.* Glasgow: Glasgow City Council.

Newman, P. and Smith, I. (2000) Cultural production, place and politics on the South Bank of the Thames. *International Journal of Urban and Regional Research*, **24**, 9–24.

Newsome, T.H. and Comer, J.C. (2000) Changing intra-urban location patterns of major league sports facilities. *Professional Geographer*, **52**, 105–120.

Noll, R.G. and Zimbalist, A. (1997) *Sports, Jobs and Taxes: The Economic Impact of Sports Teams and Stadiums.* Washington, DC: Brookings Institution Press.

Oatley, N. (1996) Sheffield's cultural industries quarter. *Local Economy*, **11**, 172–178.

OPCS (1991) (Office of Population Censuses and Surveys) *Leisure Day Visits in Great Britain 1988/9*. London: HMSO.

Oppermann, M. (1996a) Convention destination images: analysis of association meeting planner's perceptions. *Tourism Management*, **17**, 175–182.

Oppermann, M. (1996b) Convention cities – images and changing fortunes. *Journal of Tourism Studies*, **7**, 10–19.

Oppermann, M. and Chon, K.-S. (1996) Convention participation decision making process. *Annals of Tourism Research*, **24**, 178–191.

Paddison, R. (1993) City marketing, image reconstruction and urban regeneration. *Urban Studies*, **30**, 339–350.

Page, S. (1995) *Urban Tourism*. London: Routledge.

Paine, A. (1993) The university conference market. *Insights*, May, B61.

Pannell Kerr Foster (1987) *Trends in the Hotel Industry*. Pannell Kerr Foster.

Parker, R.E. (1999) Las Vegas: casino gambling and local culture. In D.R. Judd and S.S. Fainstein (eds) *The Tourist City*. New Haven, CT: Yale University Press.

Pearce, D. (1987) *Tourism Today: A Geographical Analysis*. Harlow: Longman.

Pearce, D. (1989) *Tourist Development*. Harlow: Longman.

Pearce, D. (1992) *Tourist Organization*. Harlow: Longman.

Pearce, D.G. (1997) Analysing the demand for urban tourism: issues and examples from Paris. *Tourism Analysis*, **1**, 5–18.

Pearce, D.G. (1998a) Tourist districts in Paris: structure and function. *Tourism Management*, **19**, 49–65.

Pearce, D.G. (1998b) Tourism development in Paris. *Annals of Tourism Research*, **25**, 457–476.

Pearce, D.G. (1999) Tourism in Paris: studies at the microscale. *Annals of Tourism Research*, **26**, 77–97.

Peck, J. and Tickell, A. (1995) Business goes local: dissecting the business agenda in Manchester. *International Journal of Urban and Regional Research*, **19**, 55–78.

Perloff, H. (1979) *The Arts in the Economic Life of the City*. New York: American Council for the Arts.

Petersen, D.C. (1989) *Convention Centres, Stadiums and Arenas*. Washington, DC: Urban Land Institute.

Pillsbury, R. (1987) From Hamburger Alley to Hedgerose Heights: towards a model of restaurant location dynamics. *Professional Geographer*, **39**, 326–344.

Pillsbury, R. (1990) *From Boarding House to Bistro: The American Restaurant Then and Now*. Boston: Unwin Hyman.

Plaza, B. (1999) The Guggenheim-Bilbao Museum effect: a reply to Maria V. Gomez. *International Journal of Urban and Regional Research*, **23**, 589–592.

Plaza, B. (2000a) Guggenheim Museum effectiveness to attract tourism. *Annals of Tourism Research*, **27**, 1055–1088.

Plaza, B. (2000b) Evaluating the influence of a large cultural artifact in the attractiveness of tourism: the Guggenheim Museum Bilbao case. *Urban Affairs Review*, **36**, 264–274.

Plog, S.C. (1987) Understanding psychographics in tourism research. In J.R.B. Ritchie and C.R. Goeldner (eds) *Travel, Tourism and Hospitality Research: A Handbook for Managers and Researchers*. New York: John Wiley.

Pocock, J.G.A. (1997) Deconstructing Europe. In P. Gowan and P. Anderson (eds) *The Question of Europe*, London: Verso.

Pred, A.R. (1966) *The Spatial Dynamics of US Urban-Industrial Growth, 1800–1914*. Cambridge, MA: MIT Press.

Prentice, R.C. (1989) Visitors to heritage sites: a market segmentation by visitor characteristics. In D.T. Herbert (ed.) *Heritage Sites: Strategies for Marketing and Development*. Aldershot: Avebury.

Prentice, R.C. (1993) *Tourism and Heritage Attractions*. London: Routledge.

Price Waterhouse (1991) *Annual Convention Report*. Tampa, FL: Price Waterhouse.

Pyo, S., Cook, R. and Howell, R. (1988) Summer Olympic tourist market: learning from the past. *Tourism Management*, **9** (2), 137–144.

Pysarchik, D.T. (1989) Tourism retailing. In S.F. Witt and L. Moutinho (eds) *Tourism Marketing and Management Handbook.* Englewood Cliffs, NJ: Prentice-Hall.

Queenan, L. (1992) *Conference Bureaux: An Investigation into their Structure, Marketing Strategies and Business.* Birmingham: British Association of Conference Towns.

Quilley, S. (1997) Constructing Manchester's 'New Urban Village': gay space in the entrepreneurial city. In G. Ingram, A.-M. Bouthilette and Y. Retter (eds) *Queers in Space,* Seattle: Bay Press.

Ragas, W.R., Miestchovic, I.J., Nebel, E.G., Ryan, T.P. and Lacho, K.J. (1987) Louisiana Superdome public costs and benefits, 1975–1984. *Economic Development Quarterly,* **1,** 226–239.

Redmond, G. (1991) Changing styles of sports tourism: industry/consumer interactions in Canada, the USA and Europe. In M.T.S. Sinclair and M.J. Stabler (eds) *The Tourism Industry: An International Analysis.* Wallingford: CAB International.

Renucci, J. (1992) Aperçus sur le tourisme culturel urbain en région Rhône-Alpes: l'exemple de Lyon et de Vienne. *Revue de Géographie de Lyon,* **67,** 5–18.

Rice, B.R. (1983) Atlanta: if Dixie were Atlanta. In R.M. Bernard and B.R. Rice (eds) *Sunbelt Cities: Politics and Growth since World War II.* Austin, TX: University of Texas Press.

Richards, B. (1992) *How to Market Tourist Attractions, Festivals and Special Events.* Harlow: Longman.

Richards, B. (1996) The conference market in the UK. *Insights,* March, B67–82.

Richards, G. (1994a) Developments in European cultural tourism. In A.V. Seaton (ed.) *Tourism: The State of the Art.* Chichester: John Wiley and Sons.

Richards, G. (1994b) Cultural tourism in Europe. In C.P. Cooper and A. Lockwood (ed.) *Progress in Tourism, Recreation and Hospitality Management,* vol 5. Chichester: John Wiley and Sons.

Richards, G. (1996) Production and consumption of European cultural tourism. *Annals of Tourism Research,* **23,** 261–284.

Ritchie, B. (1984) Assessing the impact of Hallmark events. *Journal of Travel Research,* **23,** 2–11.

Ritchie, J.R.B. and Smith, B.H. (1991) The impact of a mega-event on host region awareness: a longitudinal study. *Journal of Travel Research,* **30,** 3–10.

Ritter, W. (1985) Hotel location in big cities. In F.Vetter (ed.) *Big City Tourism.* Berlin: Reiner Verlag.

Robinson, K. (1994) Future for tourist attractions. *Insights,* May, D29–40.

Roche, M. (1992) Mega-events and micro-modernisation: on the sociology of the new urban tourism. *British Journal of Sociology,* **43,** 563–600.

Roche, M. (1994) Mega-events and urban policy. *Annals of Tourism Research,* **21,** 1–19.

Roche, M. (2000) *Olympics and Expos and the Growth of Global Culture.* London: Routledge.

Rogers, T. (1998) *Conferences: A Twenty-first Century Industry.* Harlow: Addison-Wesley Longman.

Rolfe, H. (1992) *Arts Festivals in the UK.* London: Policy Studies Institute.

Rosentraub, M.S. (1997) Stadiums and urban space. In R.G. Noll and A. Zimbalist (eds) *Sports, Jobs and Taxes: The Economic Impact of Sports Teams and Stadiums.* Washington, DC: Brookings Institution Press.

Rosentraub, M.S. and Nunn, S.R. (1978) Suburban city investment in professional sports. *American Behavioural Scientist,* **21,** 393–414.

Rosentraub, M.S. and Przybylski, M. (1997) Sports and downtown development: Indianapolis's effort to go from Indian Noplace to Indiana SPORTS place. In M.S. Rosentraub (ed.) *Major League Losers: The Real Cost of Sports and Who's Paying for It.* New York: Basic Books.

Rosentraub, M.S., Swindell, D., Przybylski, M. and Mullins, D.R (1994) Sport and downtown development: if you build it, will jobs come? *Journal of Urban Affairs,* **16,** 221–239.

Rouse, J. (1984) Festival marketplaces: bringing new life to the center city. *Economic Development Quarterly,* **8,** 3–8.

RPA (1985) *Conference and Exhibition Market Survey.* London: RPA Management.

Rubalcaba-Bermejo, L. and Cuadrado-Roura, J.R. (1995) Urban hierarchies and territorial competition in Europe: exploring the role of fairs and exhibitions. *Urban Studies,* **32,** 379–400.

Rutherford, D.G. (1990) *An Introduction to the Conventions, Expositions and Meetings Industry.* New York: Van Nostrand Reinhold.

Safavi, F. (1971) A cost–benefit model for convention centres. *Annals of Regional Science,* **2,** 221–237.

Salt, J. (1967) The impact of Ford and Vauxhall plants on the employment situation on Merseyside 1962–1965. *Tijdschrift voor Economische and Sociale Geographie*, **58**, 255–264.

Sanders, H.T. (1992) Building the convention city: politics, finance and public investment in urban America. *Journal of Urban Affairs*. **14**, 135–159.

Sassen, S. and Roost, F. (1999) The city: strategic site for the global entertainment industry. In D.R. Judd and S.S. Fainstein (eds) *The Tourist City*. New Haven, CT: Yale University Press.

Sawicki, D.S. (1989) The festival marketplace as public policy: guidelines for future policy decisions. *APA Journal*, **55**, 347–361.

Schimmel, K.S. (1995) Growth politics, urban development, and sport stadium construction in the United States: a case study. In J. Bale and X. Moen (eds) *The Stadium and the City*. Keele: Keele University Press.

Schouten, F. (1998) Access to museums as leisure providers: still a long way to go. In M.P. Collins and I.S. Cooper (eds) *Leisure Management: Issues and Applications*. Wallingford: CAB International.

Scotinform Ltd and Leisure Research Services (1991) *Edinburgh Festivals Study, 1990–1*. Edinburgh: Scottish Tourist Board.

Scottish Tourist Board (1991) *Visitor Attractions: A Development Guide*. Edinburgh: Scottish Tourist Board.

Searle, G. and Bounds, M. (1999) State powers, state land, and competition for global entertainment: the case of Sydney. *International Journal of Urban and Regional Research*, **23**, 165–172.

Segal Quince Wicksteed (1989) *Glasgow Tourism Review: Final Report*. Cambridge: Segal Quince Wicksteed.

Shallcross, W. (1998) The British conference market. *Insights*, January, B39–53.

Shanahan, J.L. (1980) The arts and urban development. In W. Hendon, J. Shanahan and A. McDonald (eds) *Economic Policy for the Arts*. Cambridge, MA: Abt Books.

Shaw, G. and Williams, A.M. (1994) *Critical Issues in Tourism: A Geographical Perspective*. Oxford: Blackwell.

Short, J.R. and Kim, Y.-H. (1999) *Globalization and the City*. Harlow: Longman.

Smith, C. and Jenner, P. (1999) Barcelona. *TTI City Reports*, No. **4**, 1–17.

Smith, G.V. (1989) The European conference market. *Travel and Tourism Analyst*, **4**, 60–76.

Smith, S.L.J. (1983) Restaurants and dining out: geography of a tourism business. *Annals of Tourism Research*, **10**, 515–549.

Smith, S.L.J. (1985) Location patterns of urban restaurants. *Annals of Tourism Research*, **12**, 581–602.

Spiller, J. and Ladkin, A. (2000) The growth and trends of conference centres: a case study of the UK. In M. Robinson *et al.* (eds) *Reflections on International Tourism: Management, Marketing and the Political Economy of Travel and Tourism*. Sunderland: Business Education Publishers.

Stevens, T. (1992) Barcelona: the Olympic city. *Leisure Management*, **12** (6), 26–30.

Stevens, T. (1994) Sports stadia and arenas: the sleeping giants of tourism. In A.V. Seaton. (ed.) *Tourism: The State of the Art*. Chichester: John Wiley and Sons.

Stevens, T. (2000) The future of visitor attractions. *Travel and Tourism Intelligence*, **1**, 61–85.

Stoker, G. (1995) Regime theory and urban politics. In D. Judge, G. Stoker and H. Wolman (eds) *Theories of Urban Politics*. London: Sage.

Swarbrooke, J. (1995) *The Development and Management of Visitor Attractions*. Oxford: Butterworth-Heinemann.

Syme, G.J., Shaw, B.J., Fenton, D.M. and Mueller, W.S. (1989) *The Planning and Evaluation of Hallmark Events*. Aldershot: Avebury.

Taylor, I., Evans, K. and Fraser, P. (1996) *A Tale of Two Cities: A Study of Manchester and Sheffield*. London: Routledge.

Thomas, C.J. and Bromley, R.D.F. (2000) City centre revitalization: problems of fragmentation and fear in the evening and night-time economy. *Urban Studies*, **37**, 1403–1429.

Thorne, R. and Munro-Clark, M. (1989) Hallmark events as an excuse for autocracy in urban planning: a case history. In G.J. Syme *et al.* (eds) *The Planning and Evaluation of Hallmark Events*. Aldershot: Avebury.

Tighe, A.J. (1985) Cultural tourism in the USA. *Tourism Management*, **6**, 234–251.

TMP (2000) (The Merseyside Partnership) *Digest of Merseyside Tourism*. Liverpool: The Merseyside Partnership.

Touche Ross: Greene Belfield-Smith Division (1991) *Survey of Tourist Offices in European Cities*. London: Touche Ross.

Tourism Canada (1986) *The US Travel Market Study*. Ottawa: Tourism Canada.

Towner, J. (1996) *A Historical Geography of Recreation and Tourism in the Western World, 1540–1940*. Chichester: John Wiley and Sons.

Travel Industry World Handbook (2001) *The Big Picture*. vol. 43.

Trew, J. (1999) *London: TTI City Reports*. No. 2. 1999, 37–64. London: TTI.

Trinity Research (1989) *The UK Short Break Holiday Market*. Trinity Research.

Tyler, D., Guerrier, Y. and Robertson, M. (eds) (1998) *Managing Tourism: Policy, Process and Practice*. Chichester: John Wiley and Sons.

Urry, J. (1990) *The Tourist Gaze*. London: Sage.

Van der Borg, J. (1998) Tourism management in Venice, or how to deal with success. In D. Tyler, Y. Guerrier and M. Robertson (eds) *Managing Tourism in Cities: Policy: Process and Practice*. Chichester: John Wiley and Sons.

van Bruggen, C. (1997) *F.O. Gehry: Guggenheim Museum Bilbao*. New York: Solomon R Guggenheim Foundation.

Var, T., Cessario, F. and Mauser, G. (1985) Convention tourism modelling. *Tourism Management*, **6**, 194–200

Vaughan, D.R. (1980) Does a festival pay? In W. Hendon, J. Shanahan and A. McDonald (eds) *Economic Policy for the Arts*. Cambridge, MA: Abt Books.

Vaughan, R. (1977) *The Economic Impact of the Edinburgh Festival*. Edinburgh: Scottish Tourist Board.

Vaughan, R. (1986) *Estimating the Level of Tourism Related Employment: An Assessment of Two Non-Survey Techniques*. Bournemouth: DRV Research.

Vetter, F. (1985) *Big City Tourism*. Berlin: Reimer Verlag.

Voase, R. (1995) *Tourism: The Human Perspective*. London: Hodder and Stoughton.

Waitt, G. (1999) Playing games with Sydney: marketing Sydney for the 2000 Olympics. *Urban Studies*, **36**, 1055–1077.

Walsh-Heron, J. and Stevens, T. (1990) *The Management of Visitor Attractions and Events*. Englewood Cliffs, NJ: Prentice-Hall.

Ward, K.G. (2000a) State licence, local settlements, and the politics of 'branding' the city. *Environment and Planning C: Government and Policy*, **18**, 285–300.

Ward, K.G. (2000b) From rentiers to rantiers: 'active entrepreneurs', 'structural speculators' and the politics of marketing the city. *Urban Studies*, **37**, 1093–1107.

Ward, S.V. (1998) *Selling Places: The Marketing and Promotion of Towns and Cities, 1850–2000*. London: E & FN Spon.

Waters, S.R. (annual) *Travel Industry World Yearbook: The Big Picture*. New York: Child and Waters.

Watson, S. (1991) Gilding the smokestacks: the new symbolic representations of industrialised regions. *Environment and Planning D: Society and Space*, **9**, 59–70.

Waycott, R. (1999) Marvels of the millennium or millennium madness? *Insights*, November, D15–19.

Whitehall, W.M. (1977) Recycling Quincy Market. *Ekistics*, **256**, 155–177.

Whitelegg, D. (2000) Going for Gold: Atlanta's bid for fame. *International Journal of Urban and Regional Research*, **24**, 801–817.

Whitson, D. and Macintosh, D. (1993) Becoming a world class city: hallmark events and sport franchises in the growth strategies of Western Canadian cities. *Sociology of Sport Journal*, **10**, 221–240.

Whitson, D. and Macintosh, D. (1996) The global circus: international sport, tourism and the marketing of cities. *Journal of Sport and Social Issues*, **3**, 278–295.

Whitt, J.A. (1987) Mozart in the metropolis: the arts coalition and the urban growth machine. *Urban Affairs Quarterly*, **23**, 15–36.

Whitt, J.A. (1988) The role of the arts in urban competition and growth. In S. Cummings (ed.) *Business Elites and Urban Development: Case Studies and Critical Perspectives*. Albany, NY:

State University of New York Press.

Wilkinson, J. (1990) Sport and regenerating cities. In Sports Council (ed.) *Sport: An Economic Force in Europe*. London: Sports Council.

Williams, A.M. and Shaw, G. (1988) Tourism: a candyfloss industry or job creator? *Town Planning Review*, **59**, 81–103.

Williams, C.C. (1997) *Consumer Services and Economic Development*. London: Routledge.

Wishart, R. (1991) Fashioning the future: Glasgow. In M. Fisger and V. Owen (eds) *Whose Cities?* London: Penguin.

Witt, S.F. (1988) Mega events and mega attractions. *Tourism Management*, **9**, 76–77.

Wober, K. (1997) An urban tourism database. In J.A. Mazanec (ed.) *International City Tourism: Analysis and Strategy*. London: Pinter.

Wood, A. (1998) Making sense of urban entrepreneurialism. *Scottish Geographical Magazine*, **114**, 120–123.

Wood, R.C. (1992) Hospitality industry labour trends: British and international experience. *Tourism Management*, **13**, 297–304.

Woodward, S. (2000) The market for industrial heritage sites. *Insights*, January, D21–30.

Wyne, D. (ed.) (1992) *The Culture Industry: The Arts in Urban Regeneration*. Aldershot: Avebury.

Zelinsky, W. (1994) Conventionland USA: the geography of a latterday phenomenon. *Annals of the American Association of Geographers*, **84**, 68–86.

Zeppel, H. and Hall, C.M. (1992) Arts and heritage tourism. In B. Weiler and C.M. Hall (eds) *Special Interest Tourism*. London: Belhaven.

Zukin, S. *et al.* (1998) From Coney Island to Las Vegas. *Urban Affairs Review*, **33**, 627–654.

Index

Entries in bold indicate principal treatment of a subject.